PHOTOSHOP ELEMENTS 2 TIPS AND TRICKS

George J. Kingsnorth
Gavin Cromhout
Janee Aronoff
Dan Caylor
Pete Walsh

friendsof

DESIGNER TO DESIGNER

Photoshop Elements 2
Tips and Tricks

First printed March 2003

Trademark Acknowledgements

friends of ED has endeavored to provide trademark information about all the companies and products mentioned in this book by the appropriate use of capitals. However, friends of ED cannot guarantee the accuracy of this information.

ISBN 978-1-59059-155-0   ISBN 978-1-4302-5127-9 (eBook)
DOI 10.1007/978-1-4302-5127-9

Credits

Authors
George J. Kingsnorth
Gavin Cromhout
Janee Aronoff
Dan Caylor
Pete Walsh

Commissioning Editor
Luke Harvey

Editors
Luke Harvey
Andrew Tracey
Caroline Robeson
Jake Manning

Author Agent
Chris Matterface

Project Manager
Richard Harrison
Simon Brand

Technical Reviewers
Cath O'Flynn
Nyree Costello
Denis Graham
Vicki Loader
Pete Walsh

Cover and Template Design
Katy Freer
Matt Clark

Grapic Editor
Matt Clark

Indexer
Jo Crichton

Proofing
Jo Crichton
Simon Collins

Managing Editor
Chris Hindley

CONTENTS

ABOUT THE AUTHORS

Dan Caylor I started out kind of by accident. A friend of a friend introduced me to Photoshop when I was 15. In February of 2000 I started www.thinkdan.com and it blew up (in a good way).

Since then I've worked with QUE and New Riders along with Katrin Eismann on Photoshop Restoration & Retouching, Friends of Ed on Photoshop Elements 2 Most Wanted (and a slew of technically reviewed titles), and I've been featured in a few magazines.

Gavin Cromhout lives in Cape Town, South Africa, where he works as a new media designer and digital photographer. He learnt most of what he knows about photography from carrying around his grandfather's camera case as a kid. This was known as being a photographic assistant apparently.

His past book contributions include: New Masters of Photoshop, Digital Photography with Photoshop Elements, Photoshop Face to Face, Photoshop 7 Professional Photographic Techniques, Photoshop 7 Trade Secrets and Photoshop Elements 2 Face Makeovers. You can reach him via his company website: www.lodestone.co.za.

George J. Kingsnorth, originally studied Film & Television at Bournemouth & Poole College of Art and Design, gaining an HND in 1983. Since then he has continued with his education in his spare time, gaining an Open University Degree, two Postgraduate Certificates and currently undertaking an MSc in Digital Television Technology and Production .

George has been working in postproduction for broadcast television in Ireland for about 20 years, involved in some 200 projects from current affairs, drama, documentaries, news and magazine programmes, corporate videos and animation. Recently, he has also produced nine digital video shorts, directing three of them. The most recent was screened at the 47th Cork International Film Festival in October 2002.

As a lecturer, George has been actively involved in helping numerous students begin their journey into the TV & Video Industry. Towards the end of 2002, he joined the staff at TIC (http://www.tic.ac.uk/) as the Senior Technologist/Lecturer in TV & Video Production.

Janee Aronoff Before I became a Photoshop Goddess, I taught geometry to high school students. Later, as I discovered the world of digital art and Photoshop, it seemed natural for me to want to teach what I had learned. So as I learned a new technique, I wrote it out in the form of a tutorial for my website at www.myJanee.com. I continue to maintain and build this collection on my site, along with my monthly Art Challenge, Message Board, and other digital art resources.

Aside from my "work" with my online Photoshop education community, I do freelance graphics and photo work, fine art, and technical writing, with a specialty in Photoshop and Elements. Previously, I wrote for three other Friends of ED books; Elements 2: Most Wanted, Photoshop 7: Professional Photographic Techniques, and PS 7: Trade Secrets, all published in 2002. Then in January 2003, I was proud to have an article included in SBS DigitalDesign magazine, with my artwork on the cover!

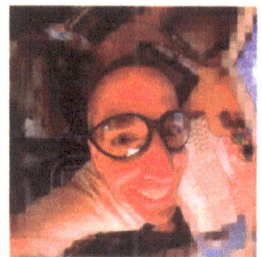

Pete Walsh sees kangaroos out of his office window and he's not hallucinating, he's Australian. He lives in the bush with his wife Selena, and two lovely daughters, Holi and Indi. They enjoy playing with crocodiles and riding in the front seat of roller coasters, not at the same time, of course.

Pete's talents include graphic design and web development. His passion for photography started while touring the outback on a mountain bike. He now uses his amazing eye (and a camera) to take breathtaking panoramic photos of Oz, which you can see at www.spacountry.com.au.

6.   Productivity   139

7.   Saving and sharing your images   149

Introduction

Welcome

How do you get the best out of Adobe Photoshop Elements 2? It's a combination of knowing what you want and knowing how to do it properly: a mixture of creativity and acumen. As you learn more, you make fewer mistakes, your workflow becomes faster, and you have more time to explore creative possibilities. This book is dedicated to accelerating your learning: providing the right information, reducing the number of mistakes you make along the way, and making your workflow more efficient. The result is you have a lot more time to be creative and look for inspiration.

The book is divided into nine chapters. To begin with we look at improving efficiency in fundamental skills areas: tools, selections and layers. Then we move into more creative areas, like image correction and special effects – you will find some short exercises here, to demonstrate real world applications. After that we look at productivity and provide some help troubleshooting. We then come to practicalities and background information on things like saving your files and sharing them on the web. Finally we look at your setup and give advice on additional hardware that might enhance your Elements experience.

Although you may choose to work through the chapters systematically, we've labeled the tips clearly and listed them all in the table of contents *and* at the beginning of each chapter, so they are easier to find. The idea behind the tips and tricks is that you'll want to use them again and again – you may flip through to find something specific, or simply browse a chapter – however you use the book, we hope our method of referencing means you can find the information you want quickly.

Platform considerations

This book is for Windows and Mac users, as Elements runs on both platforms. We only give the Windows shortcuts and screenshots in the text. This is simply because we wanted the clearest presentation possible and giving both sets of shortcuts can be longwinded and confusing. As over 90% of Elements software sold has been for Windows, we opted for this rather than the Mac – sorry, Mac users, but we hope you still enjoy the book!

The main differences between Windows and Mac, which you probably know if you're a Mac user, are:

Mac	Command/Apple Key	Option/Alt Key	Control+Click
Windows	Control Key	Alt Key	Right Click

Layout conventions

This book is designed to be user-friendly, each chapter is packed with tips and advice, and you can choose to either dip in and out of each chapter, or to work through the book in order. To keep things simple we have used a handful of layout styles, which we'll run through now:

Each individual tip will appear under the following type of heading:

Handy Tip

Most are straightforward text with bullet points where appropriate; those that contain longer exercises are numbered:

1. First do this...

2. Then do this...

3. Next, do this, etc...

You'll notice that as well as the main tips there is occasional extra information that we've written like this:

> *This is a focus point that has extra information in addition to the tip.*

As you'd expect in a book dedicated to efficiency, throughout the book we've included all the useful keyboard shortcuts that you'll need. We have kept the number of styles to a minimum to keep the presentation clear and simple, so you'll be able to pick out important words, menu commands and shortcuts easily. Here is an example:

Go to **Edit Preferences > General (Ctrl+K)** then select **Memory & Image Cache**, where you can increase the **Memory** available for Elements to use.

You'll also find some URLs that appear like this:

www.friendsofed.com

Support

None of the exercises covered in this book are dependent on a specific source file, so feel free to use any of your own images, if you would like to use our original files, then you can download many of the images used in the book from www.friendsofed.com.

If you have any queries about this book, or friends of ED in general, then please visit our web site, you'll find a range of contact details there, or you can mail feedback@friendsofed.com. We'll be happy to deal with any technical problems quickly and efficiently.

There are lots of other features on the site that may interest you – interviews with top designers, samples from all our books, and a message board where you can post queries or join in with the discussions. If you have any comments please contact us – we'd love to hear from you!

Chapter 1

Toolbox and Selections

In this chapter you'll learn to efficiently use some of the basic tools and options available in Elements. From quickly modifying selections, to familiarizing yourself with gradients, you'll become much more efficient in your workflow. The idea is to introduce (or re-introduce) you to the **how,** as well as the **when** and **why** of working with the Elements toolbox.

Selections

Use the tips and tricks below to master your use of selections. There's more to selection tools than you might think, and more selection specific shortcuts than you can shake a stick at.

1. Marquee Selections

The Marquee selection tools are the most basic selection tools. They can handle the creation of the most common geometric shapes, and therefore should be used frequently for small tasks such as cropping, and cutting/copying parts of an image.

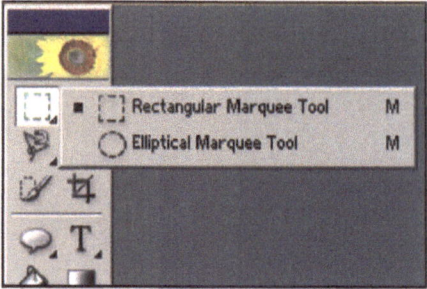

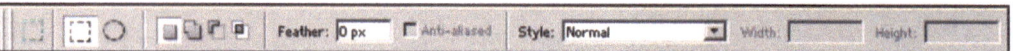

Holding the **Shift** button when using either of the marquee tools ensures a "perfect" shape (scale constrained to a 1:1 ratio). Holding the **Alt** button allows you to create your selection from the centre outwards, which is great for selecting circular/rectangular parts of an image.

Selection Styles can be set to either Fixed Aspect Ratio or Fixed Size from the **Style** menu in the toolbar. Select Fixed Aspect Ratio to constrain your selections to a desired aspect ratio. Entering values of 1 in the Width field and 2 in the Height field ensures that the height of your selection is always twice as large as the width. Select Fixed Size. Here you can set exactly how big you want your selection to be. This is great for creating thumbnail icons as shown here.

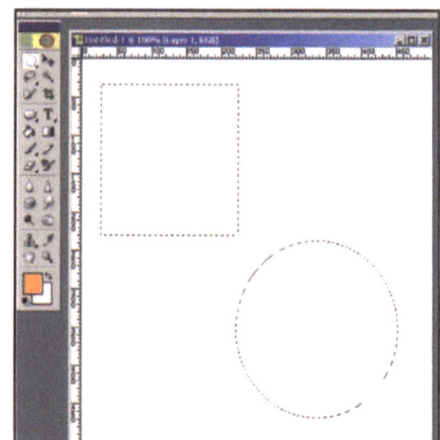

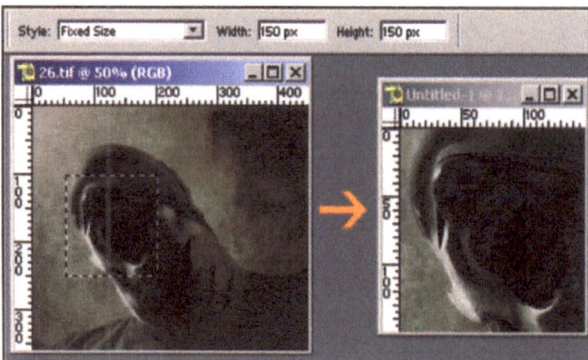

2. Lasso Selections

The Lasso selection tools are great when you need more precise selections. You can create any shape you like!

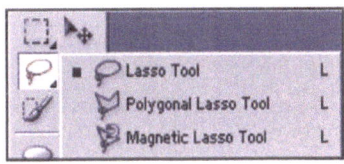

If you have a steady hand and want to avoid a lot of clicking, you can use the Lasso Selection Tool. Your selection is created all in one go, thus the need for the steady hand.

A more time-consuming option, and arguably more precise, is the Polygonal Lasso Tool, although this tool requires a lot of clicking when dealing with complex selections. This tool can be used for straight-line selections. It's also good for snipping edges and borders from images and active selections.

The Magnetic Lasso Tool attempts to do all the selecting for you. As long as there is a noticeable difference between the pixels you want to separate with a selection, this tool can usually do the job for you very easily. Use the Tolerance setting to change the sensitivity this tool has for the difference in pixels when selecting.

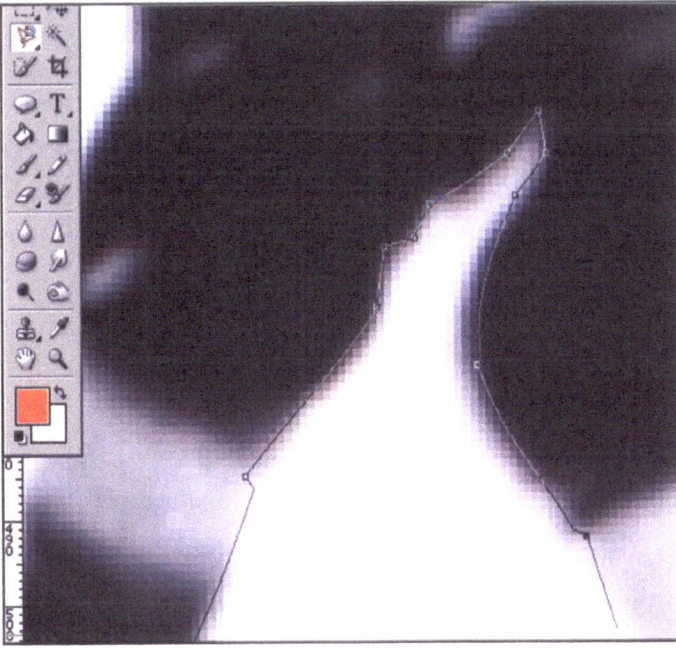

Use the Lasso selection tools when you need to make complex selections and complex adjustments to other selections.

3. Compound Selections

Selections can be added to or subtracted from each other to make a more interesting "compound selection". Normally, if you click to create a new selection you will lose any current active selection(s).

Click the Add to Selection button to keep an active selection alive while dragging a new selection and adding to it, effectively creating a "compound selection".

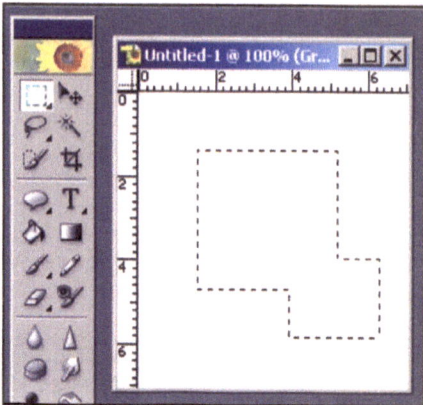

Subtract from active selections by clicking the Subtract from Selection button, and dragging out the area you wish to subtract.

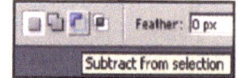

Intersected selections can be created with the Intersect with Selection button active.

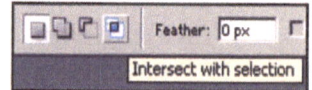

These compound selection techniques have a multitude of applications and will generally increase the efficiency of your workflow. Some real-world examples on photos could be:

- Use Add to Selection to select all the apples in a basket.

- Use Subtract from Selection to remove the triangular gaps in a selection of a wheel.

4. Selection Tips

Use these tips to become more efficient with selections. The tips shown below cover how to efficiently modify single active selections as well as the creation of complex "compound selections".

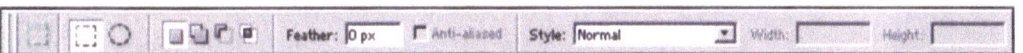

It can be cumbersome to have to use the Add to Selection, Subtract from Selection, and Intersect with Selection buttons in the toolbar all the time. To become more efficient with selections, use the shortcuts in the following table on any active selection with any selection tool in Elements:

Keyboard Shortcut	Description
Shift	Temporarily activates Add to Selection button.
Alt	Temporarily activates Subtract from Selection button.
Shift + Alt	Temporarily activates Intersect with Selection button.

Once you have your final selection you can then use the shortcuts in this next table to efficiently modify it further.

Keyboard Shortcut	Description
Ctrl + Backspace	Fills the selection with the current background colour.
Shift + Backspace	Activates the Fill dialog box enabling you to fill the selection with patterns.
Alt + Backspace	Fills active selections with current foreground colour.
Ctrl + H	Temporarily hides/un-hides the current selection in case it gets in your way.
Ctrl + T	Activates Free Transform Tool (discussed in the next section).

If you master the use of these shortcuts, you will become very efficient in your workflow in any version of Photoshop.

5. Transforming Selection Content

Transform active selections and their content via **Image > Transform > Free Transform (Ctrl + T)**. You can then use the handles on the side to easily rotate, scale, and distort the selection as you like.

Many other transform options are available when you right-click. You can switch between options and continue transforming. Press **Esc** to cancel any change made, and **Enter** to accept. Transforming objects has many applications, such as creating the illusion of 3D as illustrated in the figure opposite.

6. Softening Selections

Feather selections by entering a pixel value in the toolbar's Feather field. Feathering softens a selection, making it blend into other elements better. When you enter the value in the toolbar, any subsequent selections are feathered to that amount until you change it again.

If you want to define how much the selection is feathered *after* you make the selection, use **Select > Feather** as illustrated here.

Feathering can be used to create great vignette portrait shots. Once the selection above was made, I feathered it 50 pixels. All that was left to do was fill the selection, but if I had just done that, a soft white oval would cover the picture. Use **Select > Inverse**, and then fill the selection.

7. Magic Wand

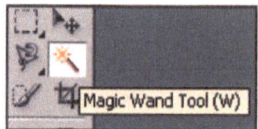

The Magic Wand Tool is the only selection tool that can make complex selections with the click of a mouse!

When you click on the canvas with the Magic Wand, your selection is dependent on the colors that you click on. The Tolerance setting lets you control how similar the colors in the resultant selection must be. In the following image, a high Tolerance setting (50) makes sure the whole sky is selected when I click on it.

"Landmark II", Al Stober Construction. Image courtesy of Chris Arlidge (http://www.steeldolphin.com)

A low Tolerance setting (10) would result in only "pockets" of blue being selected because all the shades of blue aren't the same. This is illustrated here.

With the Anti-Aliased option checked, your selections will stay smooth. Keeping the Contiguous option checked ensures that only adjacent pixels (pixels beside each other) with the same or similar colors are selected. With Use All Layers checked, you don't have to worry about selecting specific layers before you make selections.
Use the Magic Wand Tool for selections like those in the image above. Selecting complex objects with many different tonal values should be left to the Lasso selection tools.

Clone Stamp

The Clone Stamp Tool is a very powerful tool, and therefore you should familiarize yourself with its dos and don'ts. The examples used in this section are meant to give you an understanding of the tool; the real world exercises with photo retouching will follow in Chapter 3.

8. Clone Stamp Tool Basics

The Clone Stamp Tool is great tool for photographic restoration and manipulation, as you'll see in Chapter 4. It functions by using a definable part of an image as reference and stamping a clone of it within the same image or another. A crosshair icon is used to mark the part of the image currently being used as reference.

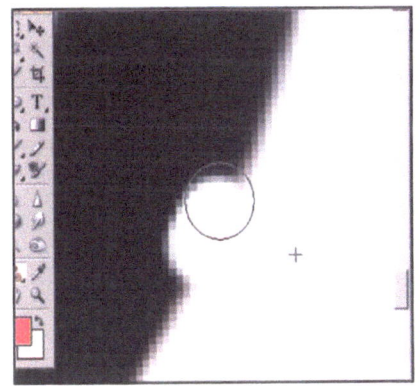

To use the Clone Stamp Tool, locate the area you want to clone, hold down the **Alt** key, left-click and drag (or simply left-click) over the area you want to sample, and release all buttons. Now that area has been sampled, all you have to do is click and drag (or simply left-click) to paint the sampled area elsewhere.

When you use the Clone Stamp Tool always duplicate your original layer and work with the duplicate. It's very easy to build up a big history (in the History palette) of clone stamps, at which point you'll have to start again if you do something you don't like.

9. Clone Stamp Tool Settings

If you want to choose your brush size from a preset of brushes use the section of the Options bar shown here.

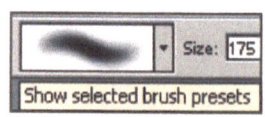

Alternatively, you can precisely define the diameter of your brush by the pixel with the Size input field. The bigger the brush, the larger an area the Clone Stamp will sample and consequently stamp. You should use small and hard brushes when working on highly detailed areas. But when you are simply working with blue sky, a large soft brush will do because the stamping effect won't be as noticeable.

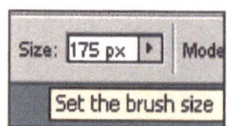

As with other brush-based tools, you can change the blending mode and opacity of the brush. If you change the painting mode, your paint strokes will interact with the layers below them, depending on which painting mode you use. Setting the opacity very low (10%) is a great way to blend in detailed areas. The following screenshot shows the result of trying to use a large soft brush with high opacity on a detailed area. It doesn't go unnoticed.

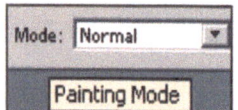

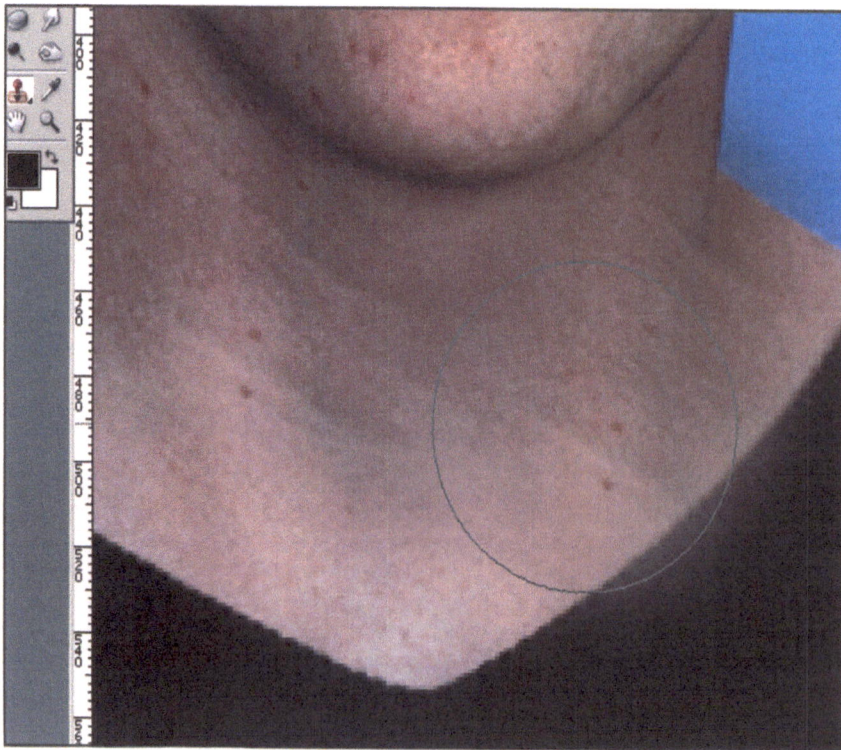

10. Clone Stamp: Using Aligned Mode

The Aligned option lets you control the sampled area that will be painted elsewhere when you stop and resume painting. When this option is deselected, the original sampling area is used each time you stop and start painting. When selected, the relative area is used. In the example below I want to remove the centred player. I've sampled the ice to his left and deselected the Align option.

If I left-click over an area of the player, white will appear. If I continue with left-clicks over the whole player, he will eventually be replaced with the ice surface. This is because the originally sampled area (the white ice surface) is used when Align is deselected.

If Align was selected, the same technique, while still achievable, would be a little more time-consuming because problems like those shown here can occur.

The Clone Stamp Tool is often used in Align mode for restoration work, as you'll see in Chapter 3, while normal mode is usually used for creating repetitive elements within an image.

Gradients

Gradients are underrated in Photoshop. They can be used to create some great effects in type, collages, interfaces, etc. Some of the examples in the following tips are a bit "cheesy", but they are merely meant to show you the door to a room of possibilities.

11. Gradient Basics

A gradient is a gradual blend between two or more colors. Elements comes with preset gradients you can use. If you click the Gradient Tool in the upper half of Elements' toolbox, you'll see the following toolbar:

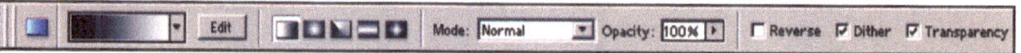

Notice the gradual blend between black and white in the left of the toolbar? That's the current gradient you have selected, the drop-down menu will reveal the rest of Elements' current range of preset of gradients. The colors in the default gradient reflect the currently selected foreground and background colors.

Linear Gradients blend from one point to another in a straight line (vertically, horizontally, or diagonally). This makes them practical for many uses such as text effects and collages, as shown here:

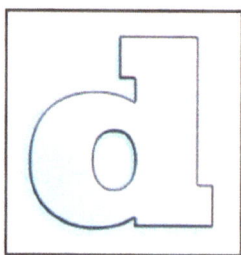

Radial Gradients blend from a center point outwards to form a circular gradient, making them especially useful for 3D spheres, and vignette effects.

Angle Gradients blend counter-clockwise to the starting point.

Reflected Gradients create the illusion of reflected symmetrical Linear Gradients.

Diamond Gradients blend from a center point outwards to form a diamond-shaped gradient. If you're looking for flashy, this is your pick.

Use the Reverse option to flip the gradient, the Dither option to eliminate banding (jaggedness), and the Transparency option to use gradients with transparency as masks.

12. Creating Custom Gradients

If you click the **Edit** button you'll see this dialog box:

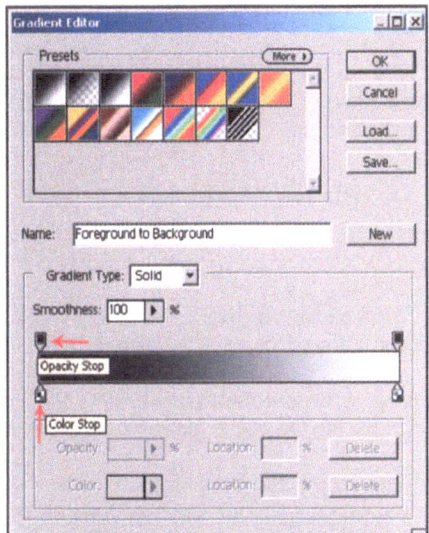

Say I want to create a gradient that evenly blends between red, orange, blue, and green. Below the selected gradient are checked boxes called Color Stops, above are solid boxes called Opacity Stops. Double-click the left Color Stop and select a red. Click just below the gradient to create an additional Color Stop. Set its color to orange, and adjust the Location field to 25%. Create a third, set it to green and 75%, and then adjust the last one to blue. In the name field type "ROGB" and then click the **New** button. Voila, I've created my gradient! Easy, isn't it?

If you want to vary the effect of a color in your gradient, modify the Opacity Stops. To remove Color Stops, simply click them and drag downwards. You'll often need to make your own custom gradients for projects that require specific elements, like a metal surface. A combination of metallic gradients and filters were used to create this metallic text effect.

13. Making Collages with Gradients

Gradients can help to create some great collages. Below, I've created a new 500x500 document with a three-color gradient blending from top left to bottom middle.

I've added some pictures from my childhood. These pictures are on separate layers (layers are discussed in Chapter 2).

I've added some shapes from Elements custom shapes library, and finished it off with some happy birthday text. The result is below. It's no work of art, but it's half bad for two minutes work. Have you noticed how much the gradient helps the piece look flashy?

Gradients, while simple, can be effective in complementing flashy effects like those above. I'll warn you to go easy with them though; effects like these are often described as "cheesy". Use gradients in a restrained manner.

Brushes

Brushes are used by most of the more powerful and extensively used tools in Elements. It's essential you learn the little tricks that can make you one with the brush.

14. Using Brushes Efficiently

Follow along for a list of keyboard shortcuts that can easily cut your brushwork time in half. These shortcuts work with all brush-based tools (Selection Brush, Pencil, Eraser, etc).

The following tips are great for touch-up work and detailed painting, as you'll constantly need to switch brush sizes and softness.

To decrease the size of the current tool's brush, hit the **[** key on your keyboard.
To increase the size of the current tool's brush, hit the **]** key on your keyboard.

This figure shows the difference in one brush size when changed with the shortcut keys shown above.

To make your brush softer, use **Shift + [**
To make your brush harder, use **Shift +]**

The next figure shows the difference in one brush softness when changed with the shortcut keys shown above.

Every time you use one of these shortcuts, your brush will move up/down one size/softness in the current brush library. This eliminates having to go to the toolbar and edit the brush (a much more time-consuming option).

To change your brush's blending mode on the fly, press **Shift + right-click** within your document. A context-sensitive menu will appear with the list of blending modes. A simple right-click within a document will reveal the edit brush menu. If you change the blending mode, your paint strokes will interact with the layers below them, depending on which painting mode you use

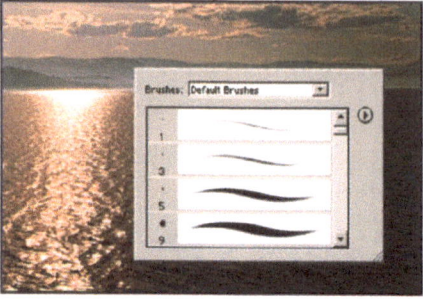

Result of SHIFT+right-clicking with brush-based tools.
Image courtesy of Chris Arlidge (http://www.steeldolphin.com)

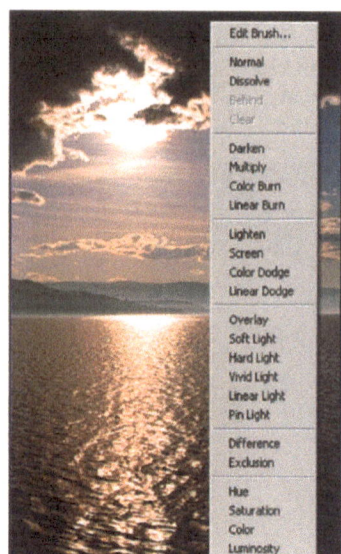

Result of right-clicking with brush-based tools.
Image courtesy of Chris Arlidge (http://www.steeldolphin.com)

15. Airbrush Introduction

The Airbrush Tool tries to mimic a physical airbrush by applying gradual tones of color. It's widely used for digital painting and image manipulation. Most magazine models have had extensive airbrush work applied to their skin. It can also be used for quick web graphics as you'll see in the three blue ball screenshots. The versatility of this tool is what makes it so popular. This gives you all the more reason to master this incredible tool.

The screenshots below show the process of about two minutes of work with the Airbrush Tool. It's very easy to create little effects like this. First a circular selection is filled with blue:

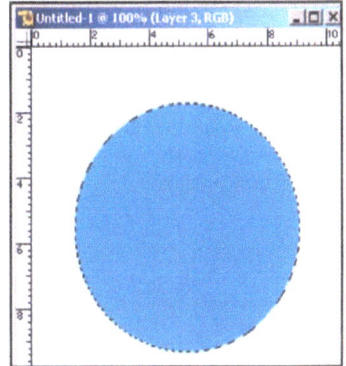

Next a dark blue is painted around the edge of the selection with a soft brush:

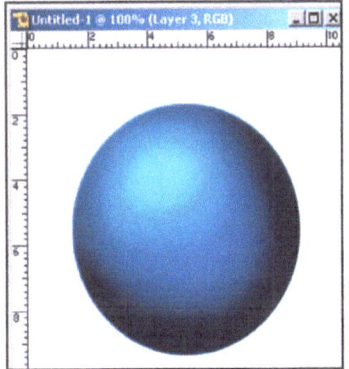

Finally a lighter blue is selected and the same soft brush is used to highlight:

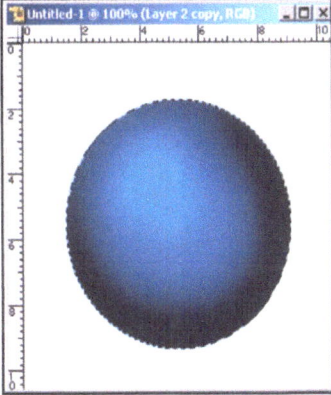

Voila, a nifty airbrush effect created in two minutes. As mentioned above, the Airbrush Tool is extremely versatile and can be used in so many different applications. I suggest you explore this tool and find your own use for it. Here you can see an example of digital painting made with the Airbrush Tool.

"Villain" by Chris Arlidge (http://www.steeldolphin.com)

16. Creating and Editing Brushes

If you want to create or edit your brushes, select the Brush Tool from the toolbox. To create your own brush, simply click the brush drop-down, followed by the right arrow button, and finally click **New Brush**.

If you hold the **Alt** key while hovering over a brush in the brush menu, the cursor changes to a pair of scissors, and you can click to delete that brush (the brush can be reloaded if you reload the brush set).

The current brush library can also be saved, replaced, or renamed, or a new library can be loaded. This is great for complex texture work. You have dozens of brush libraries that can each be used for a different kind of texture treatment.

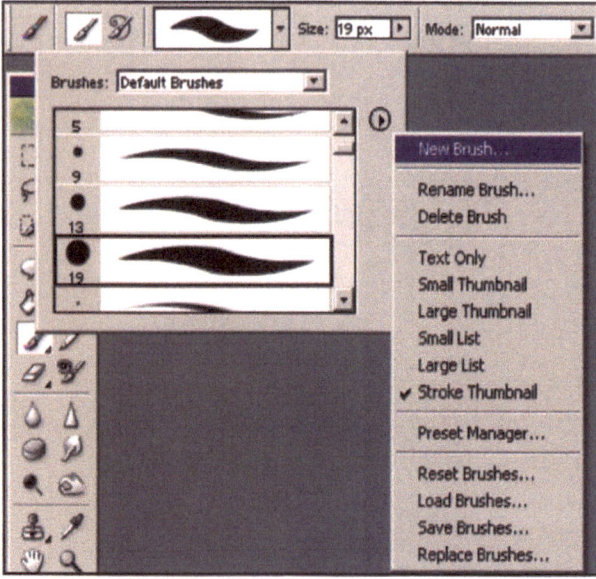

Name your brush "New Brush Example" and click **OK**.

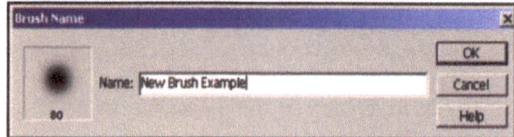

Your new brush is added to the current brush library. To modify your new brush, click the **More Options** button at the right of the toolbar to access the menu. Play with the settings and experiment with your results.

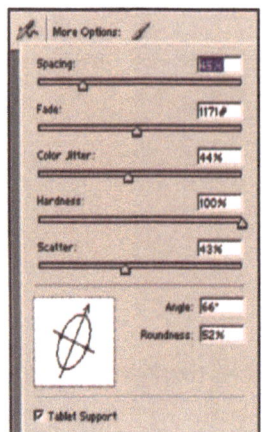

If you want a more random and rougher brush, modify the Scatter and Color Jitter options. You need to create and edit brushes and brush libraries when you start using them extensively in digital painting, texturing and retouching work. It's always good to get a good start with them now.

17. Custom Brushes

If a normal brush won't cut it, you can resort to Custom Brushes. Custom Brushes are defined with selections. Once you have your selection, choose **Edit > Define Brush**, name your brush, and click **OK**.

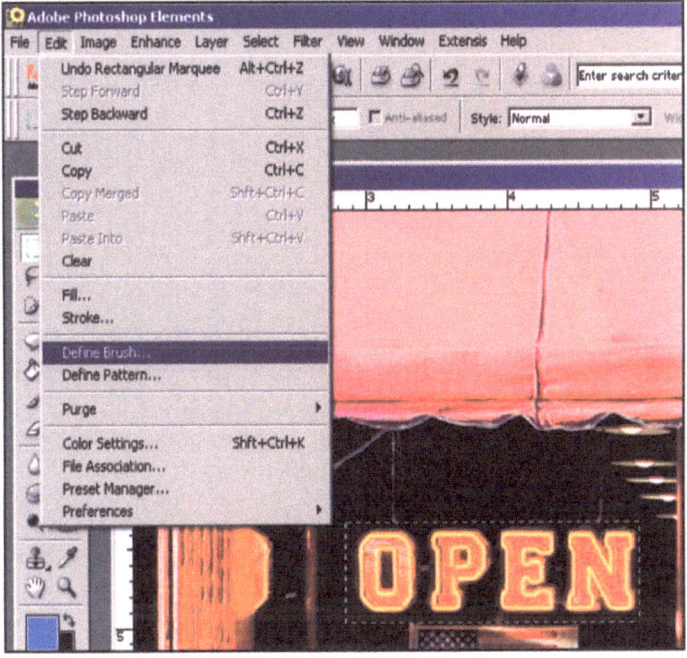

Image courtesy of Jason Morrison (http://www.dubtastic.com)

The selection will then become a new custom brush in the current brush library. You can find your new brush at the bottom of the brushes menu. It's important to note that you will lose any color information when you create your own custom brushes Think of it like a stamp. Only the foreground color will be used when you use your custom brushes.

You can modify your custom brushes just like any others. The Custom Brush above is a crude example; there are thousands of very cool custom brushes out there that can really enhance your current project. Custom Brushes are quite popular amongst some Elements and Photoshop 7 users. Images like the one to the right are heavily dependent on the use of Custom Brushes. This picture is a photo manipulation that took advantage of custom brushes for most of the texture work in the background as well for nicely blending image elements together. This is the result of hours of brushwork.

"Finding Me" courtesy of Jason Morrison (http://www.dubtastic.com)

18. Managing Presets

Choose **Edit > Preset Manager** to load the following dialog box:

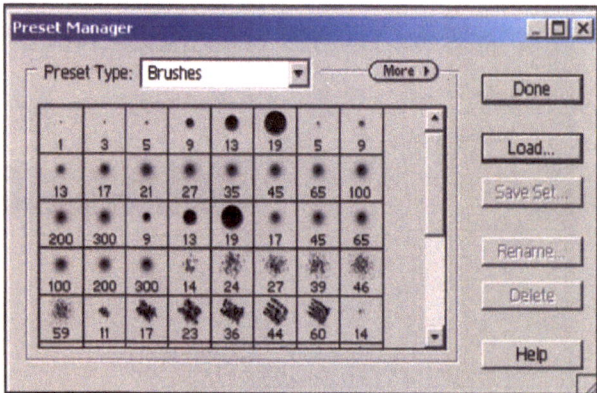

From here you can view the entire Elements preset library for all the different preset types. You can change the type from the **Preset Type** drop-down, and view more presets of the current type by clicking the **More** button. You can load, save, delete, rename, and redefine presets here as well.

Use this option if you have lots of different brush, swatch, pattern, and gradient libraries to organize. This manager is great when you need to create custom sets of brushes, for favorites, specific projects, etc.

19. Installing Brush Libraries

If you download Brush libraries from the internet (http://www.dubtastic.com), you can either place them in this folder:

[Elements Installation Directory] / Presets / Brushes

...or you can create your own folder and access them from there. Load new brushes via the **Load** button in the Preset Manager, or any edit brush menu in the Elements toolbar. The same applies for saving, renaming, and deleting brush libraries.

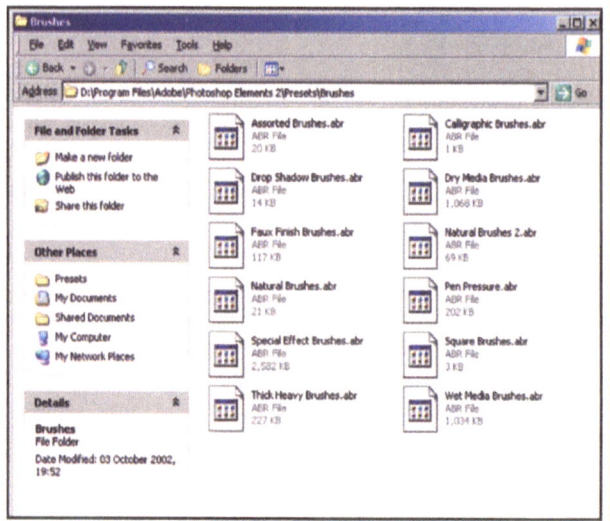

I'd recommend that you use the Brushes directory already provided for you. You should also look into getting an extensive collection of brushes; it can enhance the detail in your work a lot. If you can't find any to download, why not make your own? See tip 17 above on Customs Brushes.

Toolbox Navigation

This section contains only one tip, yet it can significantly increase your workflow. Follow along to learn how to quickly toggle between tools in the Elements toolbox.

20. Toggling Tools Efficiently

Some tools in the toolbox have others hidden beneath them. This is done to avoid a massive toolbox. You can access tools beneath others with this convention: **Shift + 0**, where **0** represents the shortcut for any tool. Switching between tools is called "toggling".

Example: To change from the Rectangular Marquee Tool to the Elliptical Marquee Tool, simply use **Shift + M** to toggle from one to the other. **M** is the shortcut for the Marquee tools.

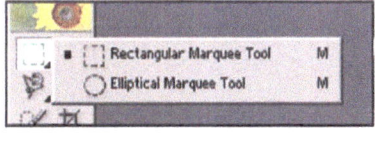

If there's a wealth of tools available to choose from, as there is under the Custom Shape Tool, you might find using the Shift method a bit annoying. Don't worry, this is easy to change.

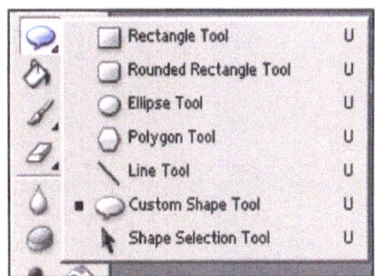

Go to **Edit > Preferences > General** and uncheck the **Use Shift Key for Tool Switch** option.

From now on, you can cycle through the tools with the shortcut alone.

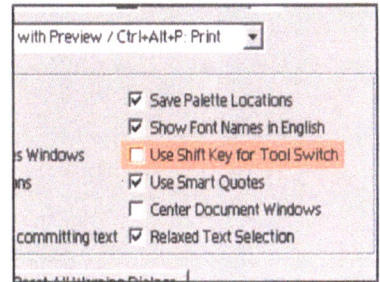

Layer Basics

1. Visualizing layers
2. Using a separate layer for each item
3. Labeling helps you to keep track of your layers
4. Adjusting the size of the of the Layer's palette's thumbnails
5. Copying a layer
6. Putting a copy of a layer into a different document
7. Filling a layer with a color or pattern
8. Revealing the names of the image layers
9. Hiding every layer but one
10. Partially hiding a layer
11. Linking layers
12. Locking layers
13. Fight the urge to merge
14. Merging layers

Layer Manipulation

15. Moving a layer from one file into another file
16. Opening an image file from the Web.
17. Cutting an object from a layer and moving it
18. Filling a shape with a photo or texture
19. Filling a shape with a pattern or gradient
20. Ctrl-click selection trick
21. Deleting a layer – three quick and dirty ways
22. Making a new merged visibles layer
23. Adjustment layers
24. Using adjustment layers to improve a photo.
25. Selective adjustments
26. Seeing the adjustment layer up close
27. Changing the effect of an adjustment layer
28. Locking a layer's transparency
29. Combining layers by masking
30. Making a vignette effect
31. More border effects with Elemasks
32. Removing troublesome backgrounds
33. Experimenting with blending modes
34. Scrolling through the blending modes
35. Layers troubleshooting tips

Chapter 2

Working with Layers

These layer tips are interrelated and many of them work together to form a basis for understanding how layers work. My advice for a novice is to read through each of the tips in this chapter once. Then read them again. As you read them the second time, they will be much more meaningful to you.

Layer Basics

Getting to grips with layers, and managing the palette.

1. Visualizing layers

Once you can visualize what layers are and how they work, you can do much more with them. I like to think of layers as plastic overlays on an overhead projector.

Unless you link them or merge them, you can manipulate the layers individually in almost limitless ways. For example, you can move one of them, flip it, stretch it, apply a blur or give it a bevel and a drop shadow, without the change affecting any other layer.

2. Using a separate layer for each item

It may seem as if more layers make things more difficult, but actually, the opposite is true! Layers afford you a great deal of flexibility. By having each of these road signs on its own layer, for example, it is a simple process to position them after they are made.

Using multiple layers frees you to experiment, correct mistakes, or just change your mind. Deleting a layer (see tip 21) is much easier than patching something that could have been on its own layer, or starting a project over!

Multiple layers also permit you flexibility with your composition.

Suppose you wanted to move the Warning sign to the front? Drag its layer to the top in the Layers palette!

Want to move it to the left? Click its layer and then type **V** for the Move Tool, and drag it to the left!

As long as each sign is on its own layer, we can do things like apply a filter to a single layer, or change a layer's opacity.

By having the signs on different layers, we can use different blending modes on the layers. Blending modes is Elements' way of combining colors mathematically on layers to arrive at sometimes surprising

results like this. I used the layers as you see in the screenshot of the Layers palette. Each layer is labeled with the blending mode applied.

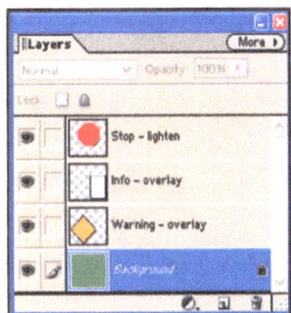

Suppose we wanted to add a crossroads symbol to the yellow warning sign. First we make the red stop sign and the white info sign invisible, by clicking their visibility eyes. Then we can create a new layer above the warning sign layer. Do this by clicking the warning sign layer in the Layers palette and then clicking the Create a New Layer icon. We can then paint the crossroads on that layer.

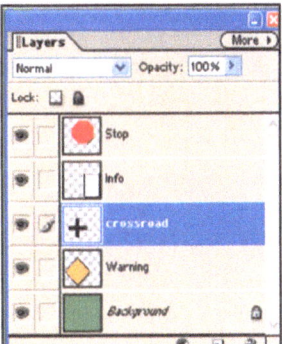

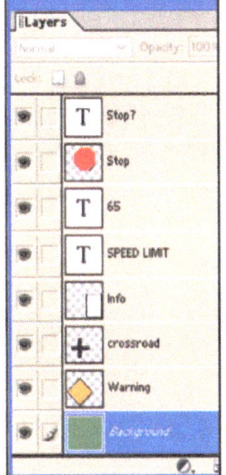

Then we can add more layers, type layers, to put the sign information on the other two signs. By putting the "Speed Limit" and the "65" on separate layers, I can position the "65" closer than the font would permit.

3. Labeling helps you to keep track of your layers

It is a good idea to keep your layers separate unless you *have* to merge them (to use a filter, for example). Even in a simple project, we can quickly accumulate eight or ten layers. With a more complex project, you can easily end up with 100 or more. So how do you deal with so many layers?

Get into the habit of labeling your layers with descriptive names, so that you can later tell, at a glance, which layer is which.

To label a layer when you first create it, **Alt**-click the Create a New Layer icon. This gives you the layer-naming dialog.

Or, you can name your layer after you have made it. In the Layers palette, double-click the current name of the layer and type in the new name.

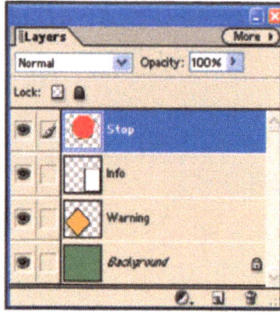

4. Adjusting the size of the Layers palette thumbnails

If you have many layers, it is handy to make the Layers palette thumbnails smaller. If you are working with layers with small things on them, you may want to have larger thumbnails, so you can more readily tell what is on the layer.

To change the size of the Layers palette thumbnails, click the **More** flyout at the top right on the Layers palette. Choose Palette Options.

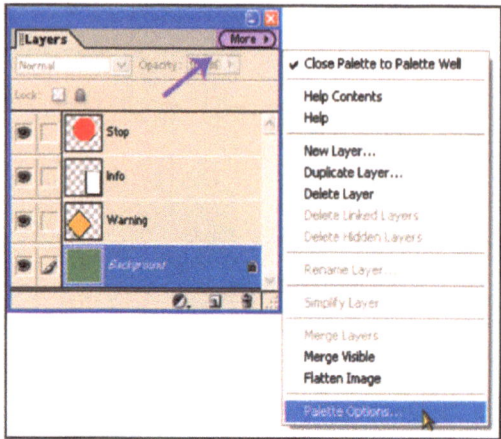
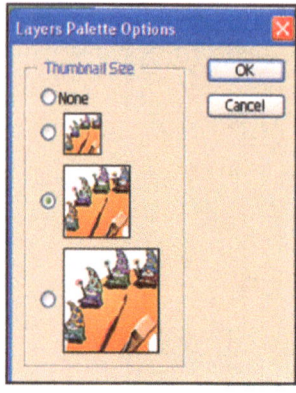

The first image below shows the palette with "None" checked for thumbnail size. The second one depicts the palette with medium thumbnails.

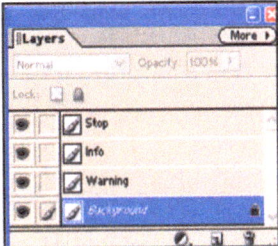 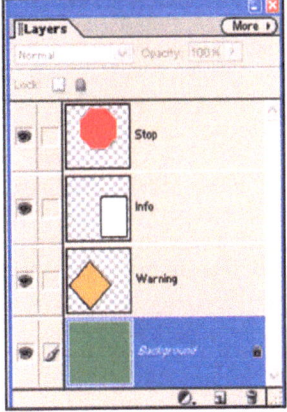

5. Copying a layer

To copy a layer in Elements, drag it down to the Create a New Layer icon in the Layers palette. And now there are two! If you want to name the copy, hold down **Alt** as you drag the layer, to bring up the layer-naming dialog box.

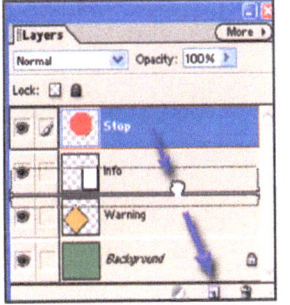

6. Putting a copy of a layer into a different document

If you want to move a copy of a layer into a new document or a different document you have open, hold **Alt** as you drag the layer to the New Layer icon. This brings up a dialog box. In this dialog box, you can name the layer, and you can specify its destination. The destination is your current document, by default, but click the drop-down menu and you see all of your opened documents, and "New".

Clicking New will give you a new document, in the same dimensions as your current one, with only the duplicated layer.

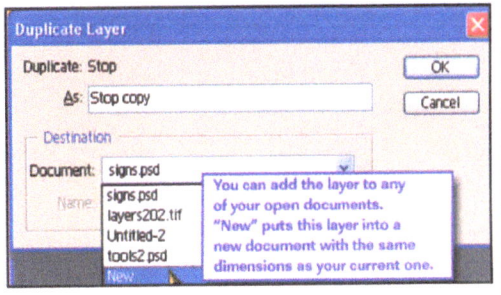

7. Filling a layer with a color or pattern

You can fill a layer with a color or a pattern. To fill with the foreground or background color, you can use **Edit > Fill...** and choose foreground or background. However, here are some handy shortcuts:

Alt+Backspace to fill the layer with the foreground color.
Ctrl+Backspace fills with the background color.
Shift+Backspace brings up the dialog box, enabling you to choose the fill (foreground color, background color, or pattern).

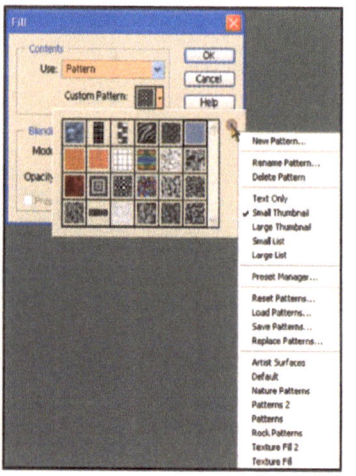

To fill a layer with a pattern, **Shift+Backspace** (or go to **Edit > Fill...** and choose **Pattern**). In that dialog box, find the pattern with which you wish to fill. Elements comes with more patterns than just the defaults! To see the other pattern libraries, click the flyout arrow on the drop-down box.

8. Revealing the names of the image layers

You can determine quickly what layers are right beneath your pointer, with this little trick:

- Type **V** to choose the Move Tool.
- Hold your pointer over the part of your image in question.
- Right-click. There you will see a listing of all the layers that contain pixels right beneath your pointer!

There are many times you may want to use this little trick. Here's one:

Suppose you have the image to the right, which is layered, and you want to make a pattern from just the apple, the stem, and the leaf on the right. You need to first isolate only the parts of the image you want in the pattern, and make any other layers invisible. You could fumble around, turning off layers till you happened to find the right ones. Or you could use this tip:

- Find the layers you want to keep by right-clicking on the places where there are more than one layer.
- Turn off the eyes for the layers you don't need.

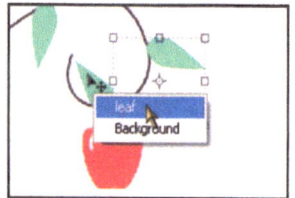

For example, I do not want this twig in the pattern, so I make it invisible.

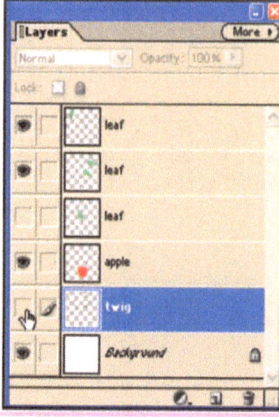

9. Hiding every layer but one

If you want to hide every layer but one, hold **Alt** as you click that layer's visibility eye. (If you have any layers invisible, you may have to **Alt-click** more than once.) **Alt-clicking** the visibility eye again will make all the layers visible.

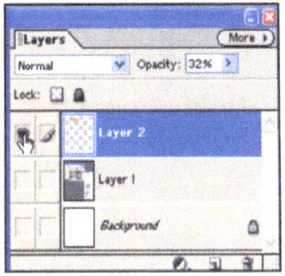

You may want to use this tip if you wish to concentrate on the details of one layer. This shortcut is very handy when you have many layers! For this example, my picture has just a few.

In this fruit picture, each fruit is on its own layer. I want to see what the effect of colorizing has on the apple. But when I colorize the whole picture, the edge of the apple gets lost in the orange.

So what we can do is to **Alt-click** the visibility eye for the apple layer, making the others disappear, and then click the eye for the Hue/Saturation Adjustment layer.

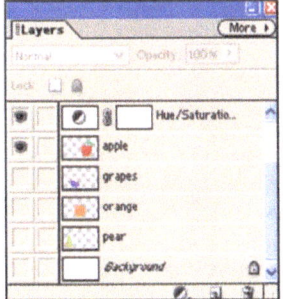

10. Partially hiding a layer

If you want to hide a layer, but not completely, you can reduce the layer's opacity in the Layers palette.

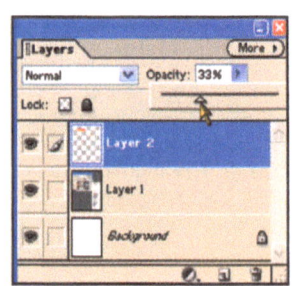

Reductions in opacity can be useful if you want to apply a filter, but don't want the effect to be so dramatic.

Here's one way to do this:

- Duplicate the original layer.
- Apply the filter to the top layer.
- Reduce the opacity on the top layer.

You can use opacity variations for artistic effect. In "Concord River Eyes," the opacity for the woman's eyes' layer was set to 25%, whilst his eye in the shadows, on its own layer, was set to 50%.

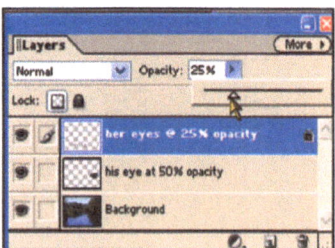

11. Linking layers

You may want to move one layer along with another, flip two of them, resize, or rotate them together. If you want to be able to separate them later, or think that you may, don't merge them. Instead, to form a temporary linkage, click the box next to the visibility eye to link any layers to the chosen layer. The little chain links tell you that the layers are linked!

For example, suppose we wanted to flip this image of the cat. His whiskers are on two separate layers, because I may want to lengthen them or color them green later.

I click the box next to the visibility eye and the layer is linked to the active layer.

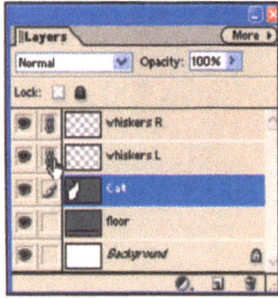

Image > Rotate > Flip Layer Horizontal flips the active layer... *and* any that are linked to it!

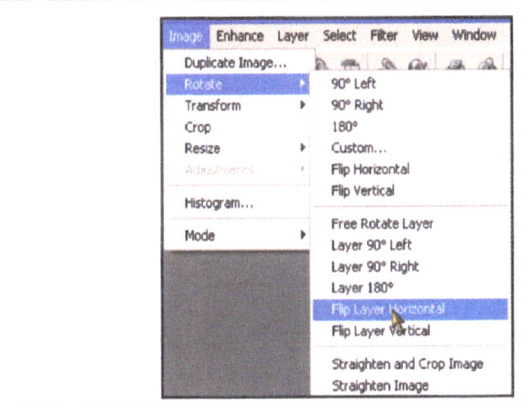

12. Locking layers

If you are in love with a layer of your document and want to make sure that you don't accidentally paint on it, move an object on it, or make other changes, you can lock it by clicking on the padlock.

Of course, if you do decide that you want to make a change, you have to unlock the layer, by clicking the top padlock again.

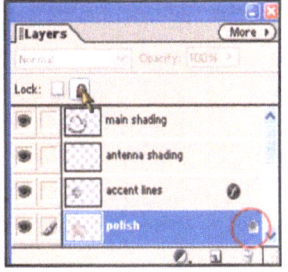

Locking can be used to secure a layer from harm. If you know, for example, that you do not want any painting to occur on this pear, but want the paint to go on the layer above it, you can click the padlock of the pear layer. This prevents you from doing any work on the pear layer! Your brush turns into that "No, you don't!" sign as you see in the second screenshot.

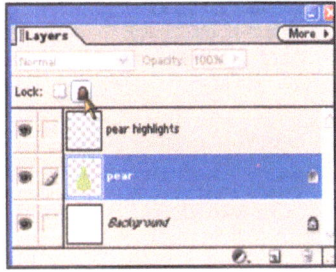

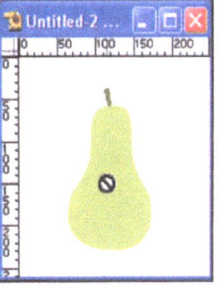

13. Fight the urge to merge

It is tempting to merge your layers when you think that you don't need to work with them individually, but resist the urge as long as you can.

I will discuss more on how to save your work in Chapter 7, but for now, I will tell you this - save in unflattened PSD format. Don't flatten anything in the PSD file, unless you are absolutely certain that you will never need to edit any part of it again.

There are several compelling reasons to keep an unflattened PSD version of your document on file.

If you need to edit something later, it is far easier to work with an object on a separate layer, than it is to change something that is part of a flattened document. In this document, if we decide we want to make "the" a different color, we can click the "the" layer, choose a color, and **Alt-Backspace** to fill. If it were a flattened image, we would have to select the letters, hope that we get all of the outlying pixels, and still, it is likely that the edges would not be perfect.

Keeping your layers separate in your PSD file is like having a library of spare parts for your images.

14. Merging layers

If you have a group of layers that you want to combine, you can merge them permanently.
Link them in the Layers palette. Then key **Ctrl+E** to merge. (Or choose **Merge Linked** from the flyout arrow to the upper right of the Layers Palette or from the Layers menu)

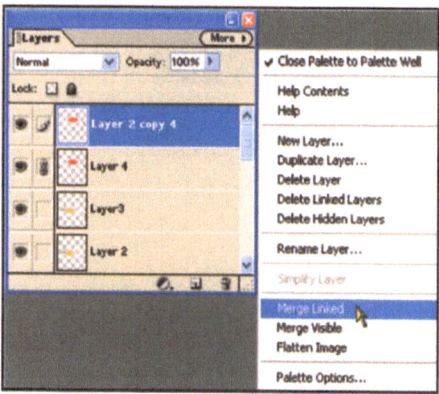

So when *do* you need to merge layers? There will be times when it is just cumbersome to work with individual layers and you are sure that you don't need them separated anymore. There are other special times when it is nice to be able to merge layers.

Here's one. If you have a layer to which you have applied a Layer Style, you are limited by the sorts of editing that you can do with it. As with shape layers and text layers, there are times when you have to simplify the layer. This will make the layer style part of the object, so that you can paint on the layer, erase it, filter it, etc.

Another thing about Layer Styles is that, when you resize your object, the Layer Style has to be resized separately (**Layer > Layer Style > Scale Effects**). Otherwise, the Layer Style can completely change its appearance, as it has here, when we reduce the size for this snowflake:

If you are finished with editing the shape and just want to resize it, it can be a nuisance to have to muck about with the Layer Style.

A problem arises when you try to simplify a Layer-Styled layer, though. See what happens if you choose **Layer > Simplify Layer**? The Layer Style flattens out in such a way that the look is totally *not* what we want!

So here's the tip. Make a plain white (in this case) backing for the Layer-Styled object. Then merge the two.

Use the Rectangular Marquee Tool to make a selection around the object.

Create a new layer and drag it to below the object in the Layers palette. Link these layers.

Then **Ctrl+E** to merge them.

Now the Layer-Styled layer is simplified and can be resized without changing the look of the style!

Layer Manipulation

Making the most of the advantages that layers give you, and some more advanced tips and tricks.

15. Moving a layer from one file into another file

Suppose you have two files open, and you want to copy a layer from the first file into the second. My favorite way to do this is by dragging. Here's how:

- Open both files and place them side by side on your workspace.
- Choose the Move Tool.
- Choose the layer in the first file.
- Drag this layer over to the second file. This will make a new layer in the second file.

If you press and hold the **Shift** key as you drag, the dragged object will be centered on the new document.

Note: The files must both be in either RGB Color mode or Grayscale. In this example, the trophy layer (a GIF file with a transparent background) has to be converted to RGB mode before it can be moved. To change the mode, in the top menu, click **Image > Mode** and choose **RGB Color**.

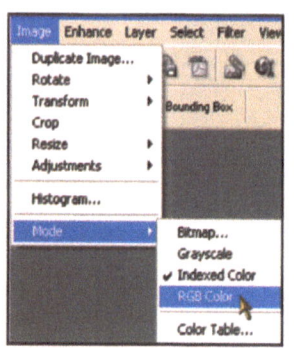

16. Opening an image file from the Web

Note: For practicing and learning, it is usually OK to use other people's images off the web, but if you are planning to publish or share your work, whether in print as a greeting card to Aunt Dotty or on your website, you must obtain permission from the copyright holder. Otherwise you are breaking international copyright laws. The notion that everything on the Web is free for the taking is false.

To "grab" an image from the Web, you can just drag it into Elements! Position your browser window beside your Elements window and click-drag the image onto the Elements desktop.

The file will open as its own file, not as simply a layer. If you want to add this as a layer to another document, you need to make sure that it is in the same mode (**Image > Mode**).

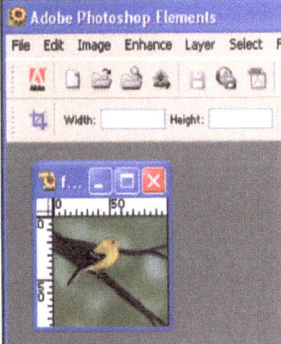

17. Cutting an object from a layer and moving it

What if we now want to move the cyan butterfly, but it is part of a layer (not on its own layer)? We can cut the butterfly out of the layer and move it:

We first select the butterfly. One way to do this is to select the whole area around the butterfly and then subtract the sky.

- Make a rectangular selection loosely around the butterfly.
- Choose the Magic Wand Tool.
- Uncheck Contiguous in the Magic Wand Options and make its Tolerance about 50. (When Contiguous is checked, it means you are selecting only the pixels that are similar in color which are touching the area you click. You need a fairly high tolerance here, because the sky, which you will be selecting, is a gradient. A higher tolerance means that there will be more shades of the color selected).

- Hold the **Alt** key and your Magic Wand has a – sign beside it. This means that you are about to subtract from your selection. Tap it on the sky. Repeat for any missed sky pixels.

Note: Depending upon your own image, your selection methods will differ from mine. I chose the Magic Wand, because of the relative homogeneity of the background colors, and the contrast between the background and the subject. Another choice here might be the Magnetic Lasso. If you need to cut a grasshopper from a leaf, and you have a steady hand, you may want to use the lasso. Or you may want to use the Selection Brush Tool, or an Elemask (see tip 30).

Once the butterfly is selected, there are three ways to move it:

Use the Move Tool and drag to move it. This will not present a problem if you are dealing with a layer that has objects that are separate from each other and the background.

However, with this butterfly example, you end up with this nasty hole where the butterfly was. And then, once it is moved, it blends in with the pixels below it, so that you can't move it again, without making *another* hole!

For more flexibility, you can put the selected butterfly onto its own layer. When you go to **Layer > New...** you see **Layer via Cut** and **Layer via Copy**.

With Layer via Cut, your butterfly is cut out of the background layer and put onto its own layer, as shown here:

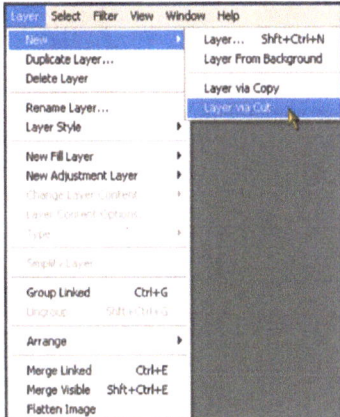 

If you use Layer via Copy, a duplicate of the butterfly is put onto its own new layer, so you can move it without leaving a hole. And, since the new butterfly is on its own layer, you can resize, rotate, or perform any of the other layer operations, without affecting the rest of the image.

18. Filling a shape with a photo or a texture

Suppose you want to fill some text or a shape with a texture or a photo. There are a number of ways to approach this. One is to make a Clipping group. That is, you use the shape to "clip out" the part of the photo you need. Unlike a stencil though, you put the photo on top of the shape.

Begin with this heart shape, or another of Elements' custom shapes. I chose this one from its Shapes library. Drag your cursor across your canvas to form the heart. Now let's fill it with Elements' Gold Sprinkles texture. Here is what we do.

Choose the heart layer by clicking on it.

Click the Effects tab and choose Textures in the drop-down menu. (**Window > Effects**, if you don't see the Effects palette).

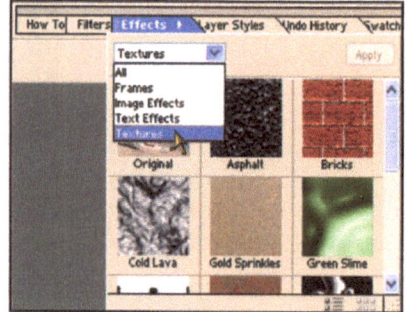

Drag the Gold Sprinkles texture onto the canvas. The layer above the heart will be filled with the gold.

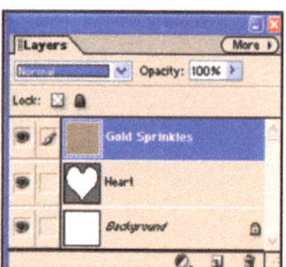

Clip the gold layer to the heart layer as follows. Hold your cursor between the two layers on the Layers palette, and hold the **Alt** key.

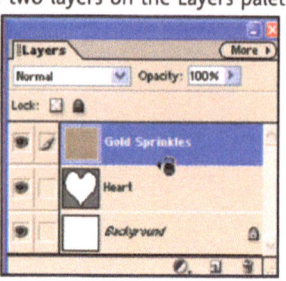

When the cursor turns into ⚫ , click.

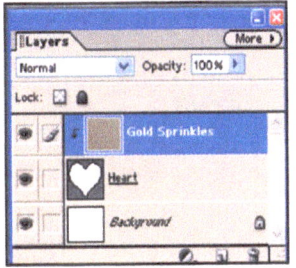

By changing the blending mode for the gold sprinkles layer to Luminosity, the red heart combines with the gold to make this metallic paint texture! (Experiment with blending modes! They can surprise you with some really cool effects!)

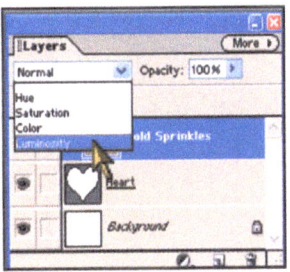

19. Filling a shape with a pattern or gradient

To fill a shape or any object on a layer with a pattern or a gradient, you proceed as follows:

Layer > New Fill Layer > and then choose the fill you want. For my parrot here, I chose Gradient.

In the dialog box, choose Group with Previous Layer. This clips it to the shape layer, as we did with the gold-sprinkled heart in the previous tip.

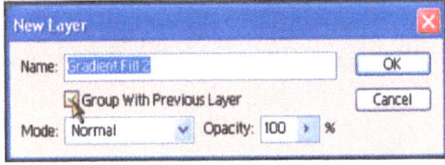

To fill with a gradient, choose the gradient you want by clicking the drop-down arrow.
For more gradient choices, click the flyout arrow in the Gradient Fill box.

To edit a gradient, you can click the gradient sample at the top. For the parrot, I used the Transparent Rainbow gradient from the Default set.

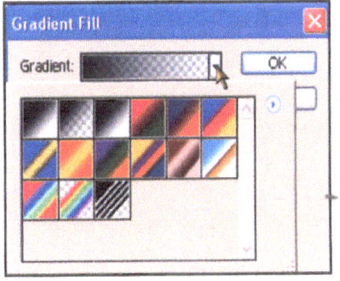

20. Ctrl-click selection trick

You can make a selection of all of the pixels on a layer, and even partially select pixels that are partially opaque. How? Hold **Ctrl** and click the layer in the Layers palette.

In order to make this sharply, but not uniformly, outlined star, here is what I did:

Begin with a yellow star, dragged out with the Custom Shape Tool. This star is in the Shapes library.

Make a new layer above the Star layer. This will be the Outline layer.

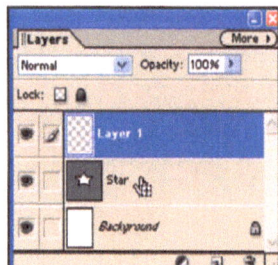

Ctrl-click the Star layer. This loads the star as a selection.

Choose a hard-edged paintbrush with the outline color. I used black.
Click the paintbrush on one point. Hold **Shift** and click it where two points join. Holding Shift makes a straight stroke with your brush from where you last clicked.

Hold **Shift** and click it on the next point.... Continue on around, till you have the outline. **Ctrl+D** to deselect.

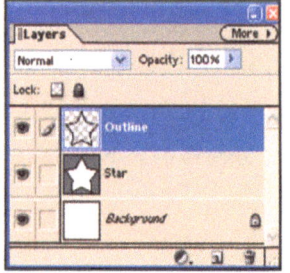

21. Deleting a layer - three quick and dirty ways

I'm not usually into "quick". For a method to work for me, I want it to be effective, but I don't want to have to reach for the manual to remember how to do it. Here are a couple of methods to delete layers that are worth knowing, and they are quick!

Drag the layer to the trash can. You can't get much more intuitive than that, but there will be times, especially if you have many layers to delete, that this is a hassle.

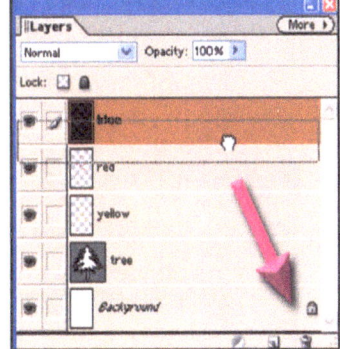

For the second method, you have to keep an eye on your Layers palette, but this is great if you want a quick and efficient way to rid yourself of many unwanted layers.

- Click the layer you want to delete.
- Hold the **Alt** key, and click the trashcan. Bang! Gone!

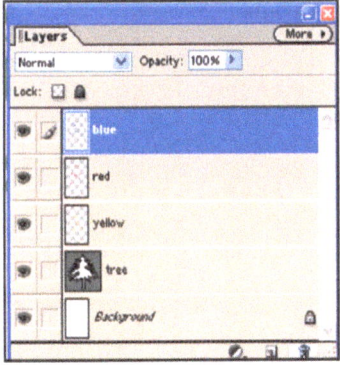

Repeat as necessary. The next visible layer down in the stack will automatically be chosen. Invisible layers will be skipped.

I like to say that there are three ways to do everything in Elements! The third quick and dirty way to delete layers, if you have many, is by first linking them:

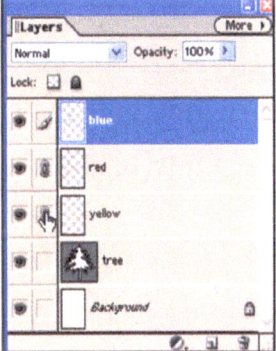

- Link all the trash-bound layers together.
- **Ctrl+E** to merge them.
- Drag the single layer of stuff that you don't want straight to the trashcan.

Sure, you can just delete the layer and make another, but that seems somehow wasteful. Here's a shortcut that is even faster. If you want to delete everything that is in a layer, do this:

- In the Layers palette, click on the layer to make it active, then **Ctrl-A** to select them all, **Del** to delete them, and then **Ctrl-D** to deselect them.

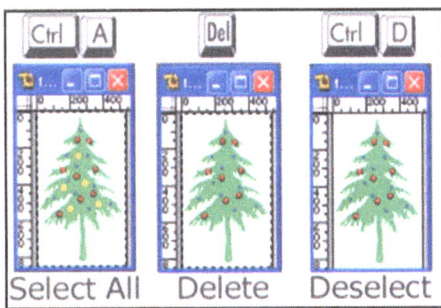

22. Making a new merged visibles layer

What if you want to merge your layers but want to keep them separate, too? This is a bit like taking an additional picture of all you see, whilst leaving all of the layers separate. This can be very handy because you keep your layers intact, but yet have them all together too.

To do this, make a layer above all the others. This is where your new merged visibles layer will go. **Ctrl-Alt-Shift-E**.

Et voilà!

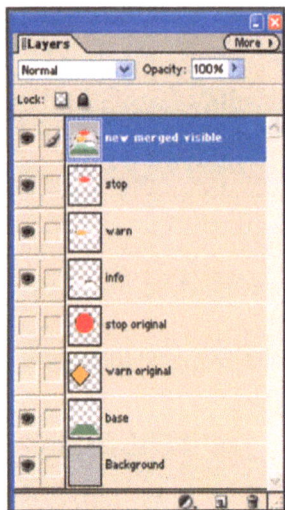

Notice that there are two layers that are not visible. These were not included in the new merged visibles layer, because this is only a merge of … visibles!

Note: You *can* make a merged visibles layer from any layer. If you do **Ctrl-Alt-Shift-E** without making a new layer, it will make whatever layer you have active into a merged visibles layer. If you forget this shortcut, you can use the menu to make a merged visibles layer, too. Go to **Layer > Merge Visible**. You will see the shortcut there in the menu. Hold down **Alt** and then click Merge Visible. If you don't hold **Alt**, it will flatten all of your visible layers, not what you want to do!

23. Adjustment layers

Ad-just-ment-la-yers… *five* syllables! But despite the difficult-sounding name, once you have tried them, you will see the reason that I am a huge fan of Adjustment layers. They are, essentially, one-step wonders!

An Adjustment layer is like a special plastic transparency. You don't just draw on it to add stuff to your image. No, this is much more special than that!

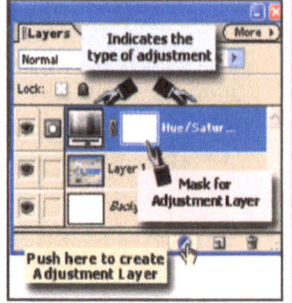

With a Levels Adjustment layer, for example, when you place it over your image, you get better contrast and you can lighten the image or darken it. With a Hue/Saturation Adjustment layer, all the hues of your layer are moved up the scale, or down, or the layer can be set to colorize the whole image so that it becomes just shades of blue, for example.

After you do a regular adjustment (**Enhance > Brightness/Contrast > Levels**, for example), your image is changed. Your pixels have been permanently altered. The only ways to back out of such a change are limited:

- Retrieve an earlier saved version of your work
- Retrieve a duplicate of your layer made before you performed the adjustment
- **Ctrl-Z** (undo) (and this option only lasts until you have used up your history states)

Note: Twenty history states is the default setting. If you want to allow more history states, you can adjust this in **Edit > Preferences > General**. You can save up to 100 history states. Keep in mind, though, that history states are kept in your RAM, so, if you are RAM-challenged, you will be well-advised to keep the number of your history states low.

But Adjustment layers allow you much more flexibility!
If you decide that you don't want the adjustment at all, you can turn off the Adjustment layer's visibility eye, or you can toss the Adjustment layer into the trashcan.

If you decide that you like the adjustment, but don't want it to be quite as intense, you can reduce the opacity of the Adjustment layer.

You can return to the Adjustment layer later and fiddle with the adjustments.
If you want the adjustment to apply to only *part* of the layer, you can mask out the rest! We'll look at this in a moment.

Note: An Adjustment layer will affect all the layers under it. If you want it to just affect a single layer, clip it to that layer. With the Adjustment layer above the layer you want it to affect, hold your cursor between the two layers on the Layers palette, and hold the Alt key. When the cursor turns into ● click.

24. Using Adjustment layers to improve a photo

In "Washington Park," my first goal is to brighten the photo to more closely resemble this crisp autumn day. Then I want to adjust the color saturation, making it even a bit extreme, to play up the idyllic fairytale scene.

Before:

After:

To lighten the photo, we can use a Levels Adjustment layer.

- Choose the photo layer in the Layers palette.
- Click the Create a New Adjustment Layer icon at the bottom of the Layers palette. ●
- Choose Levels.

- Adjust the sliders. Often, you will get good results if you pull the left (dark) slider toward the center (stopping just underneath where the histogram begins to show some points), then do the same with the right (light) slider.
- Finally, adjust the middle slider till you like the look.

I needed to make this Washington Park photo a bit lighter still, so I moved the light slider a bit further to the center. Whenever you adjust the sliders past some points in the histogram, you are relegating them to pure whiteness or blackness, and so you are, through the Adjustment layer, hiding image detail. You should therefore do this advisedly.

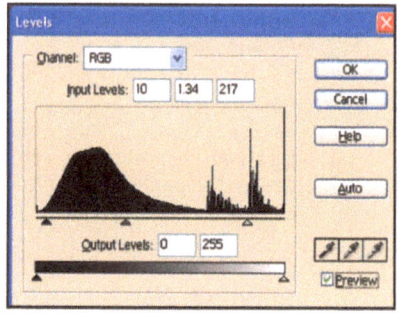

After lightening with a Levels Adjustment layer:

I next created another Adjustment layer, for Hue/Saturation. I increased saturation on the yellow, red, and green individually by selecting each of these colors in turn from the drop-down menu, to get the result in the following photo:

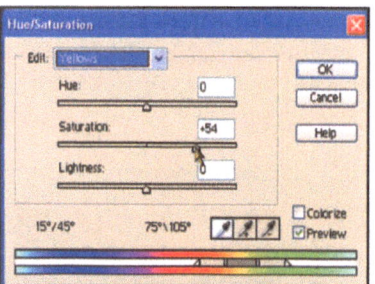

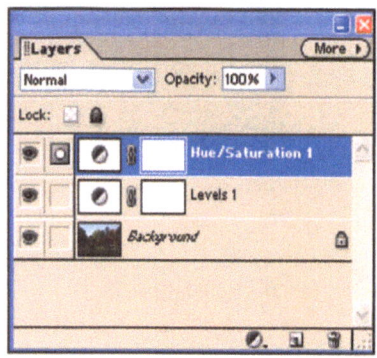

25. Selective adjustments

The sky is a bit washed out after the Levels Adjustment. What I really want is to *remove* the Levels Adjustment from the sky. See that little white square linked to each of the Adjustment layers in the Layers palette in the previous screenshot? This is a mask for that Adjustment layer. If we paint black on that, the Adjustment layer will not act upon that part of the image.

I don't want the sky to have the Levels Adjustment, so I select the sky (Magic Wand, high tolerance, contiguous unchecked) and then click the mask for the Levels Adjustment layer. Fill this selection with black using the Paint Bucket or **Alt-Backspace**.

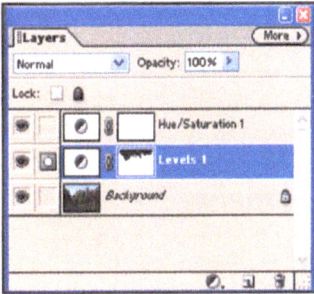

You can also paint directly onto an Adjustment layer's mask. I think the color of the foreground grass is a little too saturated. Choosing a large, soft brush and reducing the opacity, I paint a bit of black on the Hue/Saturation Adjustment layer's mask, in the areas that are oversaturated.

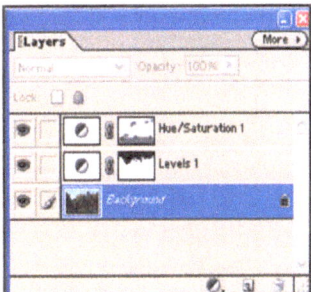

26. Seeing the Adjustment layer mask up close

If you need to fine-tune your Adjustment layer mask, you can change your view, so that you are looking directly at the grayscale mask itself.

Alt+clicking the mask for the Levels Adjustment layer for Washington Park, gives the following picture. I can then edit it in this view, by painting on the mask. **Alt+clicking** on the mask again in the Layers palette brings things back to normal view.

27. Changing the effect of an Adjustment layer

If you find the demarcation between the masked and the unmasked to be harsh, you can **Filter > Blur > Gaussian Blur** the mask, softening the edges. This does *not* blur your image itself, because you are working with just the mask.

You can also soften the effect of an Adjustment layer by reducing its opacity. Click the Adjustment layer in the Layers palette and adjust the opacity slider at the top right.

You can alter the effect of an Adjustment layer by using blending modes on this layer as well.

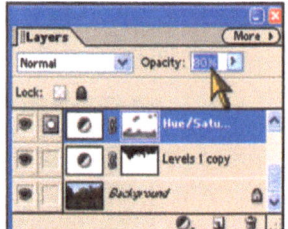

28. Locking a layer's transparency

Suppose the object on a layer is the exact shape you need. You just want to decorate it. Elements has a little trick whereby you can paint freely on the object, yet stay between the lines. You do this by locking transparent pixels.

When you click the lock transparency icon at the top of the layers palette for the selected layer, you will get a little padlock to the right.

This is not the same as locking the layer, though. When you lock a layer, you forbid *any* changes to it, including moving or distorting. Transparency locking just means you can't paint outside the lines.

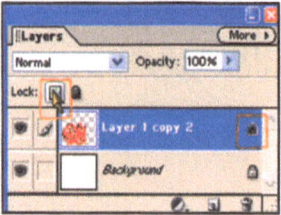

This can be useful if you want to have brushstrokes that are just on the painted part, as with these arrow brushstrokes.

It can also be used if you want to blur the inside of a border whilst keeping the edge crisp.

The outline stroked.

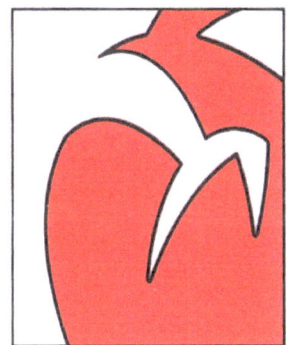

The layer blurred, with transparency locked.

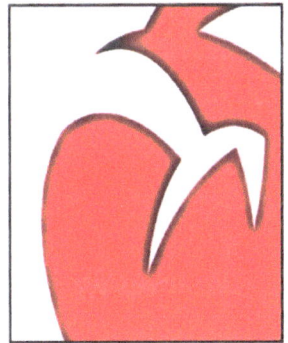

The layer blurred without transparency locked.

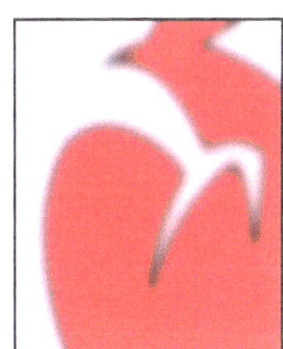

29. Combining layers by masking

We looked at Adjustment layers just a few tips ago, and we worked with the mask that comes with it. Well, how about this? We can use that mask without using the Adjustment layer! We call this an **Elemask**, and it is a very versatile tool.

In this example, I began with this elephant photo. I duplicated the photo layer, so that there were two layers.

I made the bottom photo layer into a line-drawing effect. (For details on how to achieve this effect, see Janee's Photoshop tutorials at www.myJanee.com, and find the one on making a photo into a line drawing. The tutorial works just fine for Elements!)

- For the top layer, I used the Enhance menu and colored the photo, using Hue/Saturation.
- Now, to combine them, we can put an Elemask between the two layers.
- Click the Line Drawing layer to make it active.
- Click the Create a New Adjustment layer icon at the bottom of the Layers palette.
- Choose something, say, Hue/Saturation. Click **OK** on the dialog box.
- Clip the Elemask to the top photo layer by holding the cursor between the layers in the palette and holding the **Alt** key. When you see the clipping arrow, click to clip!

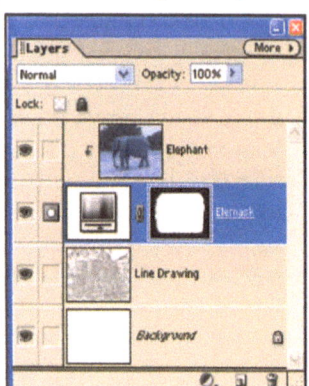

Now paint on the Elemask in black, wherever you want the top photo layer to be *hidden*. Where the mask is left white, the photo will show through onto the line drawing. Where it is painted black, the photo will be hidden, leaving just the line drawing visible.

30. Making a vignette effect

Your friends with full-version Photoshop may sneer that you can't do vignettes as well as they can. They may say that you can't, because you don't have "Layer Masks." But you have an Elemask!

For this vignette effect, begin by arranging your layers in the Layers palette.

You will need at least two layers: the photo layer and the background layer. If your photo layer *is* the background, double-click it to make it a regular layer. Then make a *new* layer, and fill it with white, or whatever you want for your background. Drag this layer beneath the photo layer in the Layers palette.

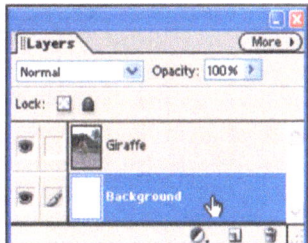

Next, choose the Elliptical Marquee Tool, and set your options so that you have some feathering. (The feathering setting will be different depending upon the size and resolution of your image, and the effect you want to have. For this image, with its finished size of about 800 pixels x 900, I used a setting of 30 pixels for feathering.)

Make the selection where you want your oval to be. I chose the head of this handsome giraffe.

Now, make the Elemask:

- Click the layer *below* your photo layer to choose it. Click the Create a New Adjustment layer icon.

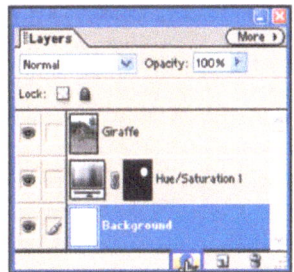

- Choose Hue/Saturation, or another of the choices, but not Gradient or Pattern. They won't work. Don't change any settings here. Just click **OK**. The selection you made is automatically transferred to the Elemask, which you can see in the Layers palette.
- In order to make the Elemask work, you must *clip it* to the photo layer. Hold your cursor right between the Elemask layer and the photo layer and hold the **Alt** key. When the cursor turns into the little clipping arrow, click to clip!

Note: The feathering option will stay where you left it, by default, so be sure to change it back to zero. Otherwise, you may wonder why your selection tools are not working with precision.

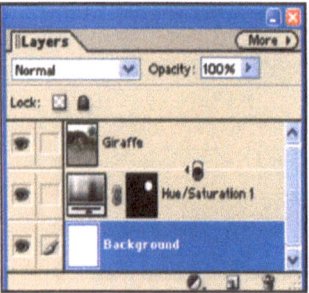

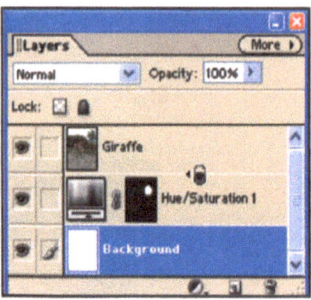

31. More border effects with Elemasks

There are many uses for Elemasks. Anything that people with "real" Photoshop can do using a Layer Mask, you can do with an Elemask. With the giraffe in the previous tip, we made a vignette border around its head. We can also do other border effects by painting on the Elemask, by applying a filter to the Layer Mask, or by using different backgrounds under the Layer Mask:

Here we see three different border effects:

Applying **Filter > Distort > Ocean Ripple** to the Elemask

Applying **Filter > Brushstrokes > Spatter** to the Elemask

Painting around the border of the Elemask with black, and a hard brush set at 50% opacity gives the border a hand-painted look.

32. Removing troublesome backgrounds

There are many ways to remove troublesome backgrounds. You can use the Background Eraser, Magic Eraser, or select with any of the selection tools, and then delete. These are all destructive methods, however, since they all destroy the original background pixels of your image.

My favorite way of changing a photo's background is with an Elemask. I really like the control you have with an Elemask, and the process is reversible, or correctible, since you are not affecting the actual pixels of the image at all, but merely hiding them!

So if, in this example, I decide that I've cut too deeply into the giraffe's neck hair, I can undo what I've done quite easily.

- If the photo is the background layer, double-click it to make it a regular layer.
- With the layer just below the photo layer selected, create an Elemask as before, placing it below the photo layer.
- Clip it to the photo layer.
- Click the Elemask so that you are sure to be painting on it and not the image itself.
- Grab a hard brush and, with black for the foreground color, paint away the background. (Be sure that your brush is at 100% opacity and Normal mode for this).

Zoom in closely and use a smaller brush, as you get closer to the edge of your subject.

Filling the background layer with black will reveal areas that you missed. Click the Elemask again and touch up these areas. If you paint into your subject, switch to white and paint away your error!

Once the background is covered, you can drag any layer in and place it above your background layer, beneath the Elemask, and make it the new background for the subject! Here, doesn't it look like he just wandered into town?

33. Experimenting with blending modes

Blending modes can be very useful for intensifying effects or creating special effects, by blending the contents of the layers mathematically. The cool thing is that you don't have to know anything about the math in order to make it work! As you experiment more with these, you begin to get a feeling for what they do, but to start with, just have fun trying them!

For this example, I used a Multiply blending mode for the pink lenses to give the "rose-colored glasses" view of Chicago's Lakeshore Drive.

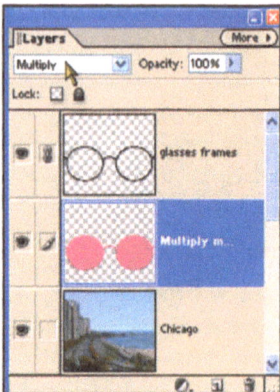

34. Scrolling through the blending modes

Remembering just what each blending mode is going to do, and predicting how it will work with the layers you have is nigh on impossible, at least for me. Here is a slick way to thumb through the blending modes:

■ Double-click the name of the blending mode in the Layers palette. By default, it is "Normal."

■ Use the arrow keys or the scroll wheel on your mouse to move down through these blending modes, and your image will change, showing the results as you go.

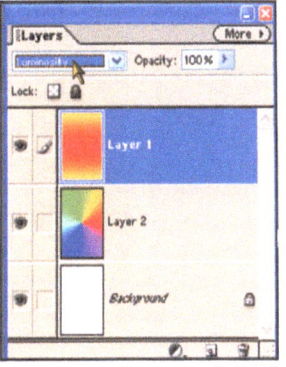

35. Layers troubleshooting tips

If things are not working as they should, here are some things to check:

■ You won't be able to drag layers from one file to another, unless you are working in the right color mode. For this, you will want to have both files in RGB mode. (**Image > Mode... > RGB Color**)

■ Make sure that all is well in the Layers palette.

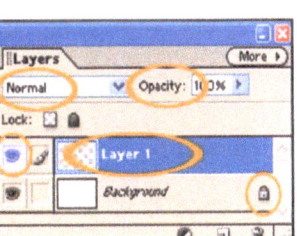

■ Your layer has to be visible in order for you to do work on it.

■ Nothing is locked which ought not to be.

■ Your opacity isn't zero.

■ You are working in the blending mode you intend to be using. Note: Some of the tools, like the Paintbrush and Gradient Tool, operate in different blending modes, too. Check your tool's options bar, if you are having trouble.

■ You might have a tiny selection going and not realize it. **Ctrl-D** to Deselect, then try your operation.

■ Can't get filters to work on a layer? Filters won't work on type layers or shape layers, unless they have been simplified. (**Layer > Simplify Layer**)

■ You also won't be able to paint or erase on a shape or type layer, unless it has been simplified.

■ If you are trying to move a layer and are having trouble, check the options for the Move Tool, and make sure that Auto Select Layer is unchecked.

■ If you are painting, and your color sampling is working oddly, type **I** and look at the options for the Eyedropper Tool. Sample Size other than "point sample" will sometimes give you unpredictable sampling.

I think that the best tip I can give you is to *experiment*. The use of layers with all of their capabilities can give you the freedom to lose your inhibitions, and to let loose your creativity! You can't hurt Elements.

As long as you are working on a copy of the image, you can't hurt it. And you can't hurt your computer. So go a little wild!

  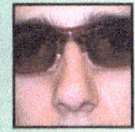 

Chapter 3

Image Correction and Retouching

Image restoration and retouching are two huge parts of the computer graphics industry. While it might seem that they are the same thing, they are actually very different from each other – as I hope will be clear from the tips in this chapter. I've started by running through simple changes you can make, mainly using the Quick Fix options that Elements offers – these are fast, but lack a degree of control. The later tips on restoration and retouching require you to put in a little more effort, but not much!

Quick Tips

1. Quick Fix dialog box

The Quick Fix dialog box allows you to make quick changes to your image. The first option is the Select Adjustment Category, which includes Brightness, Color Correction, Focus and Rotate. Each category provides a variety of adjustment options. The Auto options only require you to click on the Apply button to make the changes, while other selections require you to adjust them using sliders in the third column.

With your desired image open, click the Quick Fix icon in the Shortcuts bar, or select **Enhance > Quick Fix...**

The Quick Fix dialog box will open to reveal a before and after view of the image you are working on. Below this is a tip, which provides you with help on how to adjust the image based on which settings you choose. As it says on the tin these are quick fixes; they can be very fast and effective, but you have to rely on the inbuilt intelligence of Elements, and sometimes it may not produce the results you want. For many tasks though, they will do the job nicely.

2. Quick Fix Brightness: Fill Flash

The Fill Flash option is very useful for making quick adjustments for Brightness/Contrast, especially if you are in a hurry. It helps to lighten a dark image.

To change the brightness of an image in the **Quick Fix** dialog box:

Click on the Quick Fix icon, as shown in the previous tip. Under Select Adjustment Category, click on the Brightness radio button. Under Select Adjustment, click on Fill Flash. This will reveal two sliders under Apply Fill Flash. Drag the Lighter slider to the right to make adjustments to the desired effect.

If you are not happy with the result, you can click on the **Undo** button and start again.

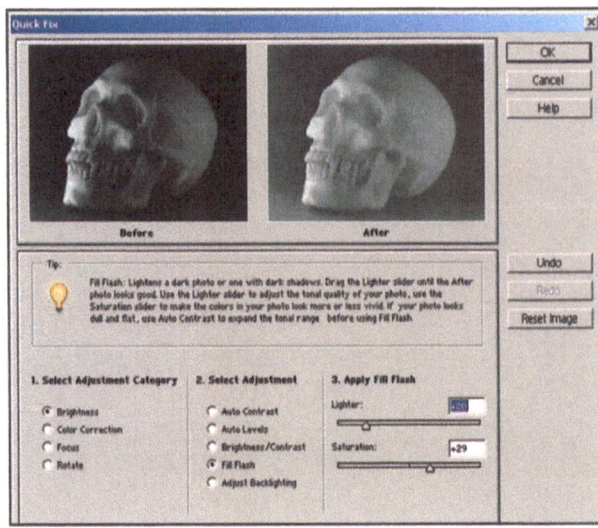

3. Quick Fix Brightness: Brightness/Contrast

There are times when the image you have scanned or transferred from a digital camera will appear flat and lacking in detail due to the low contrast between the dark and light areas of the image. To remedy this you can adjust the brightness and contrast to reveal hidden detail in the shadows and help to add depth to the shape.

Open the Quick Fix dialog box as before. Under Select Adjustment Category, click on the Brightness radio button. Then click on the Brightness/Contrast radio button. This will reveal two sliders under the Apply Brightness/Contrast column.

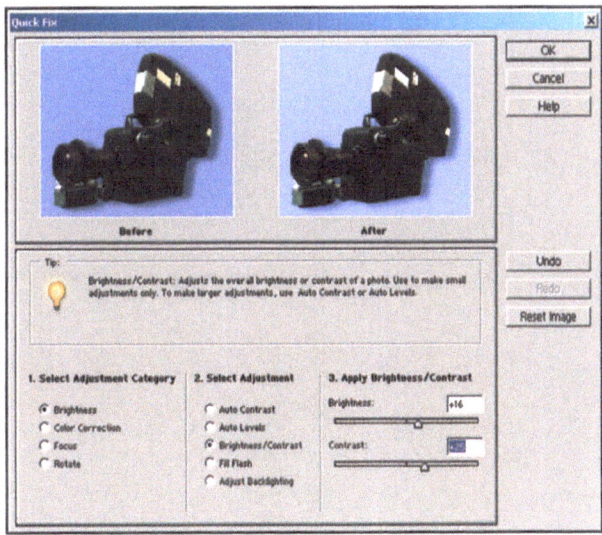

By using a combination of the Brightness slider (to lighten or darken the image) and the Contrast slider (to increase or decrease the contrast) the detail in the shadows and highlights can be modified to add character to your picture.

In the example image, the Brightness and Contrast have been adjusted to bring out the definition of the cine camera's shape and form which had previously been hidden in the blackness of the shadows.

To accept the changes you've made, click **OK**.

4. Quick Fix Brightness: Auto Contrast

The Auto Contrast is useful for broadening the contrast range between light and dark areas of your image. In this example the picture of the boy was taken in low light. By applying the Auto Contrast option in the Quick Fix dialog box, the light areas of the background are more distinguishable, with more detail coming from the darker areas. To use this feature in Elements use the following steps:

Open the Quick Fix dialog box by clicking [icon] icon in the Shortcuts bar. Click on the Brightness radio button. Click on the Auto Contrast radio button. Then click on the **Apply** button.

If you are happy with the result click **OK**.

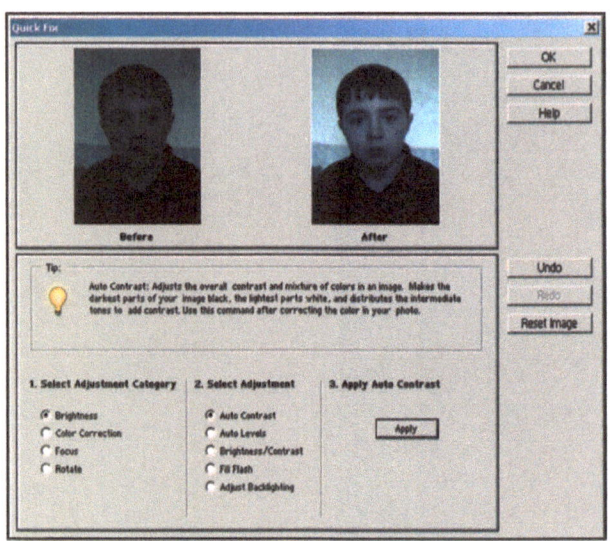

5. Quick Fix Brightness: Auto Levels

Auto Levels helps to correct color images that may have faded with a color cast or been slightly underexposed when they were taken. It will enhance the contrast of an image that has an even distribution of color.

I think you know where the Quick Fix dialog box can be found! Select Brightness from Select Adjustment Category, select Auto Levels from Select Adjustment. Then click on the **Apply** button in the Apply Auto Level column. Click **OK**.

As with the other quick fixes it's not perfect, as the Adobe Help files warn you: because Auto Levels adjusts each color channel (red, green, and blue) individually, it may remove or introduce color casts. If Auto Levels introduces an undesirable color cast, undo the command, and then try the Auto Contrast command instead.

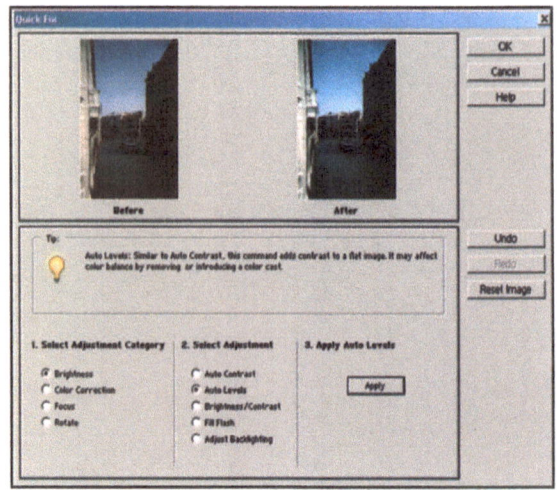

6. Quick Fix Brightness: Adjust Backlighting

In this next tip, I have scanned in an image of the interior of a French church. The visual aspect is quite pleasing but the image looks a little flat (meaning it lacks contrast), and the light coming through the window is washing everything out. To correct this in the Quick Fix dialog box, I will use the Adjust Backlighting to bring out more details in the darker areas.

With the Quick Fix dialog open, click on the radio button for Brightness in the Select Adjustment Category and on the Adjust Backlighting radio button in the Select Adjustment column. This time a slider appears in the Apply Backlight column entitled Darker. This is adjusted by dragging the slider to the right to the desired effect.

For the image of the French church the Darker slider is set to a point where the detail appears in the stained glass windows but there is still detail showing in the shaded area under the archways. Clicking on **OK** applies the adjustments to the photograph.

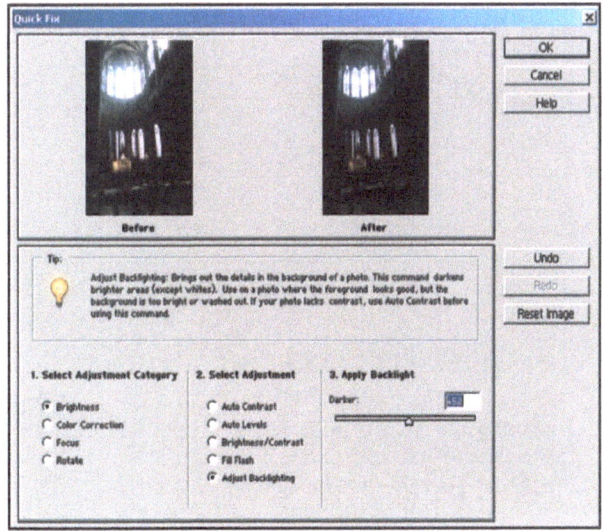

7. Quick Fix Color Correction: Hue/Saturation and Auto Color

If you have taken photographs in artificial light and the camera has not been adjusted for this form of lighting, (i.e. with digital cameras the white balance needs to be adjusted from daylight to artificial light), you will find your images coming out with an orange cast. By using Color Correction and adjusting the Hue/Saturation in Quick Fix, you can make the colors look more natural.

Again, open the Quick Fix dialog once you have opened the image that needs correction. Click on the Color Correction radio button under Select Adjustment Category. Clicking on the Auto Color radio button at this point does not really alter the image, so this is left until later on this occasion. Then click on Hue/Saturation under Selection Adjustment.

Three sliders will appear under Apply Hue/Saturation. In this example, by moving the Hue slider to +14 the orange cast has gone and the flesh tones on the face look more natural. Moving the Saturation slider to the left to about −52 reduces the yellow cast. Clicking on the Auto Color radio button again, followed by the **Apply** Button, adds a little more contrast.

Once the image has been adjusted, click **OK**. Within the Quick Fix palette there is only a limited amount of color correction that can be achieved, and images can retain a certain amount of unwanted color cast.

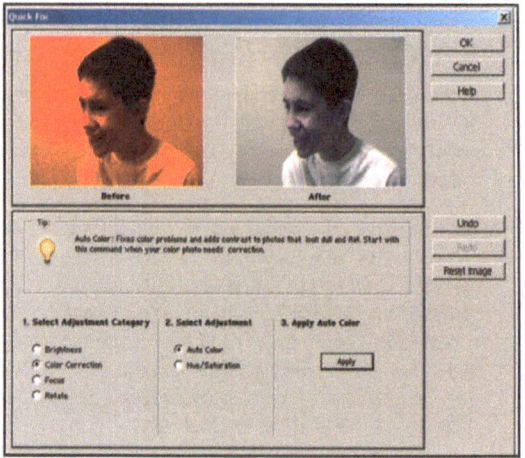

8. Quick Fix Focus: Auto Focus

The Auto Focus facility in the Quick Fix Focus category can be a little confusing. It does not allow you to automatically focus an image in the way that a camera can automatically focus on an object. Instead it simply sharpens an image that may be slightly blurred, instead of adjusting the focus.

For more precise sharpening of details, it is recommended to use **Filter > Sharpen > Unsharp Mask** from the menu bar to manipulate your image. However, if there are time constraints on you and the adjustments are minimal, then the Auto Focus option may be useful.

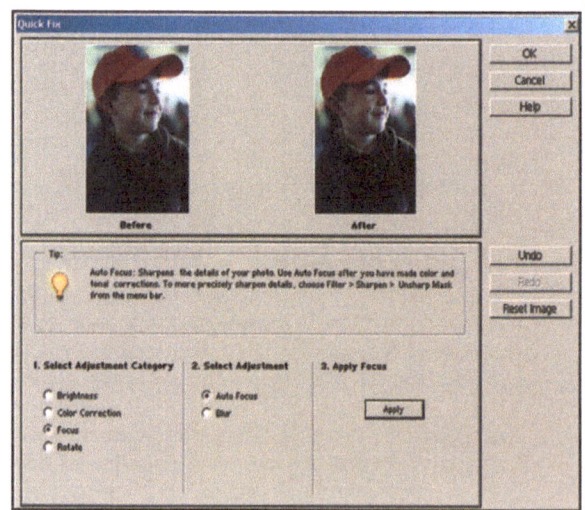

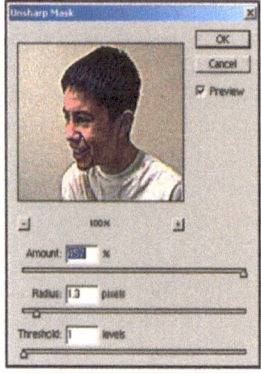

If you apply too much of this filter, you can add displeasing aspects to your image. Also, by having the settings too high, a jagged edge can be produced around the subject.

9. Quick Fix Focus: Blur

There are times when you will want to draw attention to a particular area of an image to heighten its importance by keeping it in focus and giving the impression of less important areas being further in the background by blurring them.

If you need to separate the background from the main object, select the object with a Lasso Tool. To blur the background, select the main objects using one of the Lasso Tools. Use **Select > Inverse** from the menu (or **Shift+Ctrl+I**) to reverse the selection.

Open the Quick Fix palette to blur the background.

1. Select Adjustment Category	2. Select Adjustment	3. Apply Blur
C Brightness	C Auto Focus	Apply
C Color Correction	⊙ Blur	
⊙ Focus		
C Rotate		

Once you are happy with the effect, click **OK**.

10. Correcting Perspective

Often when we are taking photographs of buildings we are forced to tilt the camera up to capture its entirety. This leads to images in which the sides of the buildings look as though they will converge somewhere up in the sky – the perspective bends the side of the building. However, this can easily be corrected in PhotoShop Elements using the magical Transform Tool in just a few steps.

Once you have the desired image open, select the edge of the image window and extend it so that there is a gray border around it by simply expanding the window. Use **Ctrl+A** or, from the menu, **Select > All** to select the whole image. From the menu select **Image > Transform > Perspective**.

Drag the top left corner control point to the left until the edges of the building on both the left-hand side and right-hand side of the picture are parallel with the edge of the image.

Double-click on the image once you are happy with the result.

*There are several tools that require you to commit the changes you have made, like the Transform and Type Tools – you can do this by double-clicking the image, pressing **Enter** or checking the tick that appears in the Options bar, BUT probably the quickest way to accept the changes is simply to move on to the next step – selecting another tool will automatically commit the changes you want to make. Simple and no extra keys or buttons to press!*

11. Create Photomerge

You may find there are times when you need to take a series of photographs to reveal the full extent of a view because it cannot be captured in one snap. A useful tool in Elements is Create Photomerge. This feature enables you to assemble a collection of images into a single picture.

To begin with, if you are using a camera which uses film, scan the photos into your computer and label them from 1 to the number of images in the sequence. If your images are already digital, store them in a folder and rename them in sequential order (though your software will probably label them sequentially for you automatically).

If you have time, adjust each image so that the brightness/contrast and any color adjustments have been made before doing the Photomerge operation. This is necessary to even out any exposure differences between images in the sequence.

Choose **File > Create Photomerge...** The Photomerge dialog box will open. Click on the **Browse...** button and select the folder you stored your images in. Left-click on the first image in the folder.

Then hold down the **Shift** key and click on the last image. All of the images will then be selected.

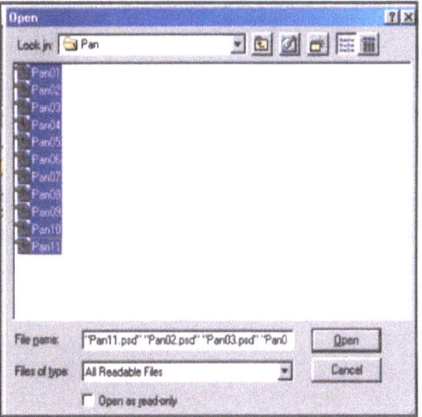

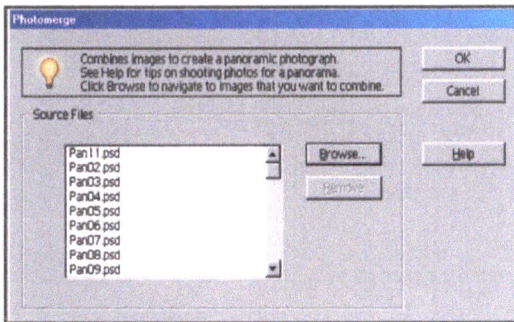

All of the images will then appear in the Photomerge Source Files field. Click **OK**.

Elements will then open each of the images, create a new image and assemble all of your images together. For the process to be successfully accomplished, there needs to be between 15% and 40% overlap between each consecutive image for Photomerge to align and merge them together.

In the example shown below, the overlaps enabled the image to be aligned and assembled horizontally. However, if the images are overlapped vertically, Photomerge will assemble the sequence of images vertically. The speed of this process will depend on the power of your machine. If any images are not automatically merged you can manually drag them into the new image and compose them yourself.

The Snap to Image facility can be deactivated if you find that the image you are trying to place is being moved to a different position when you release the mouse button.

Once you are happy with the result click the **OK** button. The new image will then be constructed and the images used closed.

The final image can then be adjusted using other features in Elements. Sometimes the sequence of images may not have lined up properly and there is a need to crop out the excessive material. Another problem, which occurred with the above image, included slight exposure changes in the sky associated with the image of the trees on the left and the sky associated with the building adjacent to the trees.

To correct this I used the Rubber Stamping Tool to even out the appearance of the blue in the sky. This method can also be used to fill in any holes that may have been created where two images were aligned unevenly, such as where the tree line needed to be extended.

Primary Restoration

Primary restoration is concerned with all of the bigger restoration problems you will find in images. Those that are immediately identifiable should be dealt with first. Through experience you'll find that if you deal with them first, you will achieve much better results in less time. Bigger restoration problems include color casts, rips or tears, and noise removal. Refer to Secondary Restoration below for tips on restoring specific areas of an image with specialized tools.

12. Image Assessment with the Histogram

If you are not sure how to approach a restoration project, the Histogram (**Image>Histogram**) can guide you along the right path.

The Histogram palette contains a graphical representation of the pixel information in an image along with statistics for individual parts below.

Typically, images are either:

1.   High-key - Contain mostly light pixels
2.   Medium-key - Contain a variation of mid-tone pixels
3.   Low-key - Contain mostly dark pixels

From the histograms you can see that one is a medium key image, which is therefore represented by a center-weighted graph. Darker (low-key) images will be weighted to the left, and lighter (high-key) images will be weighted to the right.

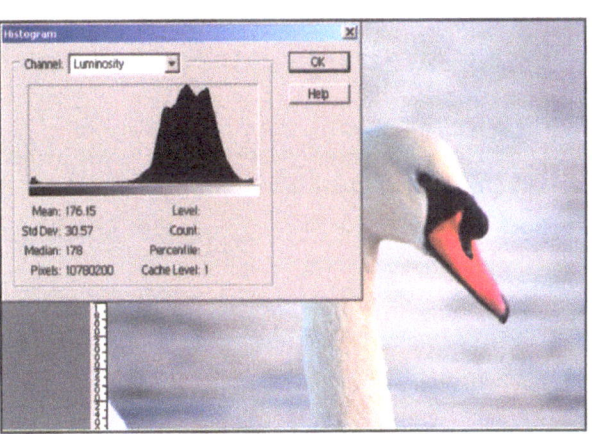

Once you know what kind of image you are working with you can move forward with a good understanding of what changes may need to be made. I recommend that you check your Histogram before making any tonal adjustments.

13. Detecting color casts

Some images clearly need color correction. In order to correct some color distortions, you need to be certain which colors the images are more saturated with. The Eyedropper Tool is your friend in this case.

Select it from the Elements toolbox and hover over a part of the image that you know should be a certain color. Here I took a reading from the towel that I knew should be white.

Take a look at the RGB values in the Info palette. The G value is a lot higher than the other indicating the cast is mostly green. There is also a small amount of blue in the cast as well.

Use this technique when you are using complementary colors to remove color casts (See "Removing casts with Variations" below).

14. Correcting color casts more effectively

In the previous section, we looked at using the Quick Fix Palette to correct color cast but with limited effect. In this section I'll show you that a more effective way of adjusting color cast is by using the **Color Cast Correction** dialog box. This is most useful when an image has been taken indoors using daylight film, which results in a photograph with an overall orange cast.

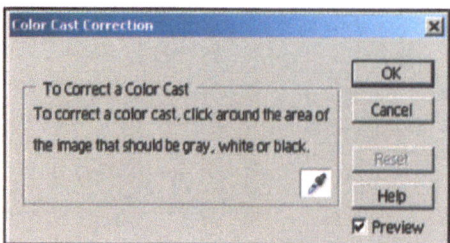

Use the eyedropper and click on an area of the image with the undesired color cast. Automatically, the image is corrected to a more natural color. Then select **Enhance > Adjust Color > Hue/Saturation...** (or **Ctrl+U**). When the Hue/Saturation dialog box appears, choose the relevant color that needs to be adjusted from the Edit menu. In this example it is cyan:

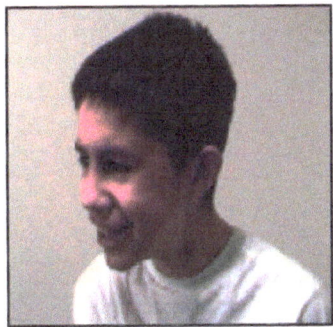 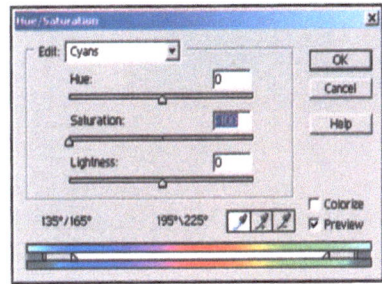

Here, I've moved the Saturation slider to –100 so that the cyan color is removed and the highlights become white. If other colors are introduced, use the Saturation slider for the intruding color to make adjustments.

15. Removing casts with Variations

Use Variations for color correction when you know what colors comprise your color cast (See "Detecting color casts"). In this picture we can see a greenish-blue cast on it:

We can correct it quickly by loading **Enhance > Adjust Color > Color Variations**. Elements provides tips on how to use the tool - Adobe have tried to make them accessible and understandable:

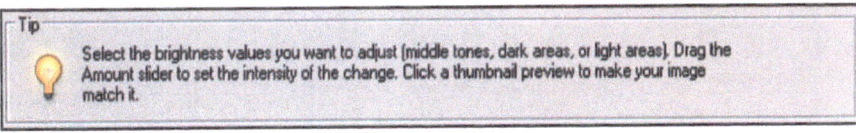

We know the image has a color cast comprised of mostly green and some blue (See "Detecting color casts" above). To correct this, decrease the green twice and the blue once.

This method is very fast and may be all you need, but due to the lack of control it doesn't produce the best results – you will have to do some correction by hand to further refine your image. In the next tip we use an adjustment layer that gives you more control, if you need it.

16. Removing casts with Levels

Using Levels is in my opinion the most precise way to correct color and tone in images in Elements. While this has the advantage of precision over both the Variations and Color Cast methods, it takes longer to achieve the results, yet as with most things, the longer you spend on something the better the result. I recommend that you read tip 12: "Image Assessment with the Histogram" before you use this tip.

This image has a strong magenta cast. Access Levels via **Layer > New Adjustment Layer > Levels (Ctrl+L)**.

To get rid of the cast we have to redefine the areas in the photo that should be black and white (see "Detecting Color Casts" above). Click the **Set Black Point** button and click on the image where you think it is the darkest (in this case it is probably between the woman's legs). Now click the **Set White Point** button and click where you think it should be the lightest (in this case somewhere in the sky is the best bet).

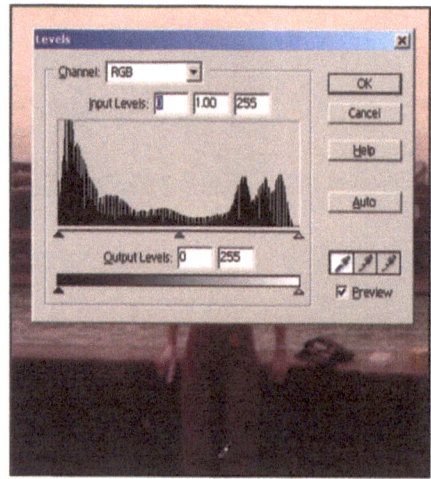
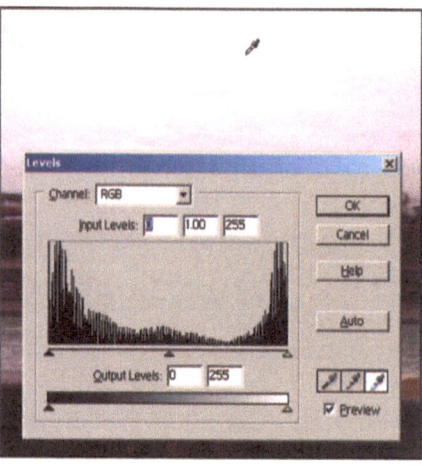

There's still a red cast to this image; for more precision you can define a gray point with the **Set Gray Point**

button (In this case the woman's shirt). Here is the result.

Although, there are further improvements you'd probably want to make to this picture, like sharpening the focus, the major problems with the color cast have been addressed. Areas that should be white are white, and areas that should be black are black. Use Levels when you have more complex toning/color correction jobs. With Levels you get a lot more precision and control.

17. Adjusting Levels "Set White" and "Set Black" points

You'll want to avoid pure whites and blacks in your tonal restoration because they will not look right come printing time. If you double-click on the **Set White Point** or **Set Black Point** button in the Levels dialog box, a Color Picker dialog box comes up. This lets you tell Elements how white the lightest highlight should be. Setting the **B** field to 95% white will ensure that you won't get pure whites in your image or final prints.

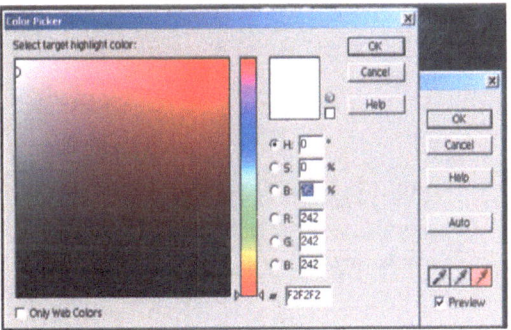

Additionally, double-clicking the **Set Black Point** button and setting the **B** field to 5% will ensure you avoid pure blacks.

This is a good technique that will help ensure you will have a lot of highlight and shadow detail. The difference between using this technique and not using it is illustrated below left:

It's very subtle on screen, but can be very noticeable in print. The image below shows a close-up of the difference in shadow detail.

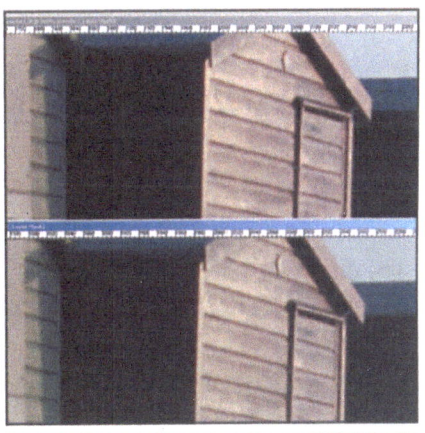

18. Noise Removal

If you have an image with a lot of static and grain (commonly called "noise"), it will most likely distract the viewer from the subject. A few passes of the Smart Blur filter can diminish the noise and result in a smoother looking image. We are blurring (and to an extent degrading) the image, in order to reduce this noise.

You can access the filter from the **Filter > Blur > Smart Blur** menu.

In this example of a "noisy" image, the image on the left is the original (A). The middle is the result of running the Smart Blur (default settings) filter once (B). The right image is the result of running the same filter twice (C).

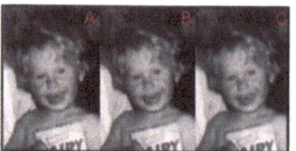

The effect is subtle, but noticeable. A similar effect can be achieved with the Median filter on default settings.

Once you have run the Smart Blur filter, you may notice that some areas still have sharp edges. Rather than keep running Smart Blur and unnecessarily blurring the areas that look fine, you can use the Unsharp Mask filter. This filter can be found via **Filter > Sharpen > Unsharp Mask**. A pass of this filter with the default settings should cure the problem.

19. Fixing Tears and Blemishes

Age affects us all! Unfortunately, with this image, time and handling has brought creases, bends, tears, stains, and fading.

We can't reproduce the information in the top right corner (unless we have the other piece) so we might as well crop it out. Refer to "Resizing Your Document" below for information on cropping your image appropriately.

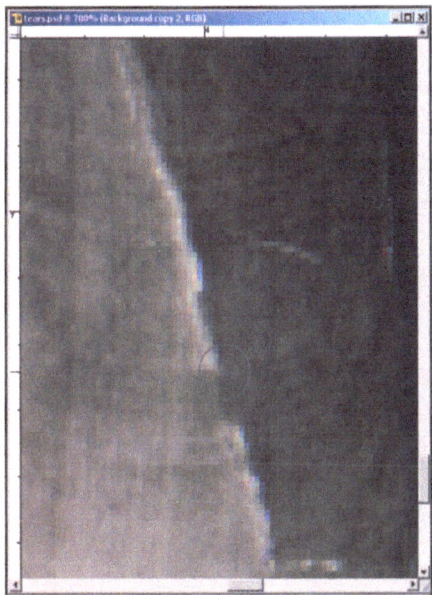

You can start removing all the tears, stains, bends, and scratches with one tool, the Clone Stamp Tool. Remember to sample lots, and use the Aligned option appropriately.

In tough areas like checkered pants, you'll need to zoom in very closely and use a smaller and harder brush to maintain the pattern. The image below is the result of about 30 minutes of touching up with the Clone Stamp Tool. I've also added some minor color correction.

Secondary Restoration

Secondary restoration is concerned with all of the smaller restoration problems you will find in images. Specific areas of an image that need restoration should be handled once all the big problems have been taken care of. Experience shows that you'll spend less time and get a better result because all of your minor restorations could be in vain if you make larger alterations later on. Some secondary restoration processes include toning specific areas, and blurring parts of an image.

20. Focus Adjustments with the Blur Filter

You can adjust the focus in your image with the help of the Blur filters. This is good for blurring selected areas that don't need a gradation in blurring. You can use the Selection Brush to separate the foreground and background elements of an image easily (See Chapter 2 for information on the Selection Tools).

With this image, the background is in focus too much and therefore fighting for attention. Start selecting the background elements by using very large brushes, and then gradually decrease your brush size as you get closer and closer to the contour of the foreground elements. Once they are "separated" with a selection, you can use the Blur filters to adjust the focus (**Filter > Gaussian Blur**).

Feather the selection a few pixels via **Select > Feather** before you use the Blur filter in order to blend everything together better.

Here we have the before (left), and after (right) example. Use filters to adjust focus when you have large areas to deal with, such as the background in this picture. Smaller focus adjustments should be left for the Blur and Sharpen Tools which we will look at shortly.

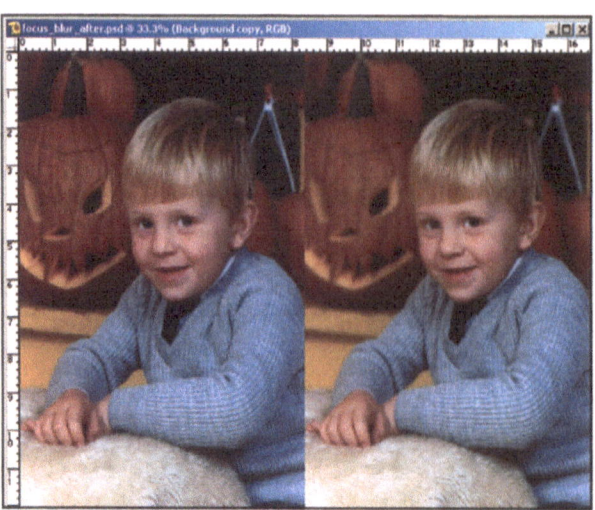

21. Toning adjustments with the Dodge and Burn Tools

These tools should be used for small toning touch-ups; full-fledged toning corrections can be handled with Levels. The toning tools are situated beside each other at the bottom of the toolbar; they are the Dodge and Burn Tools and share identical tool bar options:

Use the settings in this toolbar to enhance your efficiency with these tools. From left to right, they are:

Edit Brush – Change your current brush to change the effect of your painting.

Size – Change the size of your brush to affect a larger diameter when painting.

Range – Use Midtones to affect the middle range of grays in your image (usually your best option in most cases), use Shadows to change the dark areas of your image, and Highlights to change the light areas of your image.

Exposure – How strong the effect will be when painting. Think of it as the Dodge and Burn Tools' exclusive opacity setting. A lower setting is ideal for blending everything together. The lower the setting, the more you'll have to paint to see the result, but you'll also have more control in blending everything in.

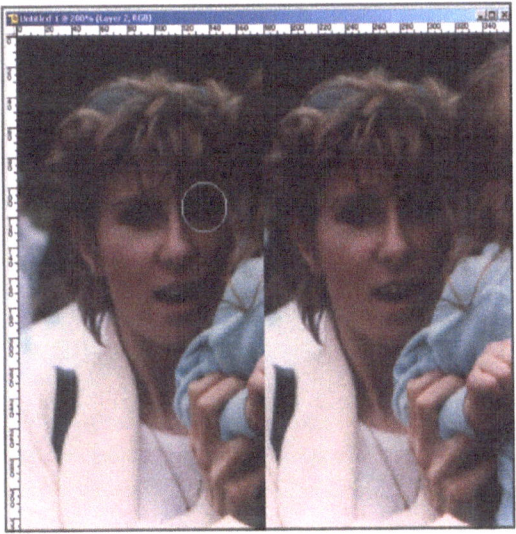

You can use the **Dodge Tool** to bring out the shadow details by lightening any area you paint:

Additionally, you can use the **Burn Tool** to bring out the highlight detail by darkening any area you paint:

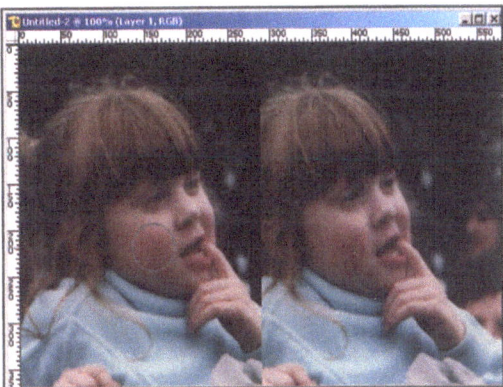

22. Focus adjustments with the Blur and Sharpen Tools

The Blur and Sharpen Tools can be used when you don't have larger focus adjustments to make. Blurring parts of an image adds character and definition in some pictures. Blurring is not always a bad thing as it creates the illusion of depth and therefore adds a third dimension. These tools can save you time, as you won't need to make complex selections before you use them, you can just use them on the fly. They can be found beside each other in the third section of the toolbar:

They operate exactly like Brush Tools in that:

- The larger the brush, the larger the area you will blur/sharpen.
- The more you paint over an area, the more it will be blurred or sharpened.

Additionally they have a **Strength** field that you can adjust accordingly - think of it like the opacity of the brush. This image illustrates blurring the contour of the bird with the Blur Tool. This is good for blending in any focus adjustments.

Retouching

Once you have done all the restoration work, you can begin to retouch your work. Retouching involves improving the image by adding or removing elements. For example, removing blemishes and editing facial features is considered retouching work. It is recommended that you perform this sort of work once the image has been cleaned of all color corrections, tonal adjustments, and focus adjustments.

23. Clone Stamp tips

When using the Clone Stamp Tool for restoration work, make sure you:

1. Duplicate your original document, or copy it to another layer. You can easily fill up the History palette with the Clone Stamp Tool (when you're making multiple small corrections) and you'll want to preserve your original.

2. Learn when to use the Aligned option. This option is explained in Chapter 1, so feel free to review if you need a refresher.

3. Continuously sample (**Alt + Click**). Restoration work usually gets printed, so the detail needs to be top notch. You'll need to constantly sample from the closest possible point from the area you wish to stamp as illustrated:

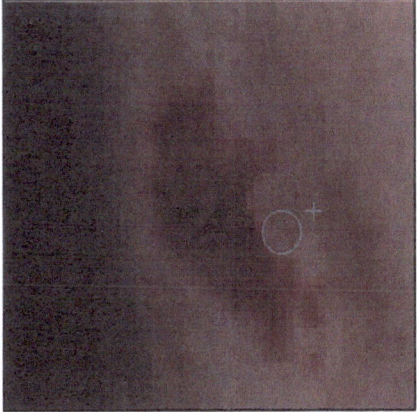

4. Zoom in and use brush sizes and softness effectively. Clone Stamping around highly detailed areas requires lots of precision, and lots of patience. For example, use smaller brushes when you get to the pixel level to increase your level of precision.

5. Using lower opacity settings mean you need to spend a lot more time retouching, but it's worth it as it gives much greater precision and control.

24. Effective image correction with the Clone Stamp

The Clone Stamp Tool is used a lot in the restoration process, so you should get very familiar with it if you plan to do image correction work. The reason it is so popular is because it's so effective, and yet so easy to use.

Removing the red mark on the baby's head is easy with the Clone Stamp Tool.

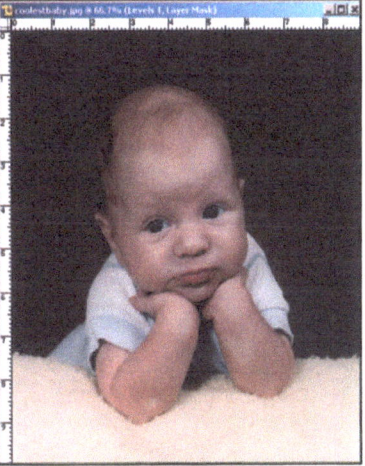

Zoom right into the problem area. If the problem area is small and detailed, use small brushes. Sample the skin surrounding the mark and proceed to stamp over it. Change to a harder brush and continue to sample and stamp if you get a mucky blurred look. To blend it all together nicely, select a large hard brush with very low opacity (10%). Sample from a wider range (from other areas of the head not immediately surrounding the previous red mark), and proceed to stamp over the problem area. This technique blends it all in better. Zoom out, and it's gone!

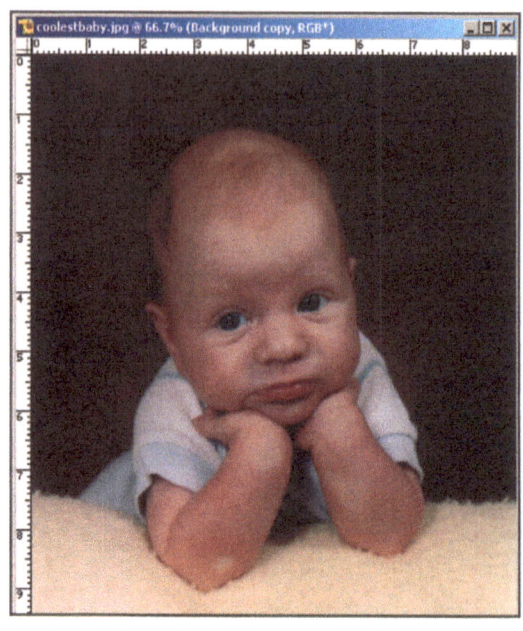

25. Resizing your Document

Image > Resize > Image lets you change the size of your document. Resizing will scale all the contents of the current document up or down.

It is recommended that you don't resize your image upwards too much or you will get blurry results. This is because Elements will resample the document information to try and create new image information. Below is an example of the dithering that occurs when scaling an image up to five times its original size.

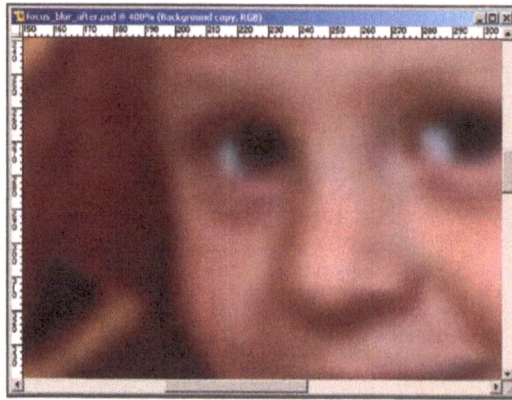

Use the **Constrain Proportions** checkbox to make sure your image maintains the same aspect ratio.

26. Resizing Your Canvas

Resizing your canvas won't have an effect on any of the document's contents; it will simply add more canvas (document space) for you to work with (maybe you want to add a frame around the image). You can specify document or canvas size in point systems from pixels to inches to picas.

You can define which way you want to "extend" your canvas using the arrow in the dialog box:

My current image width is 500 pixels. I've clicked the left middle anchor so that 500 pixels will be added to the right side of my document. Use the Relative setting to ensure that the documents aspect ratio is constant. This allows you to enter only one value (Width or Height).

Resizing your canvas is very handy when it comes to adding border artwork to your images.

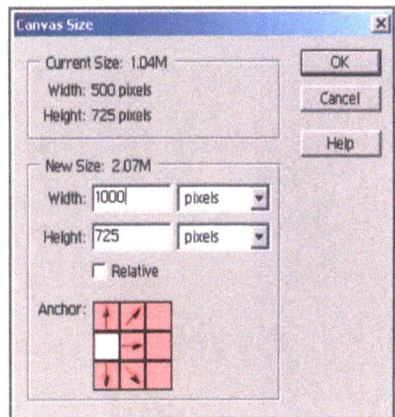

27. Cropping for Composition

Cropping an image resizes the image based on a selection. An important step in retouching your images is cropping them to create a nice composition. The pumpkin in this picture is distracting attention from the boy. If we create a tight crop, we will give the spotlight back to our subject.

Make your selection with any selection tool (the Rectangular Marquee Tool will do the job nicely here); this should be the part of the image that you want to keep.

Choose **Image > Crop**. Your image will be resized to the defined selection.

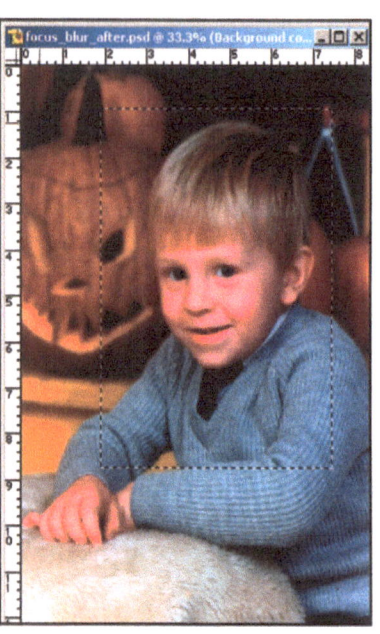

As you can see, cropping is great for creating close-up portraits. It is important to remember that you should duplicate your documents via **Image > Duplicate** before you do any cropping. Cropping is permanent, so you'll want to preserve your originals.

28. Straightening and Narrowing Noses

If you are not happy with a facial feature, you can always retouch it. In this case it will be the nose. This effect can be achieved with the help of the Liquify filter, accessible from **Filter > Distort > Liquify**.

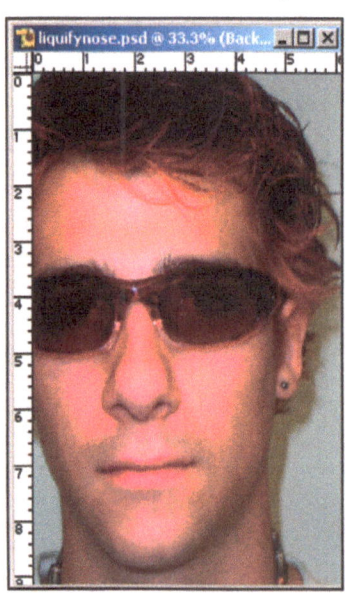

To narrow and straighten noses, use the **Pucker Tool**. Use a medium sized brush, relatively the same size as a nostril. Start on the one side and proceed to click and release, making your way slowly down the contour of the nose towards the nostrils. Do the same to the other side. Continue this until you get the shape you like. With a lot of clicking and patience you can achieve a good result.

Image courtesy of Humza Ijaz. (http://www.koolflasher.com)

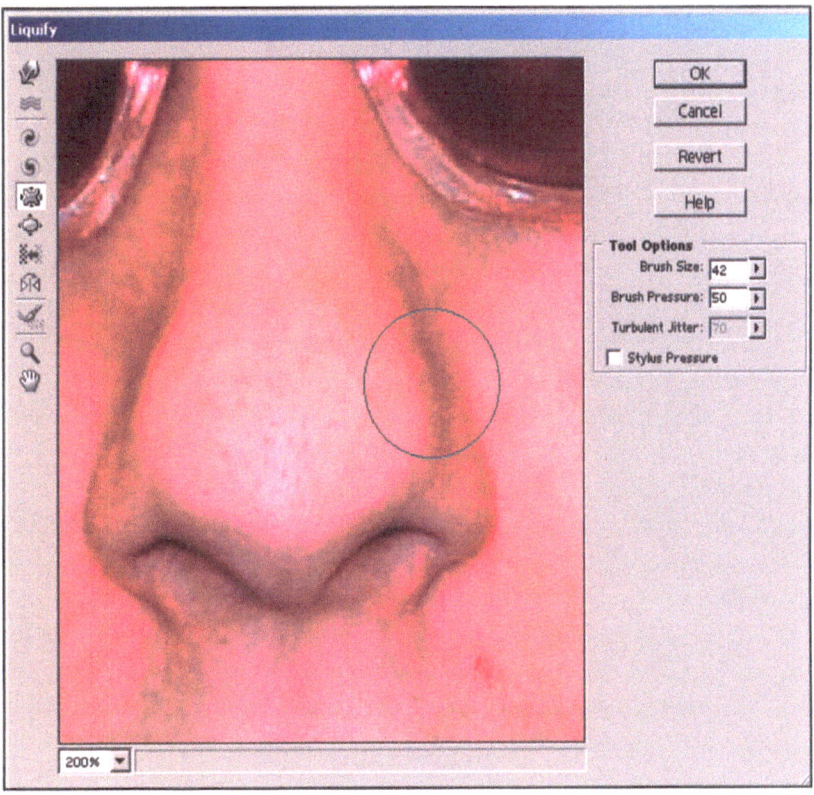

Once you have the shape you like, you could easily have an unrealistic looking nose. At this point you should use the **Bloat Tool** to puff the shape back into it a bit. If you make a mistake, you can use **Ctrl+Z** to undo it, but you can only undo the last one you made. For undo steps further back use **Ctrl+Alt+Z**. To undo all changes you've made, use the **Revert** button. Here is the improved nose:

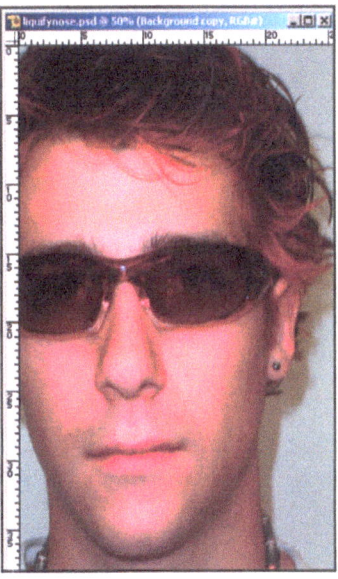

Useful and Complex Filters

1. Gaussian Blur
2. Liquify filter
3. Add Noise filter
4. 3D Transform filter
5. Unsharp Mask filter
6. Maximum and Minimum filters

Simple Effects

7. Color focus with Desaturation
8. Color focus with Monotones
9. Composite man using Selection tools and many layers
10. When to use Lighting Effects
11. Using Bump Maps with Lighting Effects
12. Photos to watercolor with filters
13. Photos to colored pencil with filters
14. Photos to HB pencil with filters

Multi-step Effects

15. Adding romance with blurs, levels and blending modes
16. Create a Private Universe using Threshold and filters
17. Transforming landscapes into faces with Liquify filter
18. Adding action with Radial blur
19. Putting your art onto canvas
20. Flowing, organic animated images with Twirl and Save for Web
21. Message on a bottle with 3D Transform
22. Depth effects using Minimum, Gaussian Blur and Emboss filters

Effects and Filters

Useful and Complex Filters

Elements ships with well over 100 plug ins, most of which can be found under the Filters menu and are therefore referred to as 'filters'. Many are self-explanatory and listing them all would be of little use, so instead we'll focus on the more complex and lesser known but very useful ones. To provide a common point of reference, the same image is used in all filters in this section – an image of four kookaburras on our bush clothes line.

For more information about plug-ins see Appendix B

1. Gaussian Blur

Filter > Blur > Gaussian Blur

The Gaussian Blur is Elements' workhorse when it comes to applying a blur to your images. Gaussian refers to the bell-shaped curve that Elements generates when it applies a weighted average to the blurred pixels. The Gaussian Blur has one setting – Radius, which determines how far the filter will look for dissimilar pixels to blur.

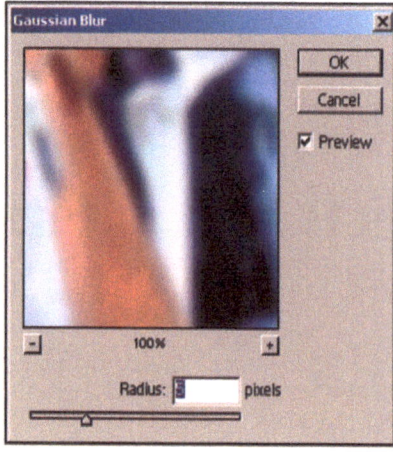

Click in the Preview area of a filter to make a before/after filter comparison (many but not all filters have this option).

2. Liquify

Filter > Distort > Liquify

Liquify is Elements' most substantial filter, as well as the most fun. It lets you apply elastic or melted effects to your images. Liquify includes its own set of tools complete with keyboard shortcuts as well as brush size and pressure options for each tool.

Warp (W)	Pushes pixels forward as you drag
Turbulence (A)	Smoothly scrambles pixels. Has additional Jitter option – the higher the value the smoother the scrambling
Twirl Clockwise (R)	Rotates pixels clockwise as mouse is held down
Twirl Counter Clockwise (L)	Rotates pixels counter – clockwise as mouse is held down
Pucker (P)	Moves pixels towards the center of the brush as mouse is held down
Bloat (B)	Pushes pixels away from the center of the brush as mouse is held down
Shift (S)	Move pixels perpendicularly to the stroke direction

Reflection (M)	Copy pixels to the brush area. ALT+click to create reflection opposite to the direction of the drag.
Reconstruct (E)	Restores distorted areas as mouse is held down
Zoom (Z)	As per Zoom in Elements
Hand (H)	As per Hand in Elements

3. Add Noise

Filter > Noise > Add Noise
A surprisingly useful, multi-purpose tool! Noise can give a more realistic look to heavily retouched areas, is an essential ingredient in most textures and can be used to reduce banding. Add Noise options include:

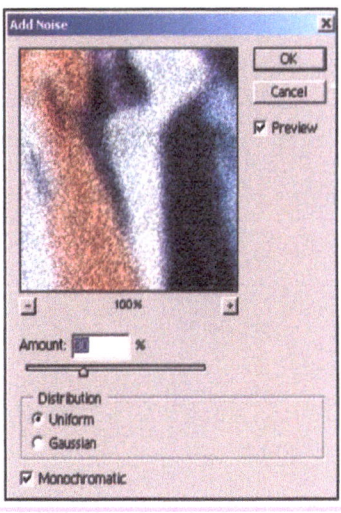

- Amount
- Distribution – Uniform creates a subtle spread of noise, Gaussian a more speckled effect.
- Monochromatic – when enabled applies noise to an image using existing tones in the image.

4. 3D Transform

Filter > Render > 3D Transform

3D Transform is a tool that will let you transform your two – dimensional designs into three – dimensional objects such as cubes, spheres and cylinders. Like the Liquify tool, 3D Transform comes complete with its own set of tools and shortcuts.

Selection (V)	Select and move entire wireframe
Direct Selection (A)	Move an anchor point
Cube(M)	Map image to cubic surface
Sphere (N)	Map image to spherical surface
Cylinder (C)	Map image to cylindrical surface
Convert Anchor Point	Change anchor point from a smooth one to a corner and vice versa
Add Anchor point (+)	Add anchor point
Delete Anchor point (-)	Delete anchor point
Pan Camera (E)	Move object
Trackball (R)	Rotate object
Zoom (Z)	As in Elements
Hand (H)	As in Elements

Anchor points must be added to the right side of the wireframe. The wireframe will turn red if you construct an impossible shape! 3D Transform options include quality settings and the ability to display or hide the background in the preview and rendered image.

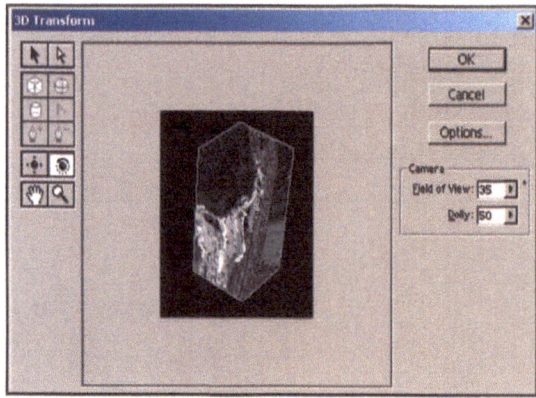

5. Unsharp Mask
Filter > Sharpen > Unsharp Mask

With an unlikely name referring to traditional film sharpening techniques, the Unsharp Mask is the tool of choice when it comes to sharpening your images. It works by locating pixels that differ from surrounding pixels by the threshold value you choose and increases the pixels' contrast by the amount you select, making the image look sharper.

There are many ways to operate the Unsharp Mask. Elements' Help files recommend using one of the following as a starting point:

- Set the Amount to 150-200%. Amount determines the increase in contrast to be applied to pixels.
- Set a Radius of 1-2 pixels. Radius determines the number of pixels (out from each pixel) to sharpen around edges.
- Experiment with a Threshold setting of 2-20. Threshold determines how different pixels must be from their surrounding area before they are seen as edge pixels and sharpened.

There are no hard and fast rules for using this filter, but these three tips hold true for all images:

1. Sharpening your image is best left to last, after all color and image corrections have been completed.
2. Excessive sharpening introduces noise and artefacts into your image.
3. Sharpening is much less noticeable in print compared to on screen.

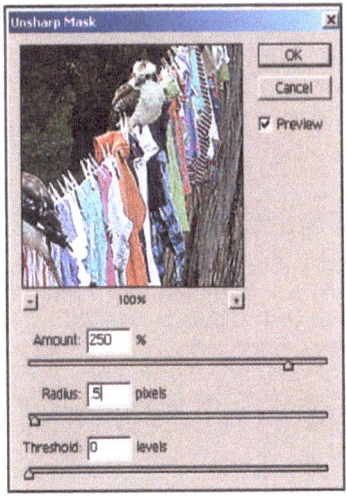

6. Minimum and Maximum

Filter > Other > Minimum/Maximum

Tucked away under the 'Other' menu it's easy to forget about Minimum and Maximum, but they are key filters when it comes to creating thick and thin masks used in the construction of many cool effects! The Minimum filter applies a spread – spreading out black areas and choking white areas. The Maximum filter applies a choke – choking black areas and spreading white. Both only have one setting – Radius. You can see this filter in action in the final tip of this chapter.

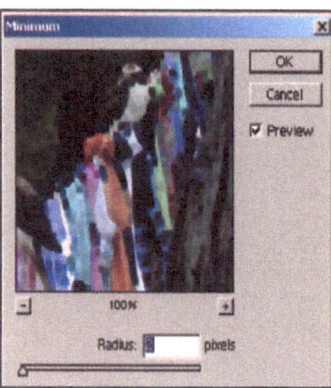 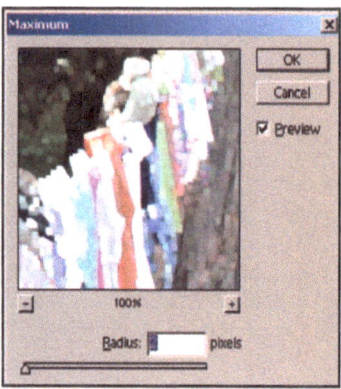

Simple Effects

Not too complicated, simple but effective.

7. Color Focus with Desaturation

If you want to draw complete attention to a certain part of an image, you can use the color focus effect. Add a **Hue/Saturation** adjustment layer to your image via **Layer > New Adjustment Layer > Hue/Saturation**. Drag the Saturation slider all the way to the left (-100), and press OK. Now simply select the layer mask (white rectangle on the right of the layer in the palette), and paint over the area you want in focus.

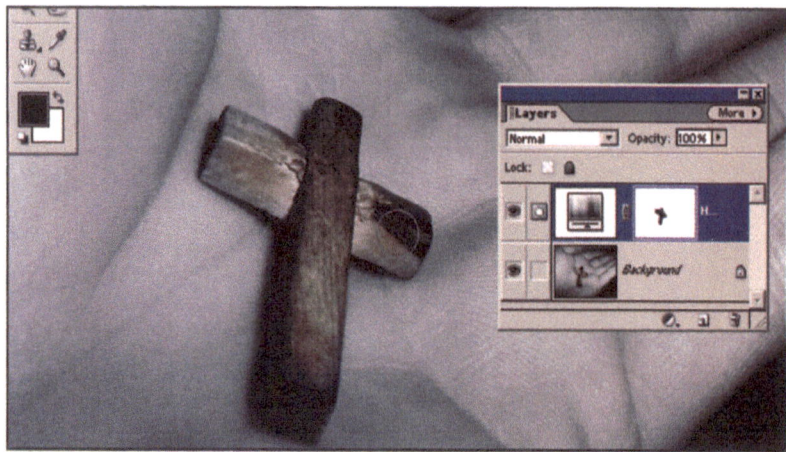

Notice how your eye is immediately drawn to the cross in the image below?

"Finding Me", courtesy of Jason Morrison (http://www.dubtastic.com)

8. Color Focus with Monotones

If you have a busy grayscale image, and you want the viewer to be drawn to a certain part of it, you can use a monotone effect. Add a **Hue/Saturation** adjustment layer via **Layer > New Adjustment Layer > Hue/Saturation**. Check the Colorize option, and press OK. You can use the Hue slider to change the color of the monotone effect. Now simply select the layer mask, and paint over the areas you don't want in focus.

You might have already seen this effect used in clothing ads in magazines, or lipstick commercials on television, it's quite popular.

9. Composite man using Selection tools and many layers

Do your partners, children or friends ever suggest you need a new look? Mine do. Grow your hair long, wear glasses, stop drinking so much coffee – if all their wishes could be combined into one composite man... what a scary thought!

Creating composite images in Elements is a snap and great fun! It's more about having the inspiration, individual parts and the patience than anything else. I'm going to create a composite man from the following pieces:

- wife's hair
- mother-in-law's eyes
- daughter's mouth before she had teeth
- my head as the glue to hold them all together!
- my front teeth!

To begin, I've dragged all the individual photos for the composite man, putting each one onto their own layer in the same PSD file.

> *When selecting images for a composite project, try and select images that have similar qualities – with similar lighting i.e. light falling at roughly the same angle, similar color balance and density. This will make the photos much easier to blend together, and a more photo-realistic result.*

The main challenge associated with creating composites is cleanly removing the background, on not one but numerous images. In Elements you have the following primary tool choices related to that process:

- Marquee Tools
- Lasso Tools
- Magic Wand
- Selection Brush
- Eraser Tools

Each tool has its own merits, and everyone has their own way of working. It's beyond the scope of this tip to explore each tool in detail (see chapter 1) – give each task your best shot, and always push yourself to try new ways of doing things - new tools - when making selections.

The image at the bottom of the stack is my wife, Selena. I've chosen to keep the bulk of the background, trimming it down to a circle using the Elliptical Marquee Tool.

I need to remove the background of the Pete image so my head is floating on the layer! Luckily the green background is very different to my face, so Elements' Background Eraser Tool should do the job nicely.

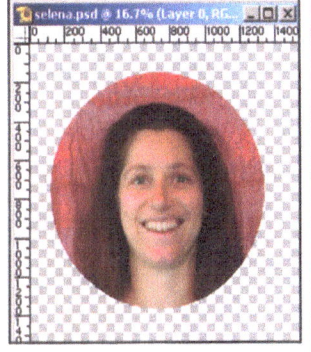

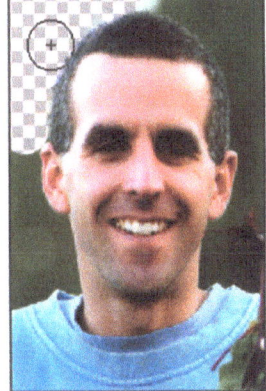

Time to fit the wig! I've grouped the Pete layer to Selena's layer by using **Layer > Group with Previous (Ctrl+G)**, and using the **Free Transform (Ctrl+T)** Tool sized my head to fit neatly over the top of hers.

And so the process of building a composite image continues – removing the background of each layer, sizing and rotating to fit using the Free Transform Tool, then zooming in and cleaning up with a soft-brushed fine eraser.

For maximum flexibility, keep each element of your composite on its own layer, as shown. Be sure to save the layered version of your composite, so you can alter it at a later date.

How the Layers palette looks when the composition is finished:

Composite man is in the building!

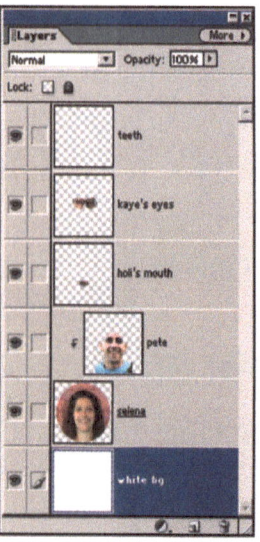

10. When to use Lighting Effects

The Lighting Effects (**Filter > Render > Lighting Effects**) filter can only be applied to layers with pixels. So for example, you cannot use Lighting Effects to tint a layer, leave that to adjustment layers. Lighting Effects is typically used on interfaces, text, and sometimes on logos.

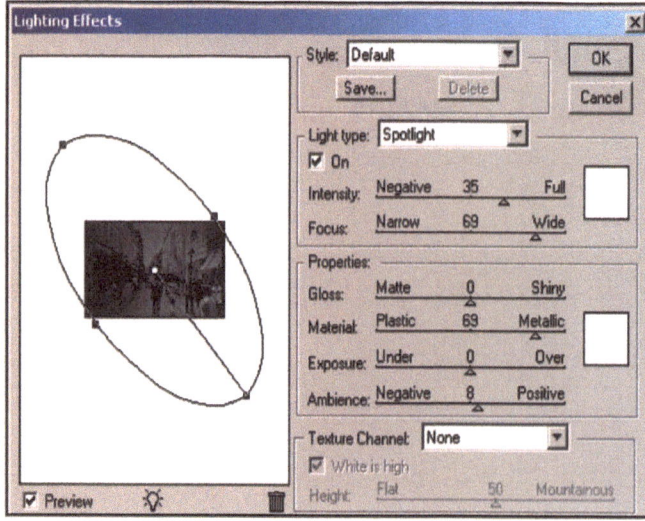

I wouldn't recommend using it on images, as there are alternatives (such as Brightness/Contrast and Levels) better suited for that. As you can see in the screenshot above, the Properties area contains a variety of settings making it possible to create a variety of unique text effects (Metallic, Plastic, etc).

11. Using Bump Maps with Lighting Effects

The Lighting Effects filter lets you load grayscale texture maps to further enhance the realism of your project. With texture maps:

- White represents high points, like the top of a mountain.
- Grays represent in-between points, the gradual blend from very light gray (top of the mountain) to very dark gray (bottom of mountain).
- Black represents low points, like a valley. There will be a complete absence of the texture where black is defined.

So if you want to create a bumpy effect across an image, you can use a large soft brush and paint on a new layer like this:

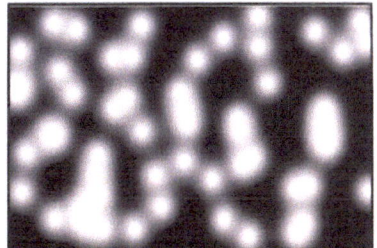

Then you can use the layer's transparency as a texture map from the **Lighting Effects** dialog box.

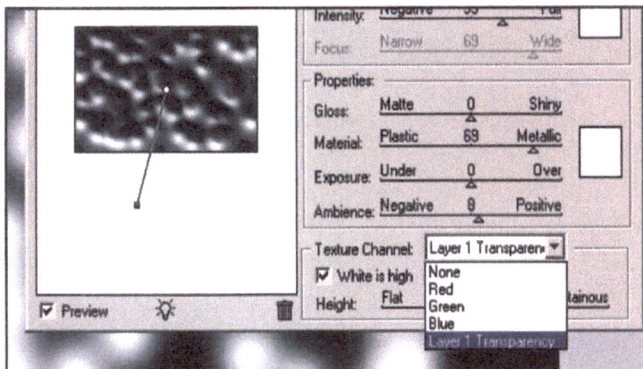

Complex textures can be created with this useful feature, so if texturing is your bag I suggest you familiarize yourself with this feature. **Texture Channels** played a big part in the creation of this goopy text effect:

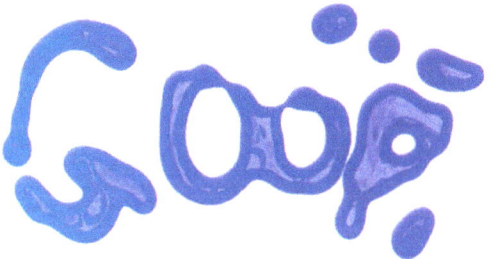

12. Photos to Watercolor with Filters

Using a combination of the Artistic and Distort filters you can turn photographs into most forms of paintings from watercolors to oil on canvas. There's even a Watercolor filter to make it that much easier.

The trick is to really look at what makes up each different style painting and use that to logically select the right filters. For example, I want to turn the image above into a watercolor painting. This would require a loss of detail, and randomness needs to be applied:

- **Filter > Distort > Wave** filter to give it some randomness.
- **Filter > Artistic > Paint Daubs** filter to give it that painted look.
- **Filter > Distort > Glass** filter to give it some more randomness.
- **Filter > Artistic > Watercolor** filter to give it the Watercolor look.

Play around with the settings to your liking, it's all about experimentation. Here's my result:

13. Photos to Colored Pencil with Filters

Using a combination of Artistic filters, you can turn an ordinary photo into a colored pencil masterpiece.

The trick is to get the pencil stroke texture right. Elements does have a Colored Pencil filter, but we'll need more than that to pull it off.

Also, colored pencils don't have as wide a range of color as digital photos do, so a Posterize adjustment layer will need to be applied along with a bit of desaturation. Experiment with the process outlined below:

- **Filter > Artistic > Paint Daubs** filter to give it a rough, textured look.
- **Filter > Artistic > Rough Pastels** filter to give it the stroked pencil texture.
- Duplicate the layer and apply the **Filter > Artistic > Colored Pencil** filter to further fine-tune the pencil effect. Set the blending mode to Overlay and opacity to 80%.
- Add a **Hue/Saturation** adjustment layer and decrease the saturation to increase the realism.
- Add a Posterize adjustment layer and set it to 15 levels to decrease the amount of tones and further increase the realism.

Altering the settings above may give you an effect you prefer. The end product will also vary depending on the type of image you start with. Here's my result:

14. Photos to HB Pencil with Filters

If you want to create an HB drawing from a photo, the process is very similar to that of colored pencils. I suggest you run through the previous tip and make the following adjustments:

- Delete the Posterize adjustment layer.
- **Enhance > Adjust Color > Hue/Saturation (Ctrl+U)** settings and decrease the saturation to –100 (you may choose to leave just a little color).
- **Filter > Blur > Blur** to soften the image a bit.

Your result should look similar to this:

Multi-step Effects

As there are many steps in these effects, I've numbered them to help you follow more easily.

15. Adding romance with blurs, levels and blending modes

Before

After

Have you ever taken a photo that didn't quite capture the mood of the subject? Or maybe you'd like to 'dress up' photos to give them a sense of dreamy timelessness? Romantics at heart, don't despair! Elements' Gaussian Blur, Adjustment Layers and Blending Modes to the rescue.

1. Begin with a black and white photo. I'm using a photo of Wallace's Hut taken in the high country of Victoria, Australia.

> *You can also begin with a color photo and convert it to a black and white image by selecting:*
>
> - ■ *Enhance > Adjust Color > Hue and Saturation (Ctrl+U) and dragging the Saturation slider all the way to the left.*
> - ■ *Enhance > Adjust Color > Remove Color (Shift+Ctrl+U)*

2. Duplicate the Background layer and name it. I've called mine Dream.

> *A quick way to duplicate a layer and name it at the same time is to **Alt**+drag it to the New Layer icon at the base of the Layers palette or to right - click on the layer and choose 'Duplicate Layer'.*

3. With the Dream layer active, open **Levels** (**Ctrl+L**). In the Levels dialog box drag the black, white and mid tone input sliders close together to remove the mid tones from the image, leaving only black and white.

> *Image > Adjustments > Threshold could also be used to create a similar effect.*

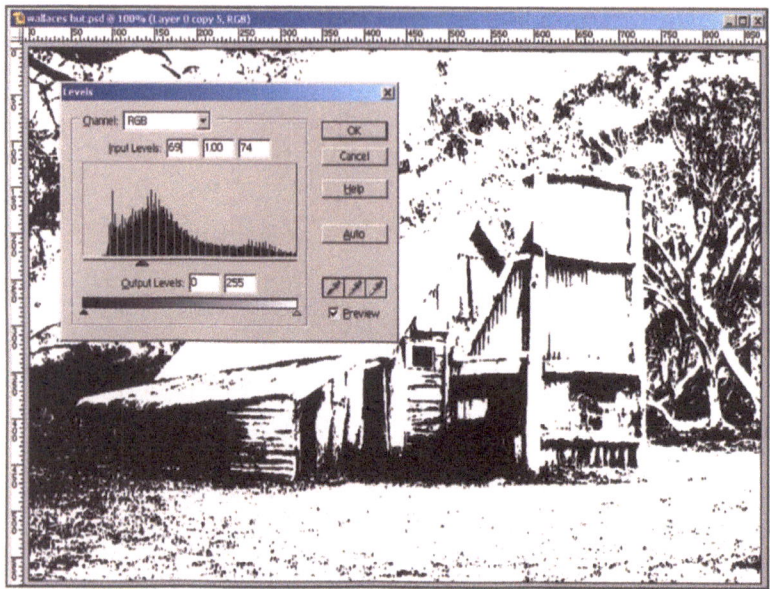

4. With the Dream layer active, select **Filter > Blur > Gaussian Blur**. Apply a significant amount of blur, such that you can no longer see details but can still identify larger shapes in the image. I've chosen a value of 10, your value will depend on the resolution of your image.

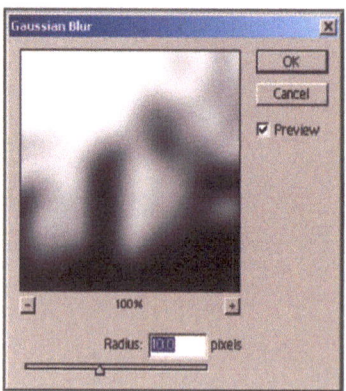

5. We need to blend the highlights and shadows of the blurred Dream layer and the original image – the answer is in layer blending modes. Try different blending modes for the Dream layer. I've chosen Hard Light, great for creating a harsh see-through lighting effect!

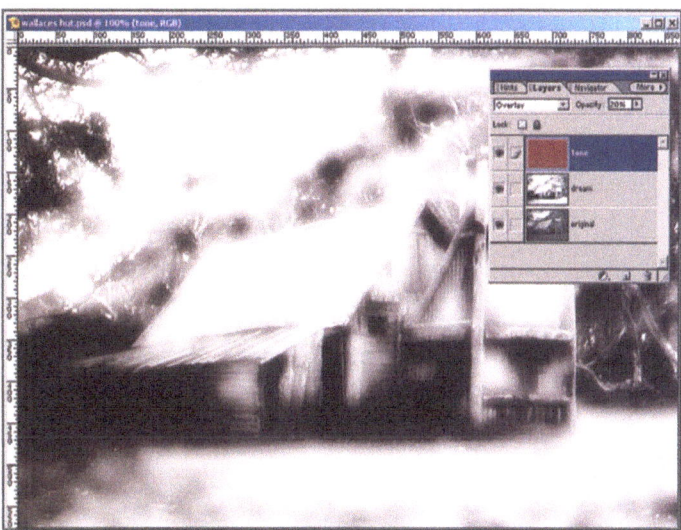

6. It's starting to look dreamy, time to add the tone!

Create a new layer, placed at the top of the layer stack and name it Tone.

> *To name and create a new layer in one hit,* **Alt+Click** *on the New Layer icon.*

7. Fill the Tone layer with the color that will form the basis of your toning, a stronger color often works best. I've chosen a strong orange/brown (R: 154, G: 64, B: 15).

8. We need to let the color of our Tone layer lay over the images below, again the answer is in the layer blending modes. Experiment with different layer blending modes for the Tone layer. I've chosen Overlay.

9. Reduce the opacity of the Tone layer to lessen the toning effect, stop when it looks good to you. I've set mine to 20%.

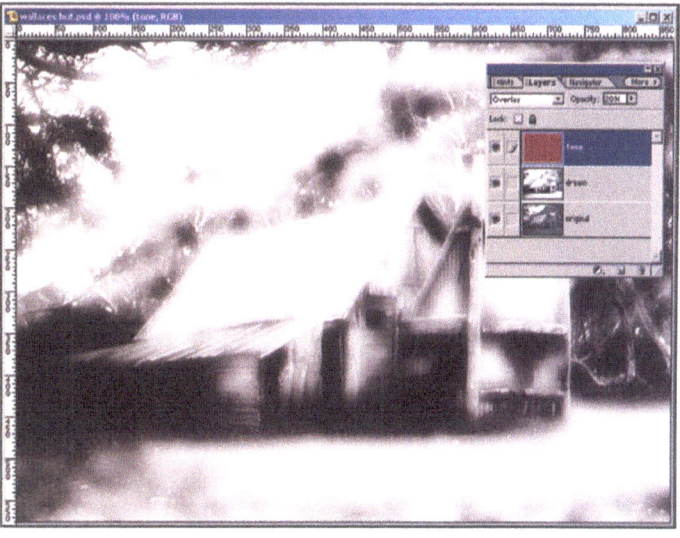

Your very own toned dreamscape!

16. Create a Private Universe using Threshold and filters

Wouldn't it be great if you could add stars to the night skies in your photos? But why stop there – why not include a galaxy or two and create your own private universe? No spaceship? No problem – we'll create it all from scratch in Elements.

1. Create a new RGB file. I've create a 600 x 400 pixel RGB file with a resolution of 72 pixels/inch, suitable for use online.

2. With Foreground and Background colors set to the default of white and black (keyboard shortcut **D** will do this for you) fill the background with black using the keyboard shortcut. **Alt+Backspace**.

    We have our black sky, but how do we add stars? If you've spent too much time in Elements, you might start to see the night sky as a black background that somebody has added noise too, that might even do the trick!

3. Select **Filter > Noise > Add Noise**. Enter a low amount – just enough to cover the background evenly with noise. I've entered 20%. Select Gaussian for Distribution and Monochromatic.

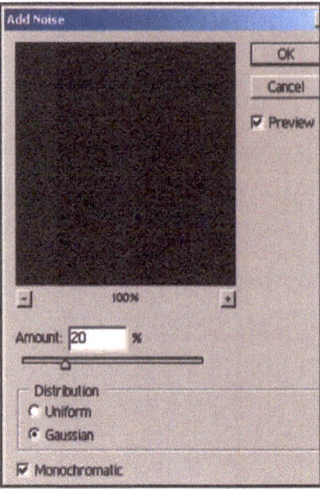

It's a good start, but the stars aren't very convincing...yet!

4. Select **Filter > Blur > Gaussian Blur**. Enter a low Radius value, just enough to blur the noise. I've entered 0.5 pixels.

5. Select **Image > Adjustments > Threshold**. Drag the Threshold slider to the left, the stars begin to appear! Stop when you are satisfied with the number of stars. I've set mine to 67.

> *The Threshold command converts color or grayscale images to high contrast black and white images. Pixels lighter than the Threshold value are converted to white, pixels darker to black.*

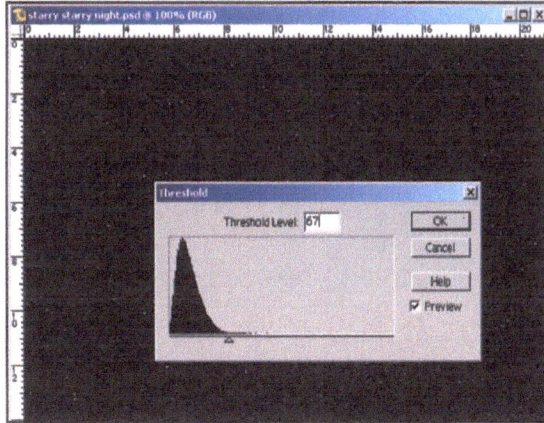

We need a fiery sun!

6. Select **Filter > Render > Lens Flare**. Click in the preview to position the Flare Center. Set Brightness and Lens Type as desired. My Brightness is set to ~160%, using the 50-300mm Lens type.

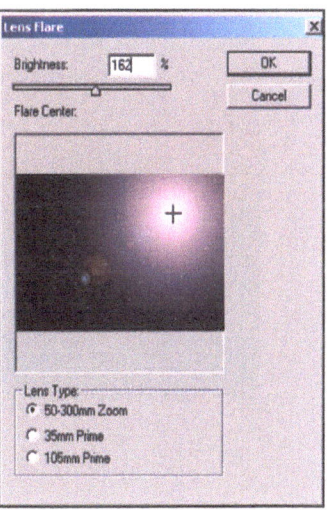

And finish off with a galaxy.

7.   Make a new layer. I've named mine Galaxy

8.   With the Galaxy layer active, select **Filter > Render > Clouds**.

9.   Change the blending mode of the Galaxy layer to Overlay. If needed, refine the effect by reducing the opacity of the Galaxy layer.

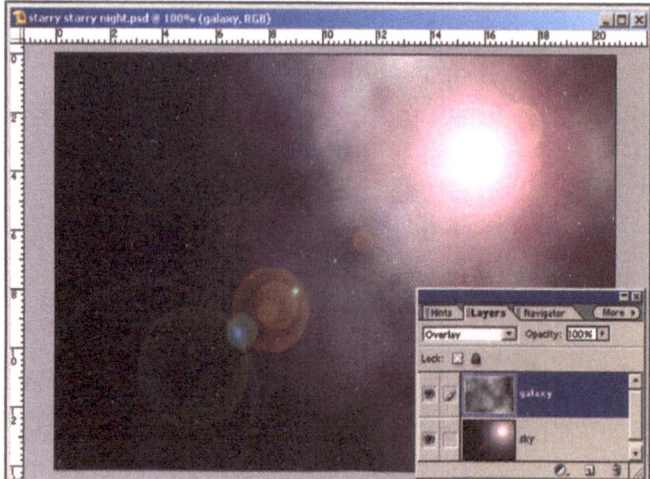

We've created our own private universe, not bad for only a few minutes work – enjoy!

17. Transforming landscapes into faces with Liquify filter

Before

After

Ever noticed human-like shapes in the clouds or landscape? Elements' Liquify filter is the perfect tool for retro-fitting such elements to your photos that will really get people wondering – maybe Lucy was in the sky after all!

I've chosen to work on a photo taken looking through a ridge on Mt Mackay, Australia at the setting sun. There isn't much to suggest a human form at the moment, but aside from that minor detail it has all the makings of a perfect candidate for the Liquify filter! The silhouetted sharp ridge contains no detail, so any distortion of pixel information created by Liquify's tools within the ridge area will be hidden in the black. Similarly the sky immediately above the ridge contains no fine details; nothing significant that will leave tell-tale distortions visible. Perfect – but how do we add the face?

If like me you find this type of manipulation difficult, use an image of the silhouette you're trying to create in your photo as a guide. Don't have one handy? Search for 'silhouette' at http://images.google.com.

Elements' Liquify filter only supports displaying one layer so unfortunately our silhouette image can't be visible at the same time as our landscape within the Liquify filter for us to trace over. But we can have it open in Elements and distort parts of the image; each time we OK a change made with the Liquify tool, we can check back with our guide image. I've dragged the silhouette into my landscape file, and used the Free Transform tool to rotate and resize it to the size and location I'd like to create the face. Lowering the opacity of the silhouette layer means I'll be able to see through it, and use it as a guide to make further alterations with the Liquify filter.

Although there are only three steps listed below, you will probably repeat them many times to create the final effect.

1. With the Landscape layer active, open Elements' Liquify filter (**Filter > Distort > Liquify**).

2. The key is to work slowly and gently! I used the Bloat Tool (**B**) at a large brush size and low pressure to gradually 'grow' the black ridge area into roughly the shape of the person's face.

3. I then used the Warp Tool (**W**) at increasingly smaller brush sizes to add the finer, sharper details.

And the final touch - just extending the nose tip a fraction!

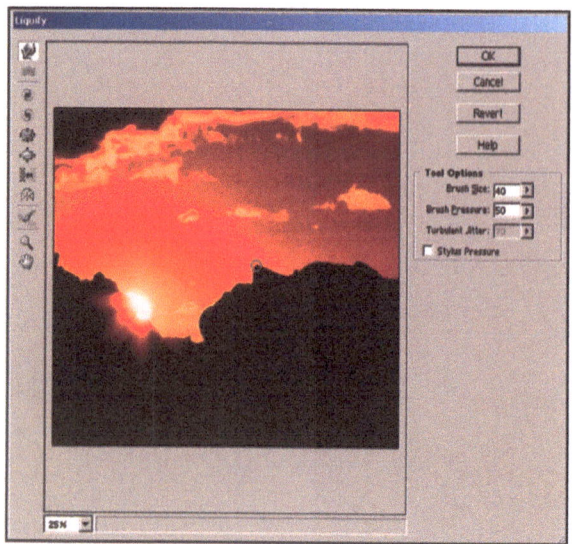

18. Adding action with Radial blur

Have you ever taken a photo that would be great – if only it contained some movement, or even better, some extreme action! Let's explore the use of Elements' Radial Blur filter.

Before

After

I'm using a photo I took of a skier in Falls Creek, Australia. Even though it had the potential to be a great skiing photo it didn't quite work out – the sense of movement and excitement is missing. There's also too much space above and below the skier, and small dust specks on the transparency, too many to clean up... if I could solve all of these problems in a few easy steps that would be great!

1. We're going to apply a filter, but not to the original photo layer as we'll need to preserve that for later use. Duplicate the photo layer. I've named my duplicate Action.

2. With the Action layer active, select **Filter > Blur > Radial Blur**.

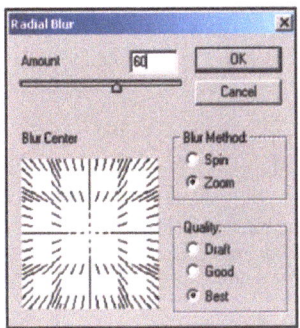

The Radial Blur filter has no preview – this is because there's heavy CPU work involved in creating the effect – so we're flying blind first time around. Because of this, the best approach when experimenting with Radial Blur is to set the Quality to Draft and click OK to apply the filter. Undo the effect and try again – when you're satisfied with the effect, re-open the filter and set Quality to Best and click OK.

After experimenting, I decided to set my amount to 60 and Blur method to Spin. Your setting may vary depending on the resolution of your file and the extent of Radial Blur you'd like to create. For example, a higher resolution file would require a higher value to achieve a similar blurred effect as shown here.

Cool. That's certainly introduced a sense of movement and excitement, plus it's hidden the dust and scratches. Unfortunately though it's destroyed a key element in many photos – a clear point of interest, in this case the person's face. We need to fix that.

3. Make the Background layer active and create an empty adjustment layer, using Levels, Brightness/Contrast or Hue/Saturation – it does-n't matter which, the main thing is we need to create an empty Adjustment layer to use as a Layer Mask. I've created a **Levels Adjustment Layer** and clicked OK in the Levels dialog without making any adjustments.

4. Group the Action layer to the adjustment layer by selecting **Layer > Group with Previous** (**Ctrl+G**).

*You can also group layers by **Alt+Clicking** the line that divides the two lay-ers in the Layers palette. Keep an eye out for the overlapped circles icon that appears!*

5. Set your Foreground and Background colors back to their default colors – white and black. (**D**).

6. Select the Gradient tool (**G**) and Radial Gradient from the Options bar. Select Foreground to Background in the Gradient Picker.

Hanging in there? Great! Here comes the fun part! We're going to apply the Radial Gradient to the empty adjust-ment layer to create what is in effect a Layer Mask – letting us gradually control how much of the layer below is revealed/hidden.

7. With the Radial Gradient tool ready to go and the Adjustment layer active, click and drag out from the center of the skier's face – not too far, we only want to reveal the skier's face. Made a mistake? No problem, keep clicking and dragging the Gradient tool on the adjustment layer until you create an effect you like.

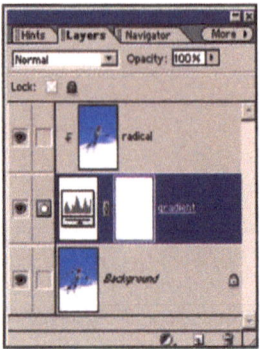

Finally let's fix that space problem – I should have taken the photo horizontally on the day, tight around the skier. A quick crop using the Crop Tool and the job's done:

19. Putting your art onto canvas

Have you ever stopped and admired a painting or print? Maybe it was the use of color, the technique, the mood or the subject that caught your eye... or could it have been the work of an Elements master painter...
If like me, your real - world painting skills are a work in progress, walk this way – with a digital camera and Elements' filters we might be able to give Van Gogh a nudge yet, or at the very least have great fun trying.

Before

After

1. Open a favorite photo that contains an obvious point of inter-est. I've chosen to use a close-up photo of an alpine flower.

At this stage you could select any one of Elements' Artistic, Brush Strokes or Sketch filters and explore the many different effects. Following the 'less is more' mantra, let's use a minimum number of fil-ters to get the job done. Too many filters could leave your image look-ing nothing like the original - though if that's the effect you're look-ing for, go for it!

2. Select **Filter > Blur > Gaussian Blur**. Enter a small Radius value, just enough to blur the sharp details – this should help give our painting a softer, less photographic look later on. I've chosen a value of 2. Your setting may vary depending on the resolution of your file – the higher the resolution of your file, the larger the radius value will need to be to achieve an equivalent effect. Click OK to apply the blur.

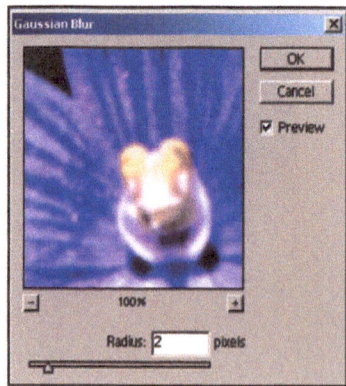

3. Select **Filter > Artistic > Dry Brush**. Settings are very much personal taste – be sure to experiment with different values. I've set the largest brush size possible (10), moderate detail (5) and minimal texture (1). Click OK to apply the Dry Brush when you're satisfied with the preview.

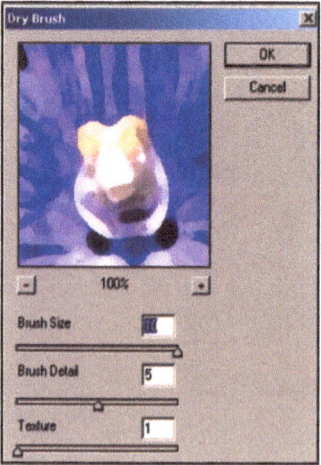

The image is certainly looking less photographic and more like a painting. We'd be able to see the texture of the canvas with a real painting - better fix that.

4. Select **Filter > Texture > Texturizer**. Again this is very much personal preference, and also dependent on the resolution of your file. I've chosen Canvas as my texture, with Scaling set to the maximum, and the light appearing to come from the bottom right. Explore each setting and texture – what looks good to you? Click OK to apply the Texturizer.

Job's done and no messy paint to clean up! Zoom in to appreciate the effect – in a small number of steps we've come a long way from the photograph of the flower.

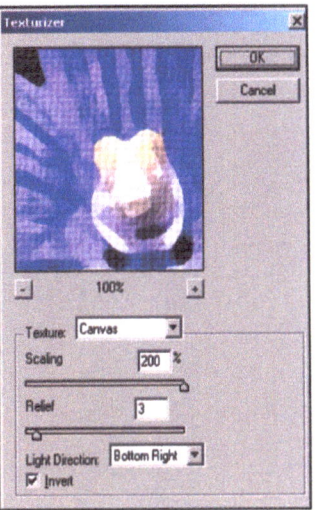

> *If you intend to print your work of art, why not try one of the many watercolor or art papers available for inkjet prints?*

20. Flowing, organic animated images with Twirl and Save for Web

Need a change from working with straight lines and single frame images? Meet Elements' Twirl filter, located in the **Filter > Distort** group – just the tool for creating cyclone animations and more...

Before

After

1. Open the image you wish to apply the Twirl to.

I'm using a 300 x 300 pixel RGB 72 pixels/inch image of a fractal I generated using the excellent Fractal Explorer (available free from http://www.eclectasy.com/Fractal-Explorer). You don't need to use a fractal image – in fact, any image that has more than one color will do.

You can download this Fractal Image at http://www.magicpixel.com.au/fractal/

As beautiful as the fractal is, it's time to twirl it!

2. Select **Filter > Distort > Twirl**. Better results are usually obtained from the Twirl filter by applying several Twirls at smaller angles versus one large pass, the latter resulting in a more dramatic destruction of pixel information. I've set my angle to -125.

Because we're applying the Twirl effect gradually, it's an ideal opportunity to create frames we can use in an animation.

When creating an animation using Save for Web, the contents of each layer become a frame of the animation, with the layer at the bottom of the stack becoming Frame 1.

Wanting to create an animation with Elements whilst using adjustment layers? They will need to be flattened with the appropriate layers below before opening Elements' Save for Web and creating animations.

3. For our cyclone the plan is to run the filter on a layer, duplicate the layer, run the filter on the duplicated layer, and repeat this several times. Each layer will then have an image that is twirled more than the previous layer - the result in our animation will be a twirl that appears to be rotating.

■ Run the Twirl filter on your original image, with a moderate to low Twirl angle. I'm using –125.
■ Create a copy of the layer.
■ **Ctrl+F** to re-run the Twirl filter on the copied layer. This applies the Twirl at the same setting.
■ Create a copy of the top layer
■ **Ctrl+F** to re-run the Twirl filter etc.

Stop when you're feeling dizzy! Your Layers palette should look something like this:

Select **File > Save for Web** (**Alt+Ctrl+Shift+S**).

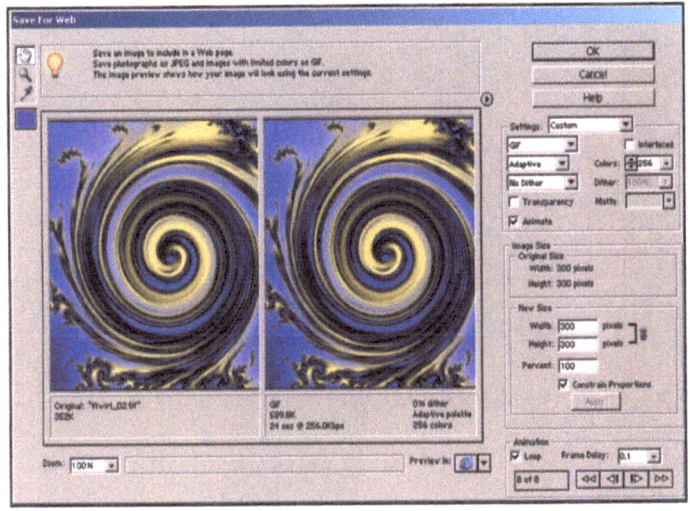

5. Select GIF from the Settings dropdown, and check the animate box.

6. Check Loop if you'd like the animation to play continuously.

7. Set the Frame Delay value. For a fluid animation like this a lower value will result in a smoother animation. I've set mine to 0.1 seconds.

8. Preview your masterpiece by clicking the Internet Explorer icon (or browser of your choice) to the left of the Animation options, and click OK to save.

You can view the finished cyclone animation at: http://www.magicpixel.com.au/fractal/

There you have it – a fractal cyclone! Don't worry if you're short on fractals, everyday photos of friends and family can create beautiful patterns when run through Elements' Twirl tool.

21. Message on a bottle with 3D Transform

Elements is packed to the gills with tools for working on two - dimensional images, but hidden away in the Filter menu is 3D Transform – a tool that will let you transform your two - dimensional designs into three - dimensional objects such as cubes, spheres and cylinders.

Before

After

What can you use such a tool for? A friend who bottles his own wine asked me to design a label for him. Rather then send the design back as a flat image; why not place it on a bottle?

1. Create the image you'd like to transform. In my case it was more than just the label for the bottle, I needed to create the image that would cover the entire bottle, including the neck. I've placed my image on a layer with transparent area on either side so there's room to position the bottle after I create it in the 3D Transform tool.

2. Select **Filter > Render > 3D Transform**.

3. Select the cube, sphere or cylinder and click and drag in the work area from the top left corner of the shape, over the image below. Really though, it doesn't matter, as you can reposition and resize your shape as you go. I've selected a cylinder as it's the closest to a bottle!

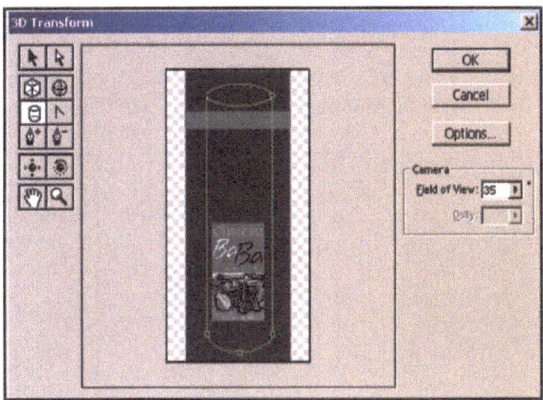

4. Select the Add Anchor Point Tool and click to add points to the wireframe. Points must be added to the right side only, and will automatically be applied 'around' the shape – like a lathe. To keep the shape easy to manage I've only added two anchors – enough to transform the cylinder into a bottle.

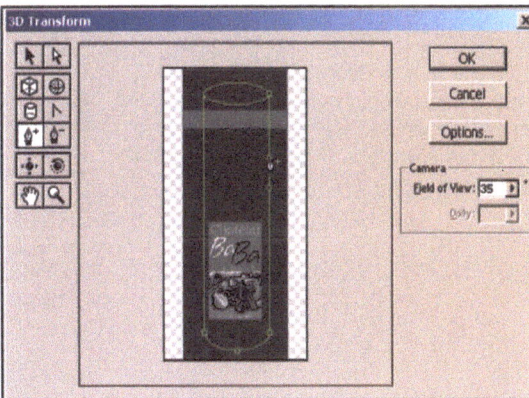

5. Select the Direct Selection Tool and click and drag any of the anchor points to create the desired shape. The bottle is taking shape!

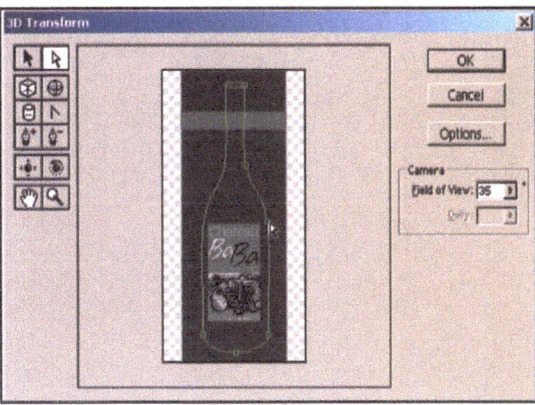

6. Select the Trackball and/or Pan Camera Tool to orientate the shape. I've chosen to lean the bottle back-wards using the Trackball, much like when a waiter presents a bottle of wine at the table.

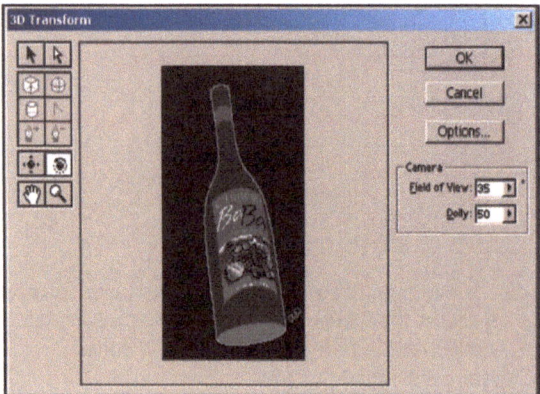

7. With the transformed image back in Elements, we need to add shadows and highlights, just as it would have in the real world. It's up to you how you do this – an easy way is to use the Dodge (O) and Burn (J) Tools with a low Exposure setting, and gradually build up the shadows and highlights.

Job done! While there are dedicated, high powered (and usually very expensive) tools for creating 3D shapes, Elements' 3D Transform Tool is a handy easy-to-use 3D alternative to have in your bag of tricks.

22. Depth effects using Minimum, Gaussian Blur and Emboss filters

Before

After

Layer Styles are cool, but what's happening behind the scenes to make stuff look bumpy?! Shut down your Styles and Effects palettes and walk this way...

There are many ways to create depth effects, in this tip we'll be relying primarily on three filters:

- Minimum
- Gaussian Blur
- Emboss

If it's your first time experimenting with creating depth from scratch, a simple shape or thick text is best to begin with. I'm using a star shape I created earlier.

> *Want to follow along using the star image? Download it from* http://www.magicpixel.com.au/depthstar

1. I've named the layer I'd like to apply the depth effect to as Star. Duplicate the Star layer twice – one layer will serve as a trimming mask later on, the other we'll use for embossing. Rename the duplicated layers Thick and Emboss.

2. With the Thick layer active, select **Filter > Other > Minimum.** The Minimum filter spreads the black and contracts the white (or transparent) area of an image. The radius you choose will depend on the resolution of your file. For my 72 pixels/inch file a radius of 2 is sufficient. The Minimum and the Maximum filter play key roles in making the masks we'll use to trim other layers.

3. Turn off the visibility of the Thick layer – we'll get back to it shortly.

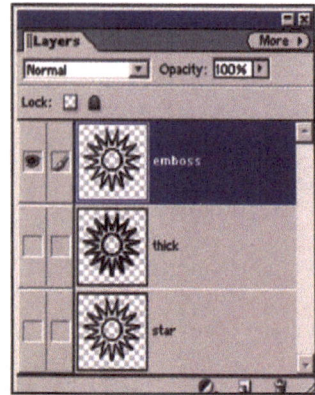

4. With the Emboss layer active, select **Filter > Blur > Gaussian Blur**. Set a small radius, the idea being to create a set of smooth tones for the Emboss filter to work on, which we'll be using shortly. I've set mine to 4. If you're working with a high resolution file, you will need to use a higher radius to achieve an equivalent effect as shown here.

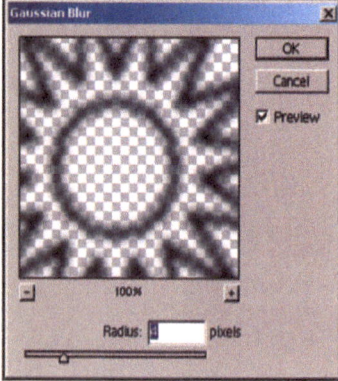

Before we run the Emboss filter, we need to place the blurred star on the Emboss layer on a white background. This is because we want the emboss effect to be applied across the entire image – the Emboss filter can do nothing to the transparent areas of the image.

5. Create a new layer and place it below the Emboss layer. We don't need to give it a special name as it'll be gone shortly! Fill the new layer with white by selecting **Edit > Fill**.

6. With the Emboss layer active, link the new layer to Emboss, as shown.

7. Select **Layer > Merge Linked** (**Ctrl+E**) – your Emboss layer should now include a white background.

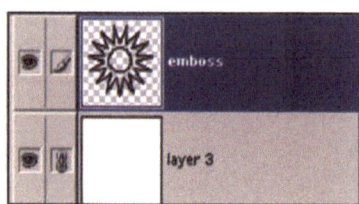

8. With the Emboss layer still active, select **Filter > Stylize > Emboss**. My settings are Angle: 150, Height 8 and Amount 150. If you're using a different image, other settings may work better for you.

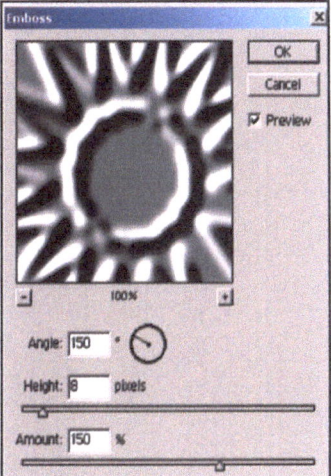

9. Duplicate the Emboss layer and rename it cutout.

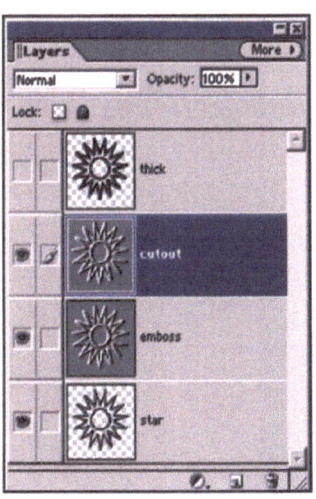

10. With cutout active, **Ctrl+Click** the Thick layer to load it as a selection. (Thick doesn't need to be visible.)

11. Choose **Select > Inverse (Shift+Ctrl+I)** to invert the selection and press delete – we're trimming Cutout with a selection loaded from Thick.

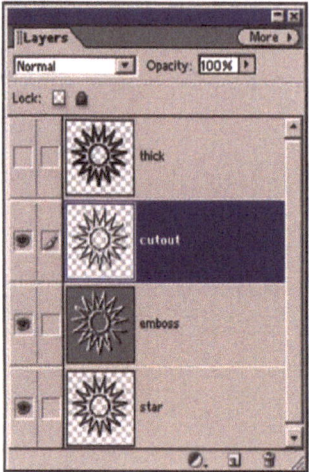 

12. With the Emboss layer active, choose **Image > Adjustments> Invert** (Ctrl+I) – *we're inverting the tones to create the illusion of depth!*

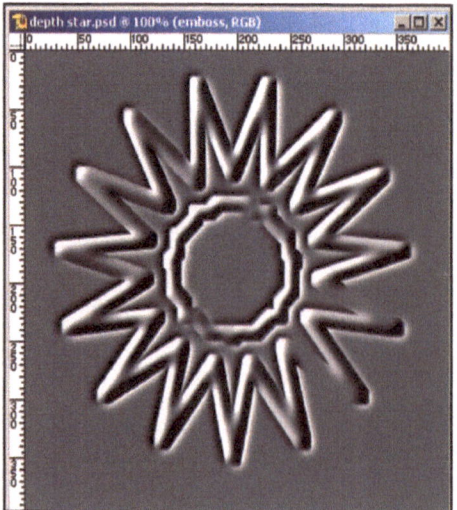

Voila! Let's review our journey:

- Create a trimming layer (Thick) using the Minimum filter.
- Use Gaussian Blur prior to embossing for quality results.
- Trim embossed image using the Thick layer.
- Invert tones to create illusion of depth.

We've created the core depth effect, now all that needs doing is dressing up. Because we have the components of the effects on different layers, we're free to apply effects any way we choose!

I've chosen to use a mix of layer groups and layer modes to apply different colors and textures to the two main effect layers. Notice at the bottom of the Layers palette the original Star layer and our thick 'trimming' layer are still preserved, ready for further exploration...

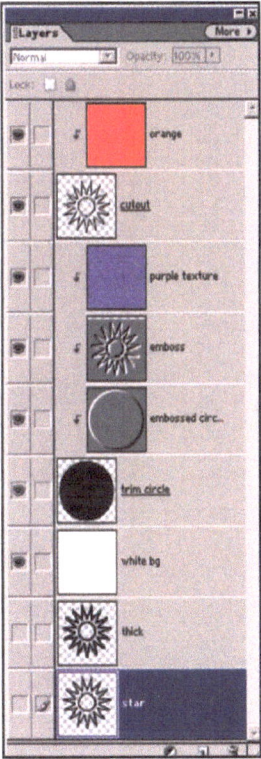

At the heart of many depth - related effects in Elements are Blur and Trim. You should now be able to apply the depth effect to your own projects, have fun!

Typing basic text

1. Creating text
2. Changing fonts
3. Resizing fonts
4. Warping text
5. Changing the text orientation
6. Using the Move Tool with type layers

Using layer styles with text

7. Applying bevels to type layers
8. Applying inner shadows
9. Applying glass buttons
10. Applying image effects
11. Applying patterns
12. Photographic effects
13. Using a combination of layer styles

The third dimension

14. The dangers of converting vector Images to raster images
15. Converting type layers into bitmap layers
16 Applying filters to text such as 3D transform

Personalities behind the mask

17. Text masks
18. Pictures inside type: method 1
19. Pictures inside type: method 2

Chapter 5

Type Tips

Through this next chapter we will be looking at how you can create and manipulate text within Elements. The new features enable you to type text in a manner similar to using a text editor. This helps to manage the creation of text in layers that can easily be altered at a later stage without much difficulty.

We will also look at how you can transform the text to create perspective and then to add filters to produce 3D effects for a more dynamic visual impression. The latter section deals with using text as a masking tool to cut out images so that you can have pictures within text.

I hope you find these tips useful and that they will lead you to devise your own imaginative creations.

Typing basic text

This section deals with the preliminary stages of using the text tools allowing you to open up the possibilities of what you might be able to do once you have got to grips with the basic tools.

1. Creating text

In Elements, text can be typed out horizontally or vertically using one of four Type Tools, which are the Horizontal Type Tool, Vertical Type Tool, Horizontal Type Mask Tool and Vertical Type Mask Tool.

The Change the Text Orientation button – which can be found on the Options tool bar when the Type tool is being used – allows you to change the orientation of any piece of text either before you begin typing or once you have typed out the text.

Once a Type Tool has been selected, the Tool Options Bar appears below the Menu Bar. This can be dragged to any part of the screen, to wherever most suits your working method.

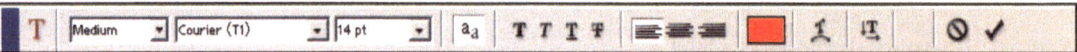

As each string of text is produced it forms a separate layer, for example the word "horizontal", shown opposite is on one text layer and the word "vertical" is on a second text layer.

It is useful to separate pieces of text into layers when you are designing something like a business card and want to be able to manipulate each piece of text – such as the name of the person, the company name and the address – so that each element has an individual character of its own.

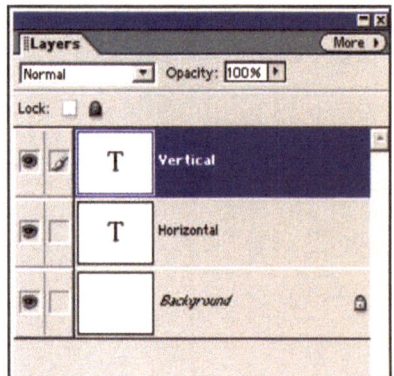

2. Changing fonts

When you type in your first piece of text, you will find that the text is in the font that you last used or is in the default setting.

To choose a different font, simply click on the Type Tool and select the text. The Tool Options will change.

To get the drop-down menu, you must click on the arrow *next* to the font name in the Type Tool bar to reveal the drop down menu. Then click on your preferred Font name.

Click on the name of the font in the Type Tool bar (giving it a blue background). Using the up and down keys, you can scroll through the fonts, with the text selection changing to show what it looks like in each font. If you are using a PC, you can also use the mouse wheel to scroll thorugh the fonts.

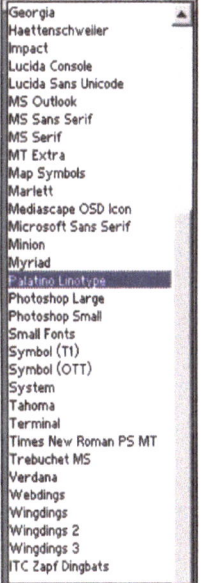

Finally deselect the text by clicking on an area away from the typed words.

3. Resizing fonts

In this section we will look at resizing the text using the Set the Font Size drop-down menu.

If the Move Tool is selected, the quickest way to access the Type Tool is by tapping **T** on the keyboard. Drag the cursor across the typed text.

Click on the Set the Font Size drop-down menu in the Type palette.

Once you click on the chosen size, the text will be resized. You can also click on the Set the font size box and, by using the arrow keys, increase or decrease the text:

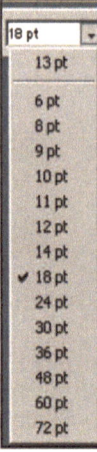

Resizing Fonts

As with changing the fonts, on a PC you can also use the mouse wheel to resize the text.

4. Warping text

The Create Warp Text button appears in the Tool Options Bar, once you have selected one of the Type Tools or via the **T** key.

There are fifteen options available in the Warp Text palette. Once you have chosen the style of warping you want to use, you can change the effect of the Style in either the horizontal or vertical plane. Further adjustments can be applied using a combination of the Bend, Horizontal Distortion and Vertical Distortion sliders in the Warp Text palette.

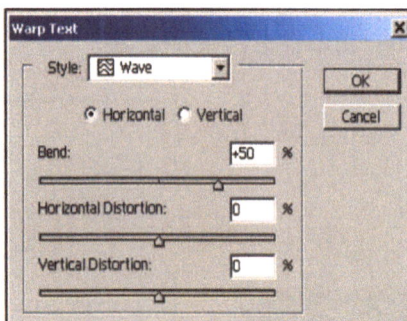

Using these sliders in a combination of different positions will produce an exciting range of different shapes for manipulating the text.

Even after you've warped your text, it remains fully editable, just as it did before.

5. Changing the text orientation

The Change the text orientation button appears in the Tool Options Bar, to the right of the Create Warp Text button , once you have selected one of the Type Tools or via the **T** key.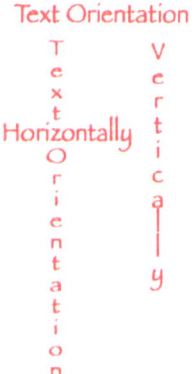

With the Type Tool selected, the Change the text orientation button will appear in the Options Bar. By clicking the button the text in the type layer will change its orientation from horizontal to vertical or vice versa depending on original orientation.

This tool is very useful because of the way we read. It is much easier for us to read text when it is horizontal than when it is vertical. Therefore, in order to ensure you make fewer mistakes when typing your text, it's a good idea to type it in horizontally, read it over so it is spelt correctly, then use the Text Orientation button to flip it round. At present there is no spellcheck in Elements, but one has been added to latest version of Photoshop, so just maybe the next version of Elements will get one.

6. Using the Move Tool with type layers

Each piece of text you type in becomes a separate layer and can therefore be manipulated in the same way as any image layer, allowing you to rotate, resize, skew and crop the text.

Rotating an image is achieved by simply moving the cursor just outside of the layers control point until it changes into the double head curved arrow icon (seen in the following screenshot). Then the type layer can be rotated in the same manner as any other layer. Alternatively, you can use **Ctrl+T** to allow you to use Free Transform.

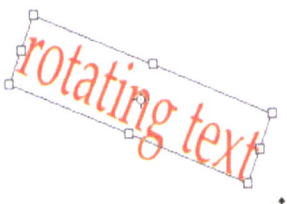

As with any layer, the skew allows you to take the corner control point to distort the image further.

Double-click on the piece of text once you are happy with its new shape. Alternatively, you can also press **Enter**, or click the arrow.

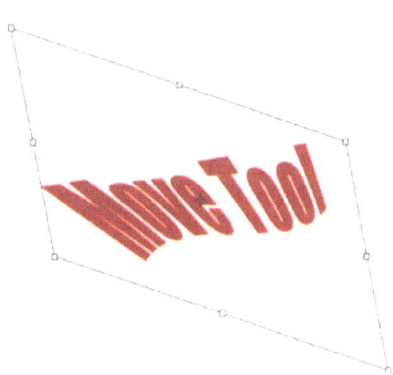

Using Layer Styles with text

This section looks at how you can use all the Layer Styles to enhance your text layers. These tips can help you easily modify your type to add some dramatic effects, especially if you are in a hurry to produce titles for video and presentations.

7. Applying Bevels to type layers

To add depth to the text, Elements provides ten different Bevels in the Layer Styles palette.

Bevels are a common design feature used to create depth to a piece of text by adding an angle to the edge of the text.

To apply any of these, click on the text layer, and then select the desired Bevels icon from the palette.

You can also apply them without selecting the type layer – simply drag and drop a layer style over your text on the canvas or the corresponding layer in the Layers palette and it will be applied, even if another layer is selected.

In the Layers palette you will notice that a small Filter icon has appeared in the Text layer.

Double-clicking on this icon will open the Style Settings window. Here the Bevel Size can be changed using the slider to increase or decrease the pixel size.

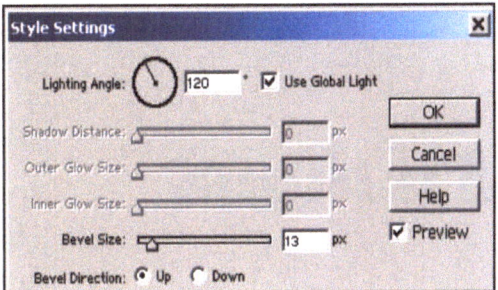

8. Applying Inner Shadows

The Inner Shadows palette provides six options.

These filters are used to add a shadow within the shape of the text to make it look more 3D.

They are great for cutout effects or making a text or shape look very indented on a background.

Clicking on the Filter icon again opens the Style Settings window.

As with the Drop Shadows filter, the Lighting Angle can be changed and you can determine whether to apply Use Global Light. The Shadow Distance can also be modified.

9. Applying Glass Buttons

The Glass Buttons filter uses a blend of Lighting Angle, Inner Glow Angle, Bevel Size and either the Up or Down Bevel Direction.

There are fourteen different Glass Button filters. Each filter can be applied by simply selecting the Type Layer and clicking on the desired Glass Button filter.

For a more 3D effect, click on the Filter Icon in the Layers window associated with the text. This will open the Styles Settings window.

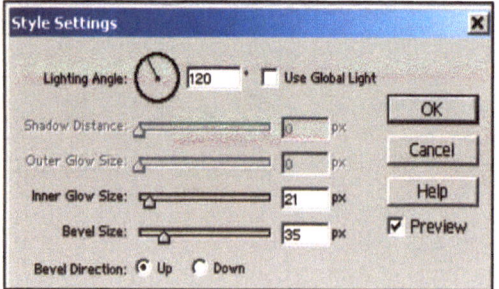
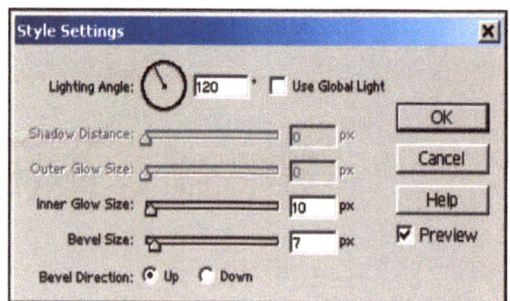

Changing the Lighting Angle enables you to reposition the highlights and shadows to best suit your design.

10. Applying Image Effects

Unlike most of the other Layer Styles filters, in the Image Effects range, only Puzzle and Tile Mosaic can be modified after they have been applied.

The reason Puzzle and Tile Mosaic can be adjusted in the Styles Settings palette that they both include a Bevel that can be adjusted. All other Image Effects are preset, so if you try to open the Styles Setting window via the Filter icon you will be presented with a notice, informing you that the Layer Style you are using is not editable.

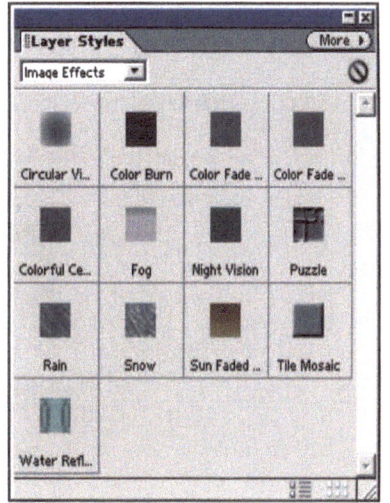

The Image Effects provided allow you to add subtle atmospheric effects to the type including Fog, Sun Faded Photo and a jigsaw puzzle beveled effect.

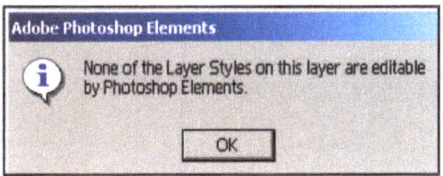

11. Applying Patterns

The Patterns palette provides twenty-six different textures that can be applied to the text:

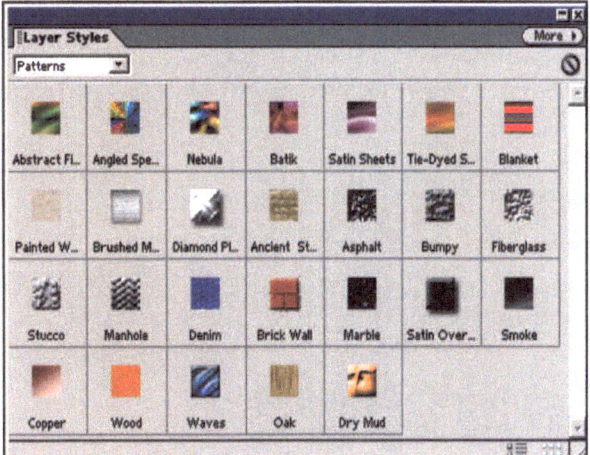

Several of the filters can be adjusted in the Style Settings window. These are the ones which are made up of relief forms, such as Asphalt and Fibreglass. A relief is a shape that is elevated from a flat surface to create texture. Examples include tarmac on a road or a tire track formed across a muddy lane. What creates the impression of a relief is the way that light falls upon an object creating highlights and shadows, as shown below.

To adjust this effect in the Style Settings, for example, with Asphalt you would want to increase or decrease the size of the shapes that form the stones in the asphalt (or Bevel size), which would give the impression of decreasing the number of objects reflecting highlights and casting shadows.

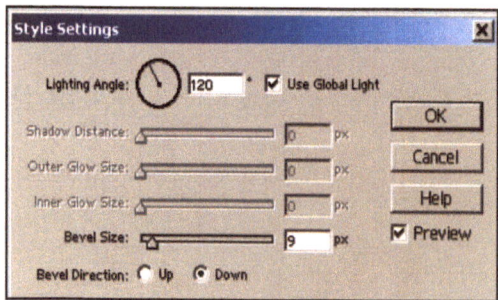

Many of the other Pattern filters function the same way as the Image Effects filters, whereby you can only apply the filter as it is, with no further adjustments being possible in the Styles Settings window.

12. Photographic Effects

The eleven Photographic Effects filters enable you to quickly add tints to your images such as Sepia Tone, Blue Tone and a variety of others.

These filters should only be used if the text has already had a texture applied to it, otherwise the effect can appear quite dull and lacking in impact.

Therefore it is best to apply one of the other Layer Styles filters before applying the Photographic Effects filter.

13. Using a combination of Layer Styles

For the most dramatic effects a variety of Layer Styles can be used together and further adjustments made using the Style Settings window.

If you find that you have been applying lots of Layer Styles and want to start again, the Clear Styles button will allow you to strip off all the Layer Styles you have applied to start from scratch again on that layer.

 This button is in the top right corner of the Layer Styles palette

The third dimension

The following three tips deal with converting vector images to raster images in order to apply Photoshop Element filters to the newly rasterized layer. Initially, we look at the dangers behind converting vectors and the importance of retaining high resolutions. Once this has been covered, we take you through the conversion process and beyond into the third dimension.

14. The dangers of converting vector images to raster images

This section looks at converting type layers from the vector shapes created using the Type Tool and converting them to bitmap images.

Vector shapes are resolution-independent, allowing them to be resized and printed out at any resolution without deteriorating the quality of the image. When they are converted to bitmap or rasterized images, rescaling to a larger size will produce lower quality images at high resolutions. This is because bitmap images are produced from a two dimensional array of pixels (think of a piece of graph paper with each square made up of colors). The higher the resolution, the more pixels are required per inch or centimeter.

The S on the left is a vector image while the S on the right has been simplified to a raster or bitmap image. As you can see, the image on the right does not have the same quality as that on the left. It is therefore important to remember that if you do simplify layers, you should start off with a high enough resolution to begin with before applying filters and effects.

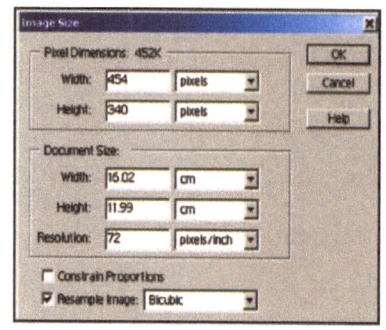 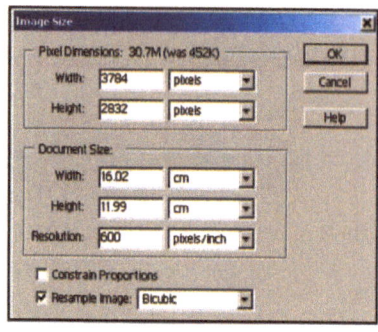 

To increase the resolution of the image, select **Image > Resize > Image Scale...**

This will open the Image Size palette. Here you can choose the resolution to suit your project. You will notice in the two examples shown above that by increasing the resolution from 72 ppi to 600 ppi, the file size has increased from 452Kb to 30.7 Mb (indicated at the top of the Image Size palette).

15. Converting type layers into bitmap layers

By duplicating the text layer and then reshaping it, you can create your own dramatic drop shadows and apply various effects.

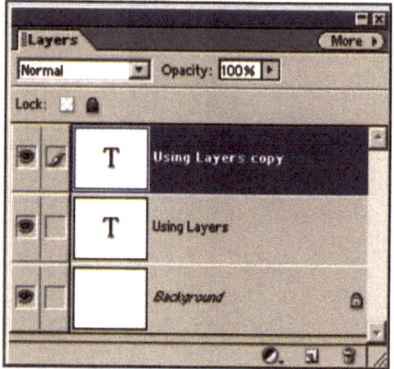

Once you have positioned the second layer of text you will need to use **Layer > Simplify Layer** so that you can apply filters and effects. PC users can also right-click on the text layer and choose **Simplify Layer**.

Once you have applied this you will notice that the Layer palette indicates the text layer has been changed to an ordinary bitmap image layer.

Depending on what you intend for the text, you may not want to simplify. Layer Styles can be used on unsimplified text, and you can still resize and change the type.

Now you can apply various filters and effects to manipulate the layer further.

Note that once you have simplified the layer, you will need to use the Undo History palette to reverse the effect so that you can change the text.

It is important to remember the default count is twenty steps. When you go backwards in the History states, you also lose any steps you made after the change.

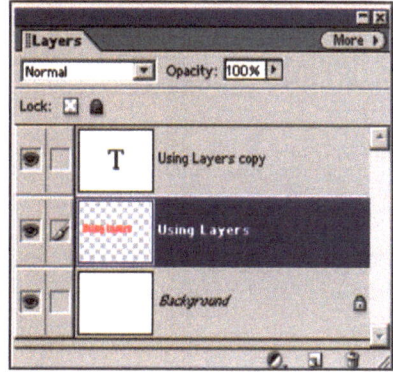

Those of you using slower machines may well have reduced the number of History states to help Elements run faster, so you will need to make sure that you have enough levels of Undo History to accomplish this.

16. Applying filters such as 3D transform to text

It is important to remember that there are many different ways to play around with text. Text doesn't have to just be purely flat and plain. Elements enables you to create your text and then add a fair amount of texture to the final design.

Once you have created a text layer, use **Layer > Simplify Layer** to turn the text into an image layer.

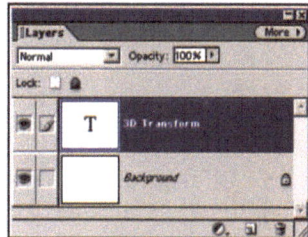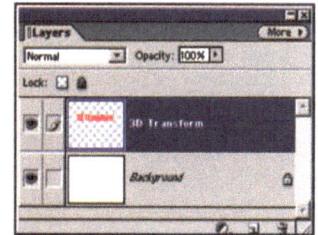

Select **Filter > Render > 3D Transform** to open the 3D Transform window. A list of the special shortcut keys for this filter are provided in the previous chapter.

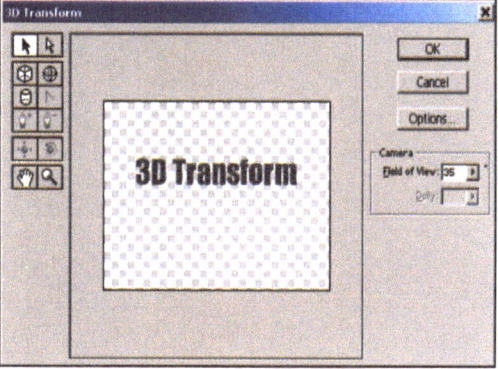

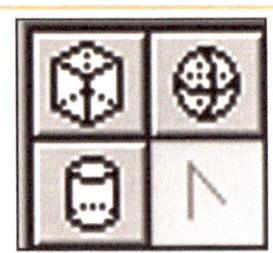

Here there are options to create spheres, cubes and cylinders to add depth to the text. This is achieved by creating the illusion that the text is wrapped around 3D objects and then rotating the objects to change the view you have of them.

There are three different primitive shapes that can be created and manipulated around the text. These are the sphere, cube, and cylinder.

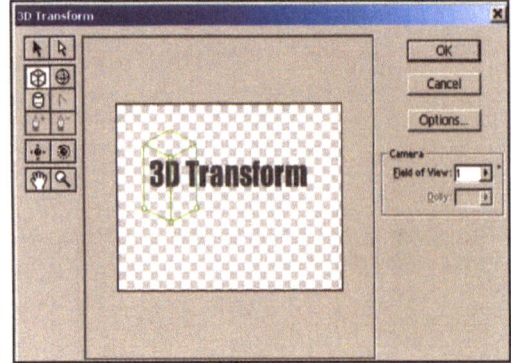

If a cube shape is used with the Field of View set at 1°, then an isometric three-dimensional shape appears as a green wire-frame when you click and drag the cursor across the text.

By changing the Field of View up to a maximum of 130°, you are able to play around with the perspective of the 3D shape.

Choosing the Direct Selection Tool from the 3D Transform palette (or pressing the **A** key) allows you to further manipulate the perspective of the primitive 3D object.

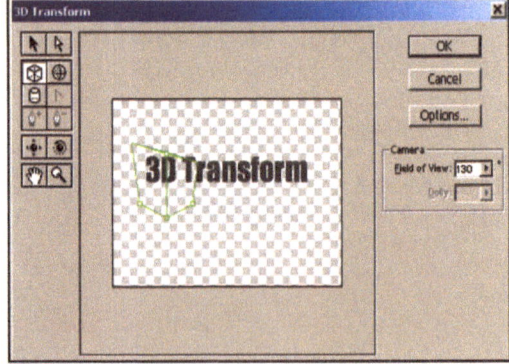

The complexity of the shape depends on the number of primitive objects you add.

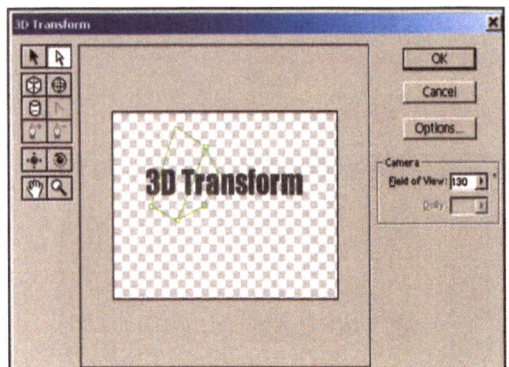

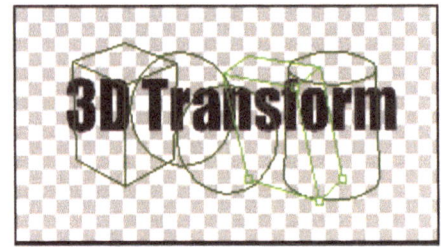

Using the Pan Camera Tool ⊕ you can move the shapes away from the original text to form a new image. Effectively this tool copies the way you can move a camera around by lifting or lowering the lens or by simply panning left or right.

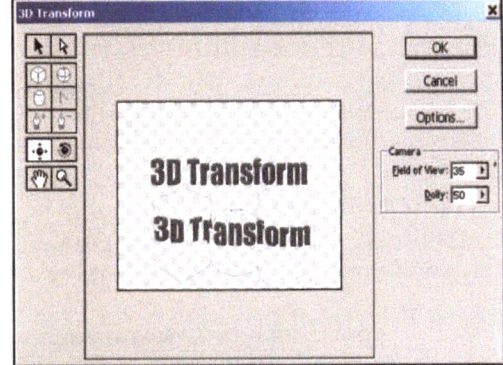

Using the Trackball Tool ⦿ the shape can be rotated as though it had been mapped onto the three-dimensional shapes created with the three primitive shape tools – sphere, cube, and cylinder. This is equivalent to simply taking a camera and moving around an object you wish to photograph to get the best view. Likewise the Trackball Tool allows you to rotate the 3D objects to look at a more visually interesting angle of the text on the 3D shapes.

The Field of View and Dolly can be changed using two separate sliders. The Options provides a window to change the Resolution and Anti-Aliasing of the final render. Once **OK** is clicked, the effect takes a few moments and is then revealed as part of the image layer.

This kind of text manipulation can be very useful for carving the shape of your words so they can fit irregular forms, such as faces or a pebble beach, where you mimic the pebbles using the 3D shapes in the 3D Transform window.

Again, various Layer Styles can be applied to add to the effect.

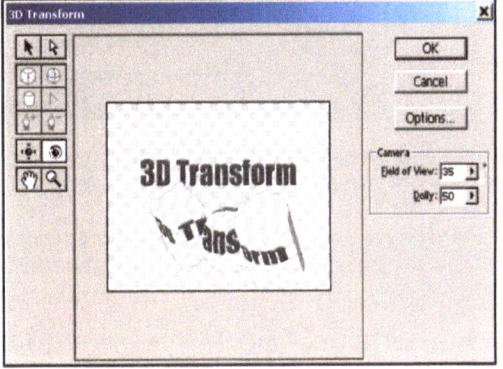

Personalities behind the mask

This section looks at using the Type Mask Tools to produce text as though you were using a stencil. We follow this with a couple of examples of how to use the Type Mask Tools to add images inside text.

17. Text masks

The two Type Mask Tools come in handy when you want to produce a piece of artwork that looks as though you have used a stencil.

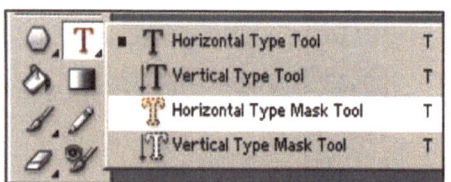

The Type Mask Tools are similar to the Selection Tools, except that they allow you to produce selections as text instead of irregular shapes, circles or squares.

To allow you to see the Type Mask as you produce the text, Elements provides a semi-transparent red background, so that you can see the text in white.

Once you have completed typing the text, the background returns to white and you can see the selection as text.

The selected area can then be filled using the Fill Tool from the palette or, if you want to be more creative, you can use a Brush to paint over the mask. To do this, select the Brush Tool from the Tool palette or by pressing B

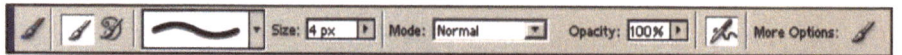

Select a brush from the Show selected brush presets drop-down menu in the Tool Box.

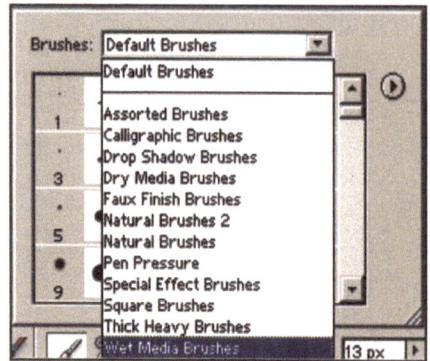

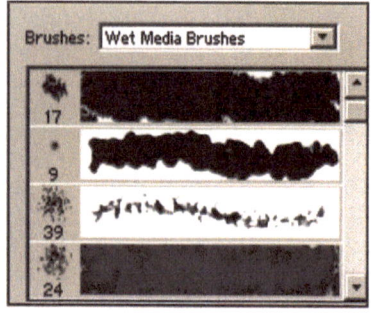

You can then choose from a further selection of brush shapes by clicking on the desired brush pattern.

If necessary, change the foreground color at the bottom of the Tools palette and the paint across the text mask area in the Image Window.

If you want the text to be in a separate layer, use **Select > Inverse** (or **Shift+Ctrl+I**) to invert the selection, press the **Delete** or **Backspace** key to clear the background, deselect and then choose **Layer > New > Layer from Background**. Then by adding a Bevel using the Layer Style, you can add depth to the text:

The text layer can then be easily dragged onto another image if necessary. This method is useful if you wish to build an image from component parts and assemble them later.

18. Pictures inside type: method 1

To place an image inside the text, simply open the image you wish to use and then select the Type Mask Tool.

If you are not happy with the position, select the text and move the type to a more suitable position.

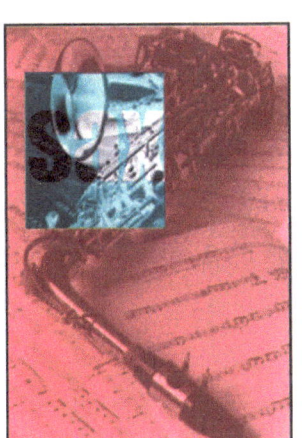

Invert the selection by using **Select > Inverse (Shift+Ctrl+I)**, Then choose **Layer > New > Background From Layer** and press **Backspace** to make the background transparent.

19. Pictures inside type: method 2

You may find the previous method too restrictive. Another method is to open the photograph you want to use as a background and then create a second layer and fill with white.

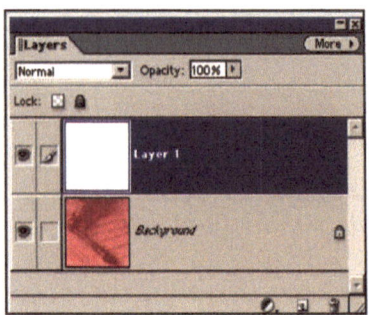

Using the Type Mask, create the desired text on the white layer, then once you see the selection line, press the **Backspace** key. Deselect the text and you'll have something like this:

Double-click on the Background layer lock icon in the Layer palette. This will open the New Layer window and name the Background layer as Layer 0. Then click **OK**.

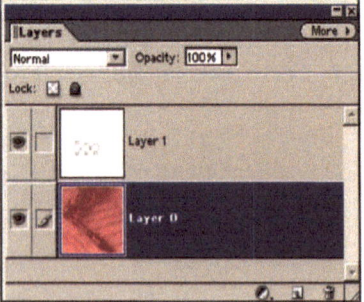

Using the Move Tool, move Layer 1 from within the text until you have the desired image visible underneath.

Choose the Magic Wand Tool to select the white area of Layer 1, then click on Layer 0 in the Layers palette and press the **Backspace** key. This will delete the unwanted part of the background image. Drag Layer 1 to the Trash can icon in the Layers palette to leave just the image inside the text.

If your text contains letters such as the lower case a in Sax, then you'll need to use the Magic Wand Tool on the section inside each letter, in order to get the right outline of the text

This method is useful if you wish to create multiple images in the background and retain the flexibility of moving them around before deleting the excess material.

Chapter 6

Productivity

Even though Elements might be one of the most versatile and relatively easy-to-use pieces of photo manipulation software out there, it doesn't mean things can't go wrong! One of the main ways to eat up time on a project is to come across some kind of technical glitch when there's no one around to help you out. You *know* it's just something small, but you can't for the life of you figure out what it is. In this chapter we're going to cover a few of the most common hiccups, and show you how to overcome them.

1. Choosing the right cursor for the job

Let's start out before we've even looked at any tools by dealing with the cursor. Elements displays a different mouse pointer depending on what you're doing. Using **Edit > Preferences > Display & Cursors** (or just double-clicking in the ruler area):

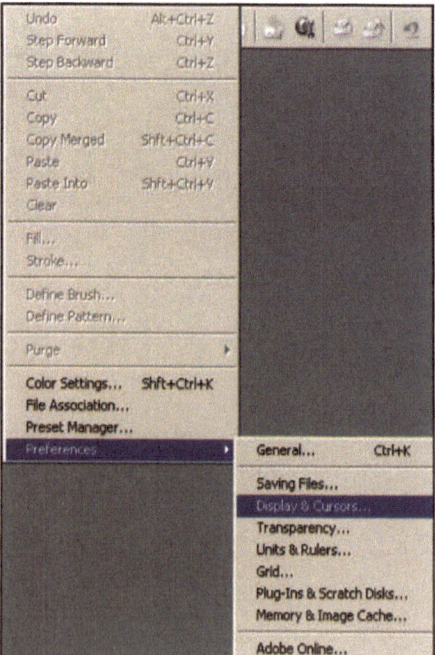

...we get the following menu:

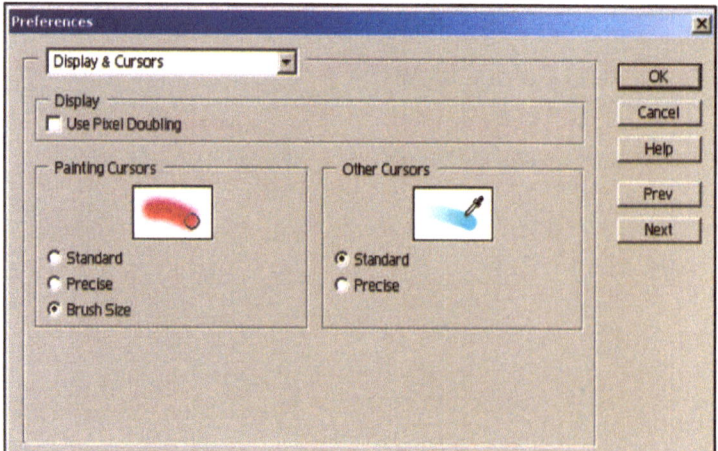

For painting cursors, it's a good idea to set the shape of the cursor to Brush Size. This means that whenever you use a painting tool, you can see the size and shape of the brush you're using. Also, if you really want control, you can use the **Caps Lock** key to toggle the cursor changing to Precise mode, which is also useful for close-up correction work.

The three settings:

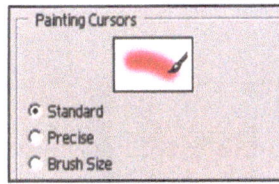 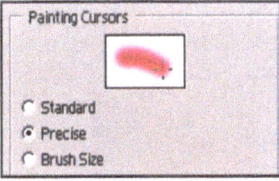

Standard: Shows you a miniature picture of the tool (for instance a paintbrush for the Brush Tool).
Precise: Shows you a miniature target as your cursor. This is useful if you want to be able to start your editing on an exact spot, but it doesn't show you the size of the brush you're using, or the shape of the brush.
Brush Size: Shows you the shape and size of the brush as the cursor. This has the advantage of letting you see what area your brush is going to affect, but you do lose a little in the precision department. Some brushes don't have an exact center – they're created a little off center – so using them in brush mode is sometimes a bit tricky if you want to use the brush with a lot of precision.

Similarly for other cursors (for example the Color Picker), set the cursor type to precise – this way you can see exactly where you're sampling from.

2. Feathering marquees

When you're creating a selection, it's useful to set your feather amount beforehand. This basically means how fuzzy the edges of the stroke (the selection line) you're making are:

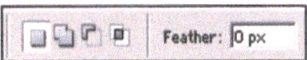

We can always apply a feather to an existing selection by using **Select > Feather** (or **Ctrl+Alt+D**). We won't always want to feather something – sometimes we want the marquee to be really tight around the object - but feathering gives us the advantage of being able to loosely select an area if we want to. For instance, if you're trying to select the area of someone's eye in a fairly small image, a precise selection will be too blocky; you'll need to feather the edges a bit. Have a look at the following image:

Let's have a look at this problem over a bigger area. Let's say we want to change the lighting coming through the window on the left. First we need to select this area:

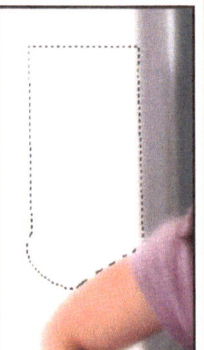

Now compare a feather on this selection to no feather:

no feather

feather

As you can see, in the image on the right, the arm blends into the red background far better as the feather closes the distance between the blurry edge of the arm and the background color.

3. Obtaining better results with the Eyedropper Tool

Here's something useful to remember about the Eyedropper Tool. Have a look at the following image:

Notice how the top left-hand corner of the sky has vertical stripes in it. This is often caused by the mechanisms of scanners. It would be great to remove those. A popular technique to achieve this is to use the Eyedropper Tool to select a blue from the area to use with the Airbrush Tool, and simply paint over it. Let's have a real close up look at this area:

Sure the sky looked a bit messed up – but not quite *this* messed up! Even if we zoom in on an area of color that looks totally flat in this image, chances are we'll find that it consists of heterogeneously colored pixels. So if we're going to try pick an average kind of blue to respray the sky, which one do we pick?

Have a look at the options for the Eyedropper Tool:

Point Sample is the default setting - when you use the Eyedropper Tool and click to obtain a color as your foreground color, Elements will select the pixel directly underneath your cursor. As we've just seen, this isn't always preferable, so you get the option of taking a 3 by 3 pixel sample which will produce an

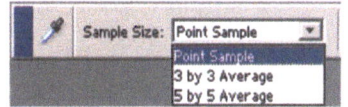

average of those colors in that area to use as your foreground color. In our case we might even want to use a 5 by 5 so that we get a really good average of the colors.

Notice the change in the top left of the image:

4. Why doesn't it work?

Sometimes you want to use a tool or an option but it's grayed out. Let's have a look at some of these in list form, and possible solutions/reasons:

Problem	Solution
Edit > Copy is grayed out	Make sure you actually have something selected first and you're on the right layer. This command works from a selection/marquee. This also goes for Paste and Paste Into.
Edit > Stroke is grayed out	This is the same problem; make sure you have some thing selected that you want to stroke. Also, if you're on a text or shape layer (which you cannot stroke) this option will be grayed out.
Turning a layer on/off does nothing	This happens a lot. You turn a layer on or off and it seems to make no change to the image. The first thing to check is which layers are active above this layer. Often these interfere with the layer you're trying to look at – especially if you have a merged layer above the one you're testing. Turn off all the layers above this point. Check theopacity of the layer. Check the blending mode of the layer. You might also want to check that there is something on the layer in the first place!
The brush shape has disappeared	Check that your **Caps Lock** key is not on Using this key

even though in **Edit > Preferences**, the cursor is set to Brush Size	toggles the brush cursor between brushsize and precise.
Define Pattern is grayed out	For this command you need a rectangular marquee. No marquee or an elliptical one will cause this option to be grayed out.
Define Brush is grayed out	This is because you don't have an area selected.
Layer > Change Layer Content is grayed out	You have to be on an Adjustment layer for this command to be active – this will allow you to change the type of adjustment being made – so if you find that you'd rather use a Levels command for greater control, rather than a Brightness/Contrast command, you can do this here. Why not delete the layer and just add the one you want? Using this command means that you keep the layer mask - which might have taken you some time to set up - and just change the effect.
Enhance > Auto Color Correction is grayed out	This is the opposite of the last problem. You need to be on a normal layer, and *not* an Adjustment layer here.
Image > Adjustments is grayed out	If you're on a type layer, this will be the case. Change to a non-type layer to make these kinds of adjustments. You can't apply a color correction to a line that you've drawn. You will need to simplify the line – click on the simplify button in the Options bar.
File > Export is grayed out	You will need a plug-in (third party software that does not ship with Elements) installed in order to export Elements files to certain file formats.

Problem	Solution
All the filters are grayed out	Make sure you have a document open. Make sure you don't have any type selected and you're not on a type layer. If you need to apply a filter to a type layer, simplify (**Layer > Simplify Layer**) this layer first.
When you create a marquee it only appears as one size	Check that the style of the marquee is set to Normal, and not fixed size (also known as Fixed Aspect Ratio). Check the options bar for these.

5. Unlocking the background layer

Sometimes you will want to drag a layer to below the background layer. As is, you can't do this because the layer is locked. To achieve this, double-click on the layer.

Doing so will bring up the following dialog box:

This will make a 'new layer' out of the background layer. The background layer will now be renamed as Layer 0 (or anything you like), and you will now be able to drag this layer around in the layer stack.

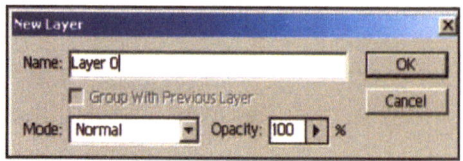

6. Simplifying shapes

Let's say you've drawn the following shape using the Custom Shape Tool:

Your layers will look something like this:

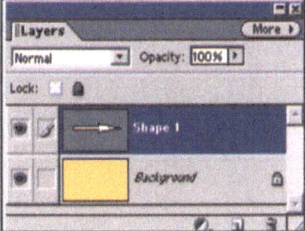

If you want to apply any enhancements to this shape (using the Enhance menu), like changing the lighting etc. you will need to simplify this shape first. This will convert the shape from a vector shape to a regular old bitmap-based layer which you can edit:

You can also right-click on the layer and choose **Simplify Layer** (or **Layer > Simplify** if you're a menu junkie).

7. Zooming with the Navigator palette

The Navigator palette is extremely useful for zooming in and out of the image you are working on so that you can make quick adjustments to the picture. If you are having problems seeing in detail in your image, this is a good way of zooming in, and the red view box allows you to move to different areas in the image with ease and precision.

With the image open, select **Window > Navigator** to access the Navigator palette. Using the slider, drag it to the right to zoom in and to the left to zoom out.

Click on the **More** button in the top right-hand corner of the Navigator palette and select **Palette Options...** to change the color of the View Box.

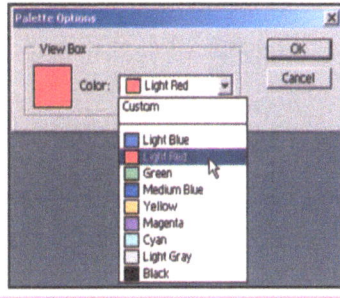

8. Improving the performance of Elements

Sometimes, especially on slower computers, Elements can get a bit sluggish. There are ways to speed things up a bit.

Use the **Edit > Purge** menu:

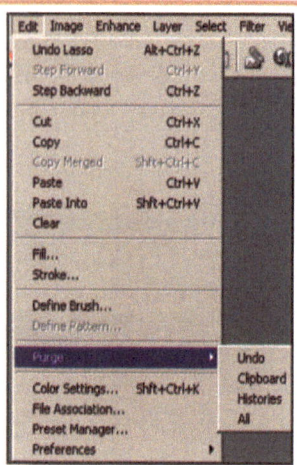

As you can see, there are a few things you can purge. Use this with caution however. Once it's gone, it's gone – there's no getting it back! Let's have a look at the options:

Undo

Elements remembers a certain number of Undo steps – quite a few, actually. This takes up memory. Purging the Undo means that this memory will become available to be used for the rest of the program – thus speeding things up.

Make sure that when you do this, you're at a state in the project that you're happy with, and not in the middle of a task. Purging Undo obviously means that you won't be able to use **Ctrl+Z** or any command to undo things you've previously done. Once you've used the command, the Undo memory will immediately start building up again as you start using the program – so you will have to do this periodically.

You can see how much memory is being used up by having 'scratch sizes' visible in the Status bar. As you use the purge commands you should see this size drop. In the bottom left of your screen is the Status bar with a small black triangle on it – click this to bring up a drop-down (or is it drop-up?!) list of things Elements can tell you on the fly:

Clipboard

This is actually quite an important one. When you use the Copy or Copy Merged command, Elements stores this information to be pasted on the clipboard. The clipboard is not something specific to Elements. You can copy text from a Word document and paste it into Elements. So, chances are there will be something on your clipboard when Elements starts.

Sometimes this can be a huge image. For instance: if you use the **Print Screen** key, a picture of your entire desktop will be placed on the clipboard. This will be a large image and will take up a fair whack of memory! Before starting work on a project, it's a good idea to purge this clipboard so that you start working with all the memory available to you.

Histories

This is a slightly more powerful version of the **Purge > Undo** command.

This will step you back through your History palette. The same caution applies here: don't be in the middle of a task when you use this command!

All
This will obviously purge all of the above in one fell swoop.

9. Customizing your workspace

If you're lucky enough to have two monitors, the good news is that you can drag all your menus over onto the right-hand screen. With two monitors, Elements can be spread across both desktops:

This way you can work on the left with your image, and not have your tools clutter your workspace. If you only have one monitor and find that all your menus are getting in the way, try using the **Tab** key, which toggles them all on and off.

You can always drag menus that you don't use that often into the palette well at the top:

This way they don't clutter your screen and you can just click on their tab to gain easy access to them. You can also place several tabs in the same palette well if you wish - you may prefer to work with related items, like filters, Effects and Layer Styles, all together in one place.

10. Two Lifesavers!

Holding down the spacebar while you're using any tool on your image gives you access to the Hand Tool, which allows you to scroll around your image. Useful when you don't want to take your eye off what's going on in the design to change tools...

Ever use a filter and then go back and wonder what settings you last used? If you hold down the **Shift** key while you use the menu, the filter will automatically come up with the last used settings.

Saving as you work
1. The four ways to save
2. Most commonly used file types
3. Save your original images
4. Save as you go
5. Base camp saves

Safe Editing
6. Put everything on different layers
7. Don't flatten - keep your layers
8. Test effects on a duplicate layer
9. Trade your eraser in for an Elemask!
10. Make notes on a hidden layer
11. Take a screenshot of your history palette
12. Let your Layers palette tell the story

Saving finished work
13. Quality v file size
14. High-quality saves
15. The difference between photos and graphics
16. Don't save photos as GIFs
17. Don't save graphics as JPGs either!
18. Don't resave JPGs
19. Create big images, then reduce them
20. Batch process to save time

Preparing for potential catastrophic loss of data
21. Managing backups
22. Backup your photos onto CD to prevent losing them forever
23. Keeping a PSD file as a library of pre-prepared elements
24. Archiving finished work

Putting your work out there
25. Printing: Garbage in, Garbage out!
26. Use the right resolution for printing
27. To resample or not to resample?
28. Making a contact sheet
29. Reduce image resolution when sending via email
30. Keep your friends - don't send them PSD files!
31. Sharing images on a website
32. Creating a PDF slideshow

Chapter 7

Saving and sharing your images

Saving as you work

Now that you have your camera and you are editing your images, you need to do something with them! Whether you hope to save them to a web photo gallery, share with friends through email, or print them, you will find how-tos and tips here.

But first, you will want to preserve your work. I will tell you about the various ways to save your work, how to protect your files from accidental harm, and how to prevent catastrophic loss of data, in the event of a hard drive crash or other disaster.

You can slave away for hours, weeks, or years, and it won't mean a thing unless your work is properly saved! How and when should you save? We will look at some answers in this section!

1. The four ways to save

There are four main types of saves you need to perform:

- **Save as you work**
- **Originals preserved** - Before you begin work on a photo, you will save your original unaltered file. This untouched original can be thought of like a "digital negative". The file format of this digital negative will depend upon what your camera or scanner produces, likely a JPG or TIF. Whatever it is, preserve it in this original format. When you want to use the file later, you will be saving a copy in another format.
- **Work in Progress** - When you first begin work on a new document, you should save your file as a "work in progress" in PSD format.
- **Ctrl+S Quick Saves** - As you work, you will want to do a **Ctrl+S** save periodically.

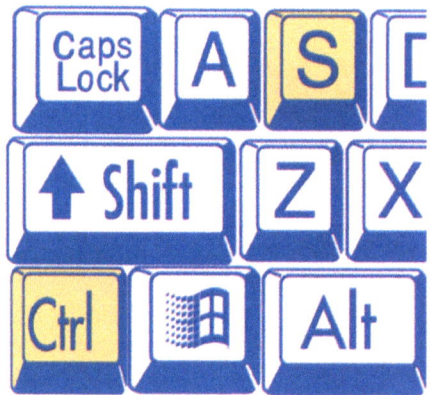

2. Most commonly used file types

No discussion of saving would be complete without a review of the file types and the purposes of each. But the fact is that you will not be using many of these file types, unless you are into specialized sorts of work. I'll tell you much more about how these file types can work for you later in the chapter, but for now, here is a summary of the main file types you will use:

PSD: This is the "work in progress" file format. This format preserves any layers and adjustment layers just as they are. You can save the file repeatedly without any degradation of the image. Because PSD format preserves all layers in their original highest quality, these files can get very large.

JPEG (or JPG): Many of the images you see on the web are JPGs because they can be made in relatively small file sizes. JPEG format allows for unlimited color display and is, therefore, best for images which use gradations of colors, such as photos. The disadvantage to this format, however, is that it is *lossy*, that is, it compresses the file with each repeated save. Therefore, you do not want to edit a jpg, save it as a jpg, and repeat this. You will notice a difference in the quality of the image after just a couple of repeated saves!

JPEG 2000: Using a freeware plug-in currently available from www.fnordware.com, you can take advantage of the emerging JPEG 2000 technology. This compression method takes into account the visual range of colors, and is, therefore, able to compress files smaller, but in notably better quality, than with standard JPEG.

GIF: This is another file format which you see for images on the web, because they can be made in small file sizes. GIF is not lossy; repeated saves will not reduce image quality. If you need to have the background transparent for a web graphic, you will likely use GIF. Also, if you want to make an image on your website move, you probably want an animated GIF. Another place where GIF really shines is in saving files which have crisp graphic edges or text. GIF, for example, is usually the best format for which to save screenshots of computer dialog boxes.

However, because GIF works by saving images in only a limited palette of colors, this format is *not* good for photos, or images with gradations of colors.

TIF: TIF is a file type which is generally non-lossy, so it is good for saving finished work. TIF files are useful for transferring across other programs, too. If you are doing a picture for publication in a print medium, such as in a newspaper or magazine, they will likely need your file in TIF format. You can save layers in TIF files, and these will be preserved when the file is re-opened in Photoshop, ImageReady, or Elements. If the file is opened in another program, though, the file will open as a flattened document (no layers).

Images in TIF format are likely to be quite large in file size, even larger than PSDs.

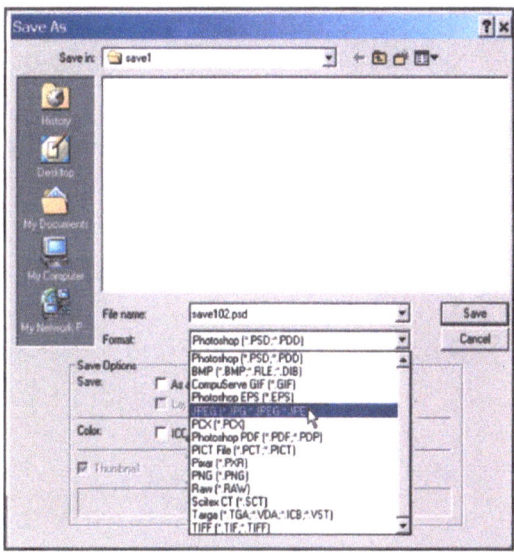

Other file types: There are other file types which you may encounter. One is PNG, which is used in saving images for the web. It is not as common as JPEG and GIF, and is not supported on all browsers, a decided disadvantage. There are other file formats which are good for specialized work. You can get a full rundown of these from Help. (To access Help, hit **F1** on your keyboard. Choose **Index > F > File Format**.)

3. Save your original images

With a film camera, should your prints get ruined, you have your negatives. With a digital camera, you have your original unaltered photos, just as they came from your camera. Any file among these, whether you can use all of it or just a part of it, should be archived. (See Archiving Digital Negatives, later in this chapter.) Consider these your digital negatives.

Save any of your digital images which you think may have some redeeming value later. If you have two shots of the same scene, from the same angle, you can trash the worst one. But sometimes you may want to keep even a bad photo, as a basis for some other project. A horrible photo might just supply you with a great background for a work of photo art!

I kept this one.

Although I didn't like this one as well as the first, I might still use some part of it.

You may want to make a seamless tile from the pattern in a shirt!

Just as you can use a film negative to make new prints of a photo, you can use your digital negatives to reproduce the photo. You can also use it in other photo manipulations, as well.

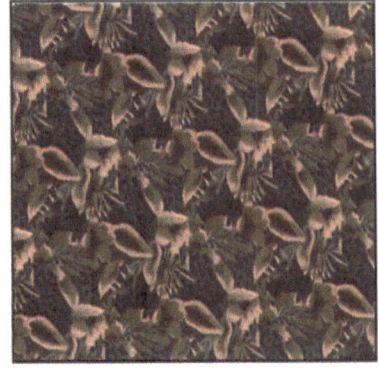

4. Save as you go

Elements will not automatically save as you work! Why not?

You would not want an auto-save feature. Especially when you are working with very large documents. Saving a large document can mean several seconds of downtime for each save, so be grateful that Elements makes you save on your own.

Save at the beginning when creating a new document

If you are making a new document, you should begin saving it even before you open it! In the New File dialog box, name your file, and specify its contents, size, etc., in the box.

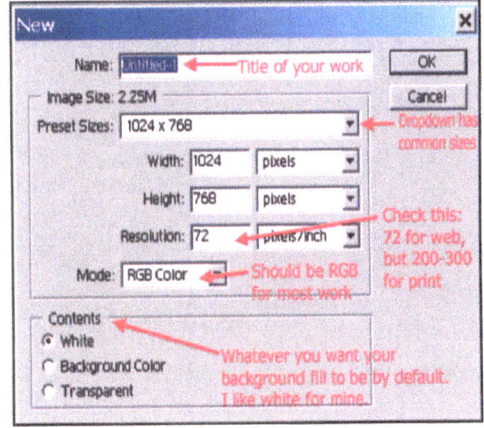

At this point, the document is not yet saved.

Select **File > Save As** (or **Shift+Ctrl+S**). Choose your file type (probably PSD) and choose a folder location for the file.

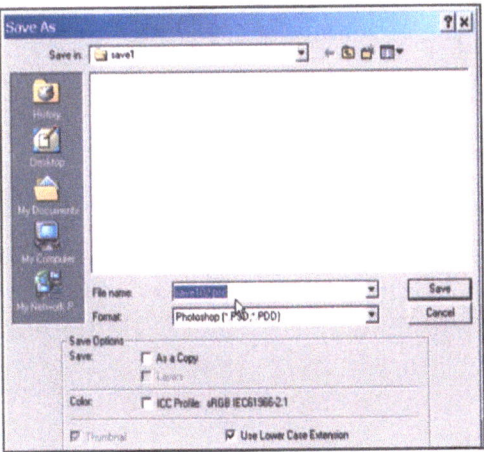

This little bit of saving setup enables you to do a **Ctrl+S** quick-save at regular intervals, potentially saving you much grief!

Save before editing a photo

When you first begin to edit a photo, it is likely that you will be working on your digital negative, that is, your unaltered original. Always begin such an editing session with a **Shift+Ctrl+S** or **File > Save As**. Choose PSD for your file type. This will maintain any layering that you do, and will not compress your image. Moreover, by choosing Save As... you do not save over your digital negative. It remains where it was, pristine and pure for posterity.

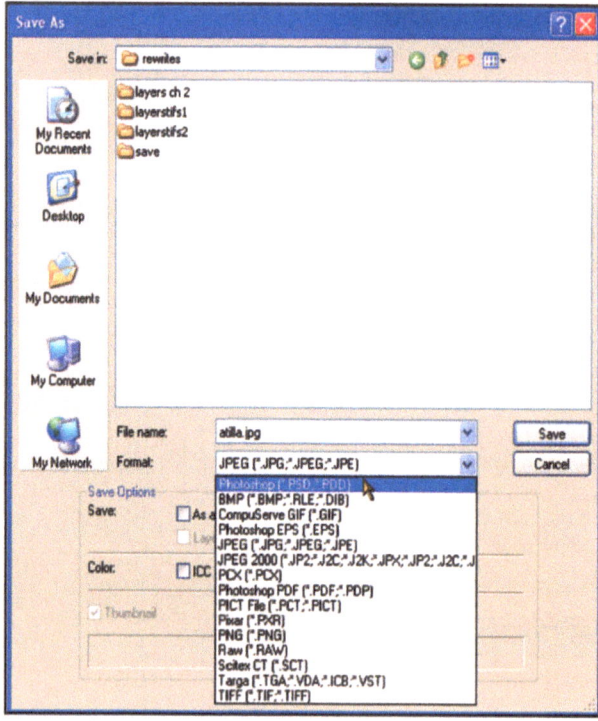

Saving on the fly

I feel your pain. Who has time to save stuff? You are working (or playing) and get involved in your project. Who wants to disturb the flow for a bunch of boring file-saving menu commands?

Well, I have your answer. The Ctrl-S Quick Save. A little roll of the left wrist, and your save is updated.

It is important to do this from time to time. Why? A power fluctuation shuts your computer down for an instant. Bam. Or your computer chokes on a big byte and you get the dreaded blue screen of death. <gulp>

When you open Elements again, your work will be where it was at your last save. If you have to think about how long ago that was, it has been too long. I **Ctrl+S** every time I do anything that makes me think, "That's kinda cool."

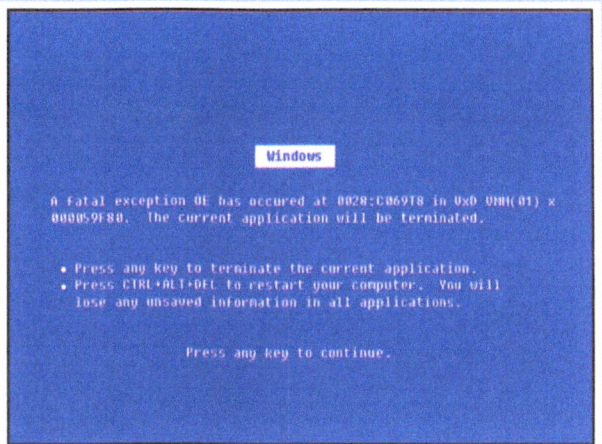

5. Base camp saves

In addition, to be super-safe, now and then make what I call a "Base Camp Save". This is a new PSD version of your file, and you make it with the Save As command. As you move along, if you really mess something up and have already **Ctrl+S** saved it, you can then return to your last base camp. (**File > Open Recent**...) In this way, you end up with several PSD file versions of your work.

So the flow of your work will be this:

Open file. **Ctrl+Shift+S** and name it `file1.psd` ... work ... **Ctrl+S**... work ... **Ctrl+S** ... work ... **Ctrl+Shift+S** and name it `file2.psd` ... work ... **Ctrl+S** ... and so on.

For the sake of storage space, be sure to go back and delete the extraneous base camps, once you are satisfied with your project.

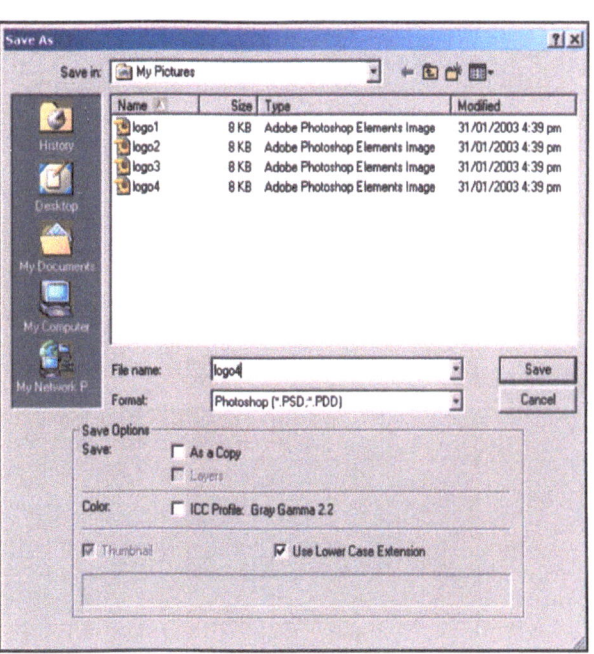

Safe Editing

The next section details some tips for you to use so that you can easily edit your images to your heart's content without risking damaging the work you've already done, or be able to quickly and easily change elements of your images with minimum fuss

6. Put everything on different layers

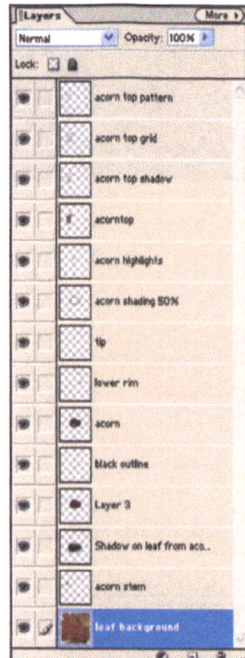

Use a new layer for every new thing you put on your image. For this acorn, I used a total of 13 layers, not counting the leaves in the background.

Using many layers makes it trivial to make changes later! By putting this white highlight on its own layer, for example, if I decide that I want to move it or shrink it or blur it, I can click that layer and do what I want. Such an operation would be well-nigh impossible if the white highlight were painted right onto the acorn base layer!

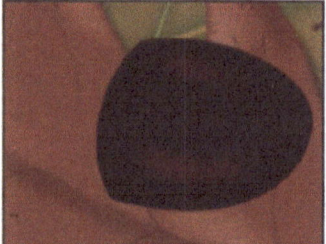

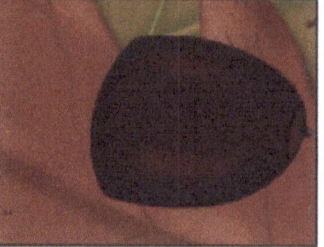

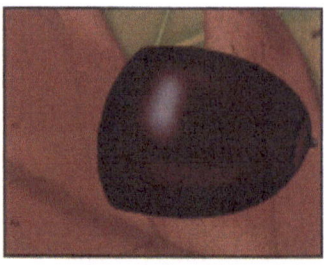

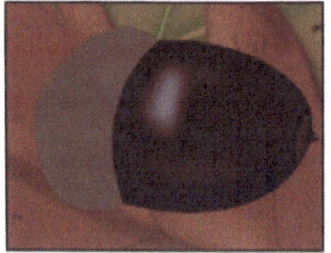

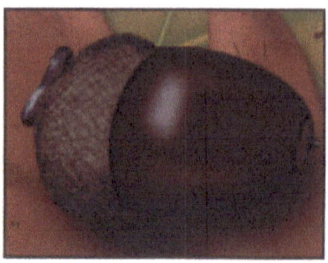

7. Don't flatten - keep your layers

Maintaining many layers will make your files considerably larger. This will mean that they will use more disk space and, perhaps, take longer to save. However, if you don't have to flatten your work, don't! Ok, there will be times when you are working with several objects, one of them is complete and you know you won't need its components separately. At those times, it is tidier to merge those layers. (To merge a few layers, link them in the Layers palette 🔗 and then **Ctrl+E**.)

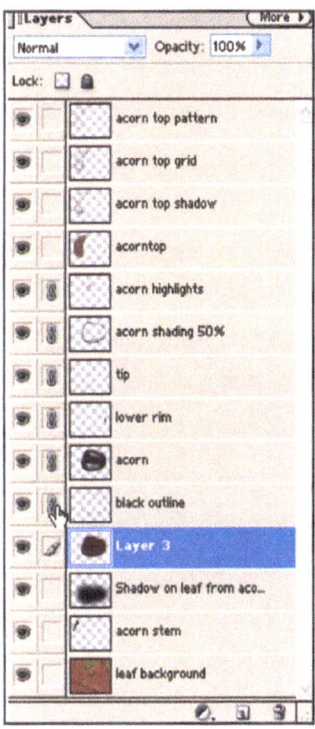

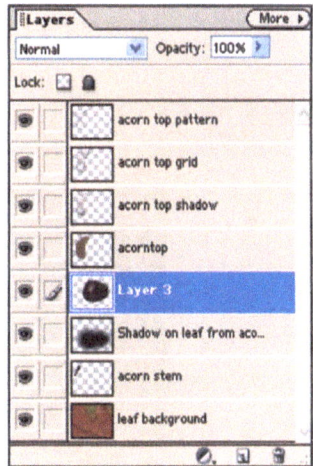

Here's a trick to reducing file size when you are working with many layers: This is another use for Base Camps! Here's how it works: You are working on `file1.psd` *and you have 15 layers. You really want to merge 5 of them to tidy things up a bit.*

1. *Ctrl+S to save this file as it is.*
2. *Then Ctrl+Shift+S (File > Save As) and name it* `file2.psd`.
3. *Now merge those 5 layers and continue to work on this new file, Ctrl+S-ing as you go. This new file will be smaller than the other!*

Then, when you are finished with the project, before you crop it, you can consolidate all of these layers into one master PSD file and get rid of all the extra PSDs. To do this, hold Shift as you drag each new layer you want to keep onto the older PSD file. This centers the contents of the layer on the new document. That is, it places the new stuff in the same position on the old one.

8. Test effects on a duplicate layer

Elements makes it easy to use the Enhance, Image, and Filter commands in the menu bar. However, if you must use these commands, you should only use them on copies of layers. That is, drag the layer you are working with to the New Layer icon at the bottom of the Layers palette to duplicate it. then apply your command.

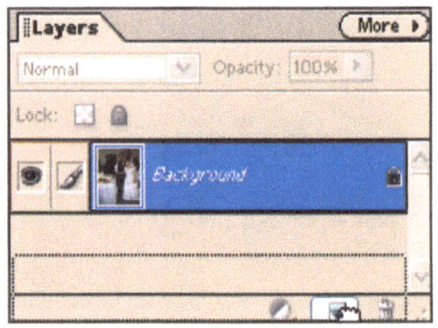

Why? Because these menu commands are permanent and "destructive". Once you apply a filter and then do some other work on that layer, if you then decide you don't like the filter's effect, you can only undo as far as your history states will allow. If you have done some painting or cloning on the layer, these history steps add up fast, too! Furthermore, once you close your document, you cannot undo the effects of that filter.

Suppose, for example, you sharpen your image. When you open the file later to work on it further, you discover you got it just a teensy bit too sharp, like Hogan here. Can you undo this?

If you have used a copy of your layer, you can!

First, if you don't like the effect at all, you can toss the layer into the bin, and no one will be the wiser!

Also, if you like the effect, but it is a bit extreme, you can keep this layer, but reduce its opacity or use a blending mode to combine its effects with the original, untouched layer.

This same advice follows for working with Elements' Effects palette. Duplicate your layer first. These effects change your layer, and are, therefore, destructive. (Layer Styles, on the other hand, are add-ons which are not destructive.)

9. Trade your eraser in for an Elemask!

Suppose you are working on merging two photos together, for example, Hogan, my black cat, and Oliver, his orange brother. You check to be sure both files are in RGB mode (**Image > Mode**) and then drag Ollie's photo onto Hogan's. Now you erase the part of Ollie's photo that you want trimmed away. Your strokes are small and swift.

After a while, you look at the part you did in the beginning, and realize that you erased part of Ollie's ear by mistake! So you have to either start all over or try to replace the part you erased. Big job!

But not if you had done this "erasing" with an Elemask! With an Elemask, you can "erase" part of the image by hiding it. Painting on the mask with black hides that part of the clipped picture. If you paint on the mask with white, you reveal that part of the picture once again! As you can see in the Layers palette thumbnails here, the photo of Ollie is still intact. If I discover that I've cut off too much of the hair around his neck, I can "replace" it, by painting white back onto the Elemask.

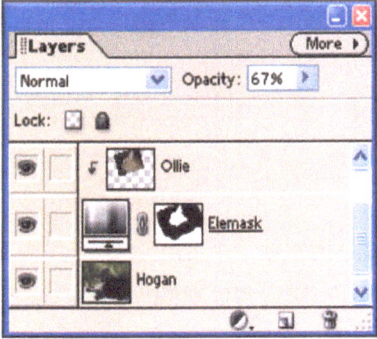

The full lowdown on Elemasks was in Chapter 2, but I thought I'd mention them again here, incase you missed it earlier.

10. Make notes on a hidden layer

Do you ever do something really cool in Elements and then try in vain to remember those steps later? Here's a tip that can help you with remembering your steps. Make a layer above all the rest of them and, using your Type Tool, list the steps you used in creating your image. (Of course, you can turn off the visibility eye for this layer, when you don't need to see it.)

 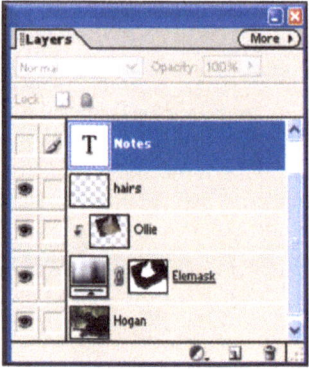

11. Take a screenshot of your history palette

You can also make yourself a reminder of your steps by taking a screenshot of your History palette and including it as a hidden layer in your PSD file. Here's how to take a screenshot with a PC

With the window you are shooting active, Alt+Print Screen. This copies the current window view to the clipboard.
Then, in Elements, File > New. The new file will be the same size as the window you are shooting.
Ctrl+V to paste the screenshot into the window.

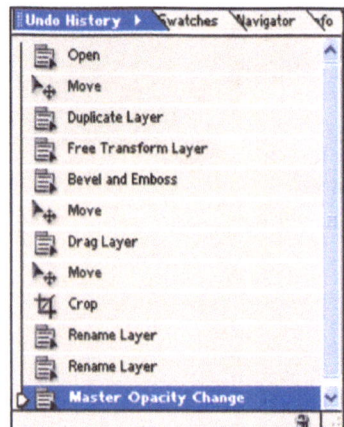 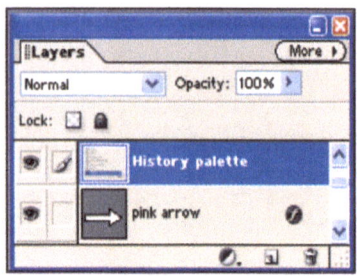

12. Let your Layers palette tell the story

If you make a new layer for each step and carefully label your Layers palette, you can tell the story of your image creation in your Layers palette. Then, when you save your file as an unflattened PSD, your Layers palette will remain as a visual charting of your steps.

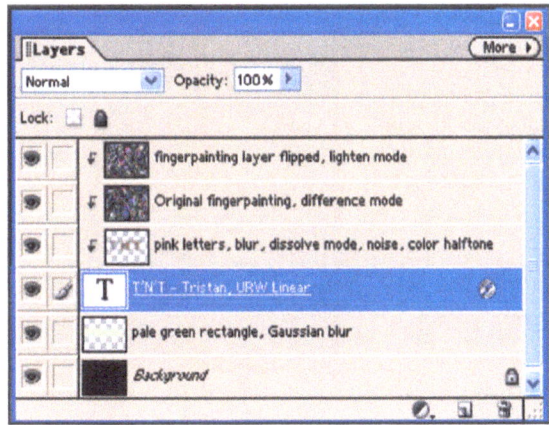

Saving finished work

This section concerns tips for when you've finished your work and covers the practical differences between the various file formats, along with other topics.

13. Quality v file size

In short, you usually cannot have both. If you need high quality, such as for printing, you most often will have a big file. If you want a small file, like for use on your website, you will often need to sacrifice quality, especially with photos. Your mission is to consider your needs, and to come to a happy balance where your quality is good enough, and your file small enough.

Quality level: 0 - File size: 3K

Quality level: 100 - File size: 33K

14. High-quality saves

In all likelihood, you will save finished work in TIFF, JPG, or GIF format. Where high-quality and cross-application compatibility is desired, such as for printing, or for using the file in page-editing software, you will probably want to use TIFF (Tagged-Image File Format). With TIFF, you can use no compression, a non-lossy compression, or JPEG compression, which is lossy. With the non-lossy compressions (or no compression) you won't lose image data when you save. Therefore, TIFF is a good format for archiving finished work, too.

When you do a **File > Save As**... and choose TIFF, you'll get this dialog box asking you to choose TIFF options. You get to choose among four types of image compression, the byte ordering, layer compression, and whether or not you want to save the image pyramid. These are explained in detail in the manual under **Index > F > File Formats > Choosing > Saving in TIFF format.**

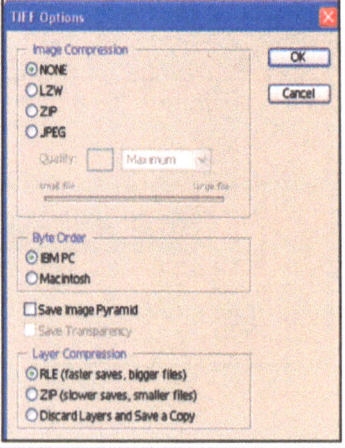

15. The difference between photos and graphics

Photos generally have many colors, gradations, and gentle shadings. Graphics, on the other hand, are usually just a few colors. Because of this difference, we save them into different file formats. Photos are saved as JPEGs (JPG) and graphics are saved as GIFs.

Graphic

Photo

It is easy to remember which file format to use, if you remember what each of these abbreviations means:
JPEG is Joint Photographic Experts Group.
GIF is Graphics Interchange Format.

16. Don't save photos as GIFs

As a general rule, GIF is not the preferable format in which to save photos. Here is an example. The photo on the left was saved as a JPG. The one on the right is the same file size, saved as a GIF. Notice how pixelly the GIF image is! That is because the indexing of the colors does not allow for the subtle gradations of color required by this photo.

You can save a photo as a GIF. In fact, if the photographic image requires a transparent background or if it is to be part of an animation, you will save it as a GIF. Or you may want the pixelly effect for its own artistic value for your project. In general, though, GIF won't be best for photos.

17. Don't save graphics as JPGs either!

Because of the compression methods used in JPG format, you get funky artifacts left behind in JPG images. This is not noticeable with high-quality (and high file size) JPGs, but in lower quality, the artifacts can be really awful.

In a graphic, where you want the edges to be nice and crisp, you can easily wreck things by saving as a JPG. I saved the left-hand image with GIF, and the one on the right, in a similar file size, using JPG. Which would you rather take home for dinner?

18. Don't resave JPGs

So photos are best as JPG and graphics are best as GIF. Now here's another consideration: JPG is lossy, that is, its compression loses some data for each subsequent save.

The scenario: You open a JPG file. You do some work. You **Ctrl+S** to save. You do more work. You **Ctrl+S** to save. Good... right?

NO! Each time you resave a JPG, you lose some data. It might not be noticeable, but it does build up, and it may be noticeable at high resolution.

Better: You open a JPG file. You click **File > Save As**.. and choose PSD for the file type. You do work. You **Ctrl+S** to save. You do more work. You **Ctrl+S** to save. When you are all ready to make this a JPG again, **File > Save As** ... and make it a JPG.

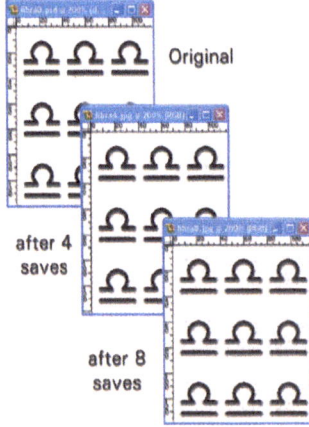

Original

after 4 saves

after 8 saves

19. Create big images, then reduce them

The reason is that when you enlarge an image in Elements, however you do it, the image is resampled. You are effectively stretching the distance between pixels, and so Elements has to figure out what goes in there. Elements does this by averaging the values of all the surrounding pixels. The resulting image will look blurred. The fact is that Elements cannot create image data that is not there, and that is what you are asking when you try to stretch an image!

See what happens to this cute little anchor, when I try to enlarge it?

You can sometimes fix this blurring somewhat by using **Filter > Sharpen > Unsharp Mask.** But you are best off to make your images large and then reduce them, if you have to.

20. Batch process to save time

This only sounds difficult. This utility is an enormously efficient time-saver. And besides, it is fun to do!

You can run this process on either all files you have open at the moment, or all the files in a folder. This utility will resize all of the images within the constraints you specify, save copies of each of them in the format and quality you have chosen, name them, if you want their name changed, add a sequence number, and put the saved copies all in the destination folder of your choice. Very slick.

Batch Processing
can be a big help in
saving and organizing
your photos!

To do Batch Processing, begin by putting all of the photos you want to process into a folder, or, alternatively, open them in Elements. Click **File > Batch Processing**, and this dialog box will appear. Fill in your choices, click OK, and watch it go!

> Batch Processing will close any files that you have open. Therefore, if you are working in PSD, be sure to **Ctrl+S** to update your PSD version before you run Batch Processing.

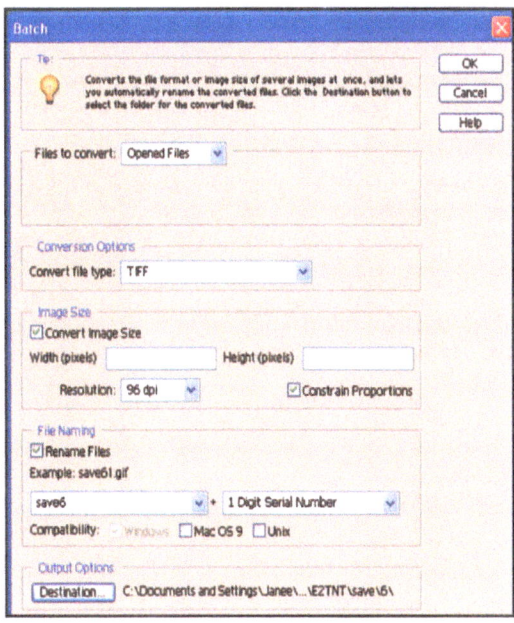

Preparing for potential catastrophic loss of data

I have heard that it is not a question of if your hard drive will crash, it is a question of when! This doesn't mean that you should be afraid to use your computer. You just have to use it wisely. You have a plan for how to get out of your house in the event of a fire. You fasten your seatbelt in the event that you should have an auto accident. A crash of your hard drive is another potential disaster for which you should prepare. Please believe me.

I'm not referring to those "My computer crashed," moments when your OS freezes up, requiring you to reboot. A true crash of your hard drive is very different. When your hard-drive crashes, you turn your computer one sunny morning, and, as it is booting up, you will get a message: "Hard Drive not found," or something equally inspiring. <gulp> Now what?

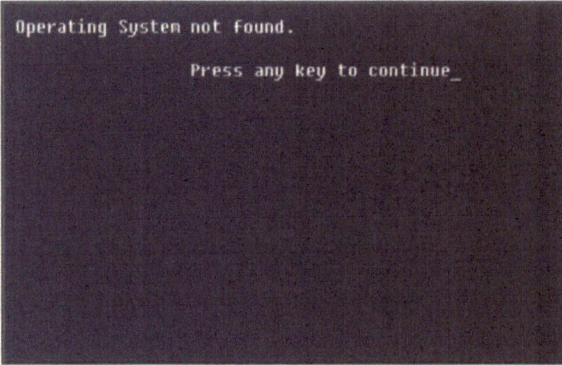

Don't panic right away. First be sure your system is plugged in right. Turn the box around and be sure that all the connections are tight. Turn your computer off and then on again. Still nothing? Ok, *now* you may panic.

Once your computer guru has established that your drive is broken, then comes the shock. If this drive contained all of your data, your life's work, all of your vacation photos and every photo taken of your baby who is now 5 years old, and you have no backups, you may have to kiss that portion of your life goodbye. There are some data recovery outfits, but you will likely be paying well into the thousands of dollars to get your work back. And then, there are no guarantees! Let's work *now* to ensure that you will not have this sort of shock in your life. Ever.

21. Managing backups

Ok, so you are convinced you need to back up your work, and to keep it backed up routinely. How do you do this? You are likely to need your backups at some point, so they should be accessible and usable. In addition, it is important that your backup procedure is easy to follow, if it is not automatic. If it is complicated and difficult, you won't do it. And if you don't do it, it won't work. Here are some backup methods:

Because of the way my mind works (or doesn't), I prefer an automatic backup. There are many good software packages which will handle this for you, usually backing up to a second hard drive.

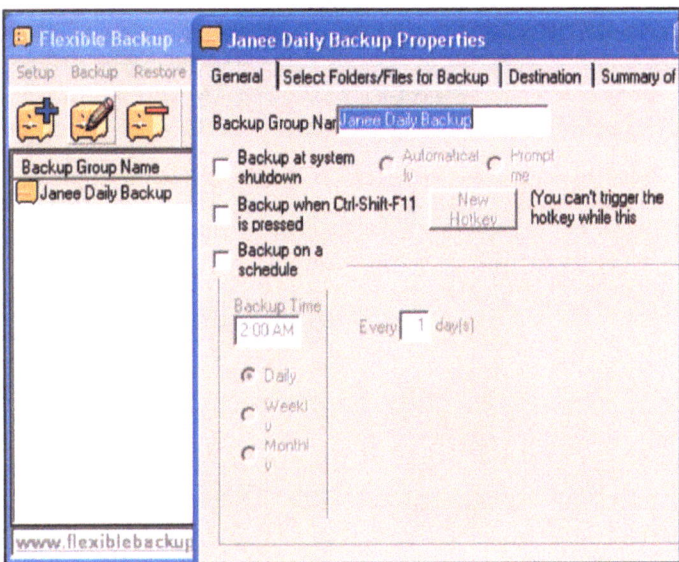

Backing up daily to Zip disk can be practical for some applications, but I don't think that it is particularly useful for the large file sizes that you get with images.

Backing up to CD or DVD is generally considered to be a good thing, and in fact, is so good, that I talk about this under Archiving.

Whatever means you choose to back up your work, ask yourself from time to time, "Where would I be, if my system were to crash right now?"

22. Backup your photos onto CD to prevent losing them forever

There are several ways to store your digital negatives, and your choice will depend mostly upon your storage medium. It is best to have at least two different backups for your photos – a hard drive backup and a portable medium backup. By "portable medium", I am referring to such media as CDs, DVDs, or Zip disks.

When a person's house burns, the things that they invariably miss most are their family photos. Digital negatives are good insurance from that loss, if you make a habit of keeping a backup away from home. CDs are inexpensive. A handful of them can store years of photos and will take up little space in your safe-deposit box, in a safe place at work, or at a family member's house.

CDs are often targets for burglars. If you keep a copy of your family photo CDs away from your other computer CDs or music CDs, you are less likely to lose them to theft.

23. Keeping a PSD file as a library of pre-prepared elements

The PSD file can be viewed as a little library of spare parts. This little spare parts library is only as useful as it is easy to find and use, however.

You might find it helpful to group like objects together in a layered PSD file, if you want to be able to choose among them easily. I have a file I use nearly every day called `tools.psd`. Each of the objects is on its own layer, ready to drag to another file, should I wish to demonstrate something and just need an arrow or a pen tool. Though it would not take up more disk space to maintain separated PSD files for each of these objects, it is much easier for me to find just what I want here.

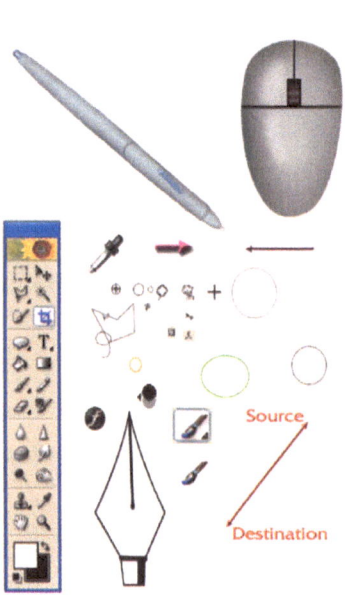

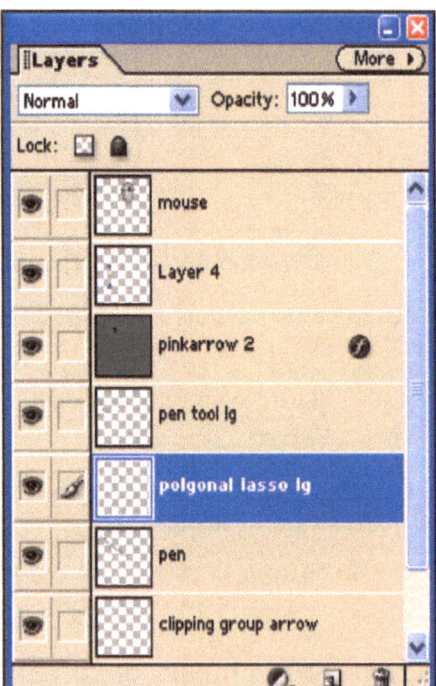

24. Archiving finished work

I have a problem with the concept of "finished work". This is because, when I first began using image editors, I was so excited about the work that I did on my pictures, that I deleted all the originals and kept only my "finished" JPGs.

So what was wrong with that? First of all, I saved these JPGs at 72 ppi, a good resolution for monitor-viewing, but horrible for printing. And also, *no matter how good you are now, you are not as good as you are going to be*. I look back at my pathetic attempts and wish I could have that girl (me) back so I could shake some sense into her! The originals with which I worked are gone now, replaced by my attempts at "improvement".

Therefore, if you have a choice between archiving as "work in progress" PSDs or finished work as TIFs or JPGs, I'd say to archive the layered PSDs. (Do not flatten). PSDs are compressed using RLE, a lossless compression method, and they save all of your image data. TIFF can save layers, but the file either will be compressed, or, if uncompressed, the file will be much larger than the PSD.

*You think you're good
but soon you'll see...
You're not as good
as you're going to be!*

Putting your work out there

So what good is it to do all of this fabulous work, if no one will see it? I have compiled some tips for putting your work out where you and others can enjoy it, both by printing and by sharing on the internet. For tips specific to using your images on your own website, check out the next chapter, too!

25. Printing: Garbage in, Garbage out!

There is one fundamental rule for printing: GIGO, or Garbage In, Garbage Out. You cannot expect a bad image to look good, just because it is printed. In fact, the opposite is more likely to be true. We are accustomed to lower quality images on our monitors, but we expect a lot from the quality of our prints!

So if your image is to be printed, first take time to be sure that it is as good as you want it to be.

26. Use the right resolution for printing

For printing, your files should be at least 200 - 300 ppi (pixels per inch). (This will translate into dpi on your printer.) There are at least three ways to set your resolution of your file.

When you create a new file (**File > New**), you are asked to specify the resolution. If you choose one of the "print sizes", like 8x10 or A4, the resolution will be set to 300.

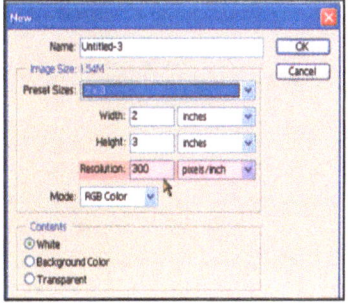

If you use **File > Save for Web**, the resolution of the image will automatically be set to 72 ppi, which is good for the web, since most monitors have a screen resolution of just 72 anyway.

If you go to **Image > Resize > Image Size**, you can change the resolution there. Beware the resampling question, because this is important. Read on to find out about resampling.

27. To resample or not to resample?

In this tip, we begin with an image which has a resolution of 72 ppi, typical of one you might find on the web. What happens if we decide that we want to print this image?

We can print it as it is, at 72 ppi (which your printer will translate into 72 dpi(dots per inch)), but this is low resolution and so your picture will look pixellated and rough.

We can go to the Image Size dialog box (**Image > Resize > Image Size**) and change the resolution there to a better resolution for print, say 300 ppi.

In the Image Size dialog box, you need to change the resolution to 300. You will also have to make an important decision about whether or not to resample. Resampling is Elements' way of adding or taking away pixels which it thinks you don't need. If you have to resample, you can choose among three different kinds of resampling. These are nearest neighbor, bilinear, and bicubic, with bicubic giving the smoothest results. You will find, though, that, because of the inevitable loss of quality, you should avoid resampling if possible.

In the following image, see what happens to an image which has its resolution changed from 72 (web resolution) to 300 (a good print resolution). Whether you want a teensy print, a resampled print, which is likely to appear blurred, or a low-resolution print, which will be pixellated, is up to you and your purposes. But if you have just a few pixels to start with, you will not be able to make a large crisp image with them.

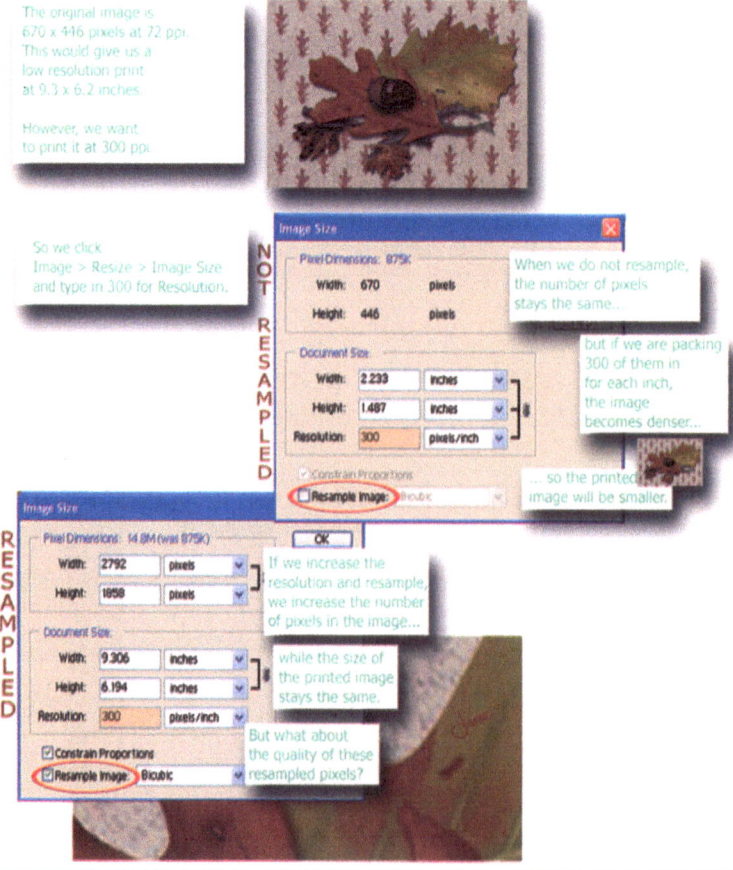

28. Making a contact sheet

A contact sheet is a page of thumbnails. You could use this to show proofs of a collection of shots, from which your client could choose. To make one, first put all the pictures you want to use into a folder. Click **File > Print Layouts > Contact Sheet** to bring up the Contact Sheet dialog box. Then choose your options, hit **OK**, and kick back and watch! Even if you don't *need* a contact sheet, this is cool, just because it is fun to watch Elements work.

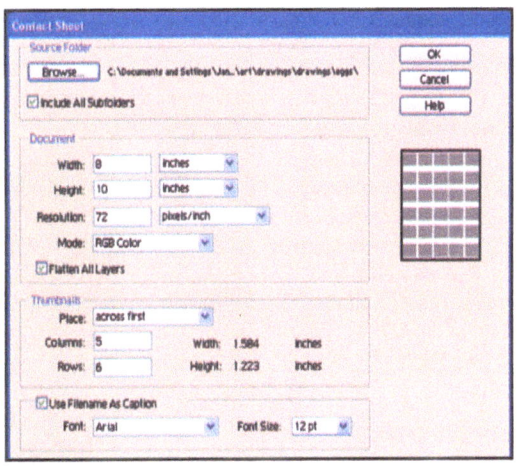

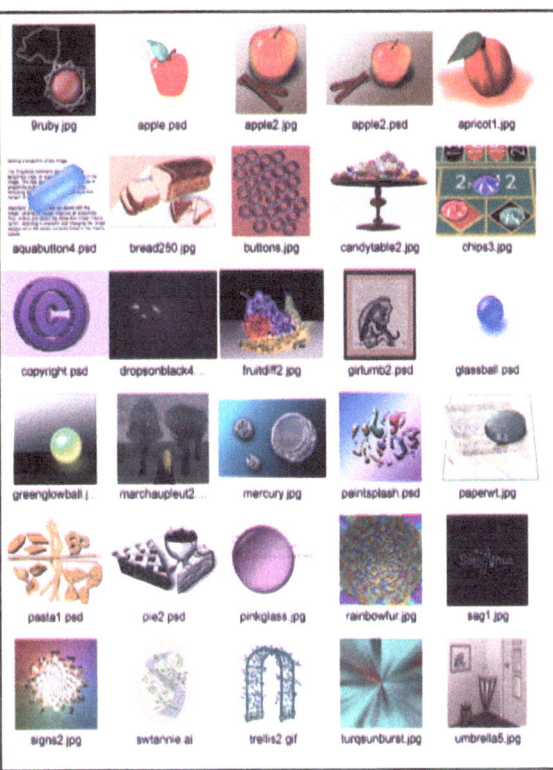

29. Reduce image resolution when sending via email

Whether you are retouching family photos, taking pictures of your new baby, or making collages or other art on your computer, it is fun and personally rewarding to share it! The Internet has given us the ability to share not only with family and friends, but also with people from all over the world!

Being able to share image files through email is one of the rewards of having a computer and an image editor like Elements! Elements not only helps you in making your images presentable, but also enables you to save them in the proper quality, size, and file format for sending.

Sure, you *can* send files just as they come from your scanner or your camera, but this is not the best approach. First, the photos that you start with will probably be too large to be comfortably viewed on a monitor. Say your camera takes pictures that are 1600 x 1200, a common size for digital cameras. And suppose your friend's monitor is set at 800 x 600 resolution, a common resolution. If your picture is 1600 pixels wide, his monitor can only look at a quarter of it at a time!

30. Keep your friends - don't send them PSD files!

You may have noticed by now that PSD files, the layered files which you create as you are editing an image, can be *huge*. It is not uncommon for a PSD file to become several megabytes in size. You are herewith forbidden to email a friend a PSD file unless they want to see the layers of your file. What you will do instead is save your image in a format which they can use as they wish, for example, a JPEG, GIF, or, if they need the best quality and don't mind a larger file, a TIFF.

In this example, the PSD file, with only three layers, is 615KB. The same file in a JPG of medium quality is just 58KB!

For photos for the web or for email, I keep this as my personal rule of thumb: *60K in file size and 600 x 500 in pixel dimensions.* Unless your recipient has a specific need otherwise, you should stick to 72 ppi resolution.

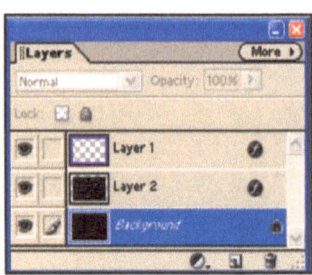

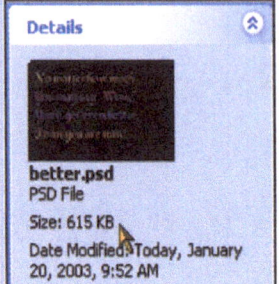

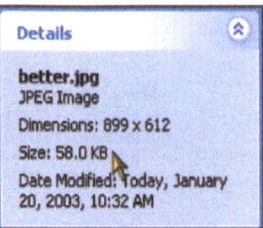

31. Sharing images on a website

Having your own personal website can be an immensely rewarding creative endeavor, and, actually, with several hours of work, you can have your own shingle on the World Wide Web! There are many resources available with how-tos for putting together your own site. One of these is the Website Creation FAQ at http://www.kellysweb-studio.com/studio/website_faq.html.

But even before you set up your own site, you can share your images online! There are many image-sharing communities set up just for this purpose. Some are online galleries, whilst others are more interactive, run as "Art Challenges" and the like. (There is an Art Challenge, for example, at www.myJanee.com). For a listing of many online photo-sharing services, do a search for "photo sharing".

On these services, you will typically have to register. Most of the services are free, but some will charge, depending upon the amenities you want. Then you go to an upload screen, which gives you a Browse button. From there, you find the image files you want to post. Some of them offer choices of background color or framing.

One popular option for a photo-sharing community is Shutterfly, and Elements makes it easy for you to upload your images directly to this service. To do this, click **File > Online Services**. You will see the various options for online services, one of which is to upload images to Shutterfly! If you have trouble with Adobe's link for registration, you can register directly from www.shutterfly.com.

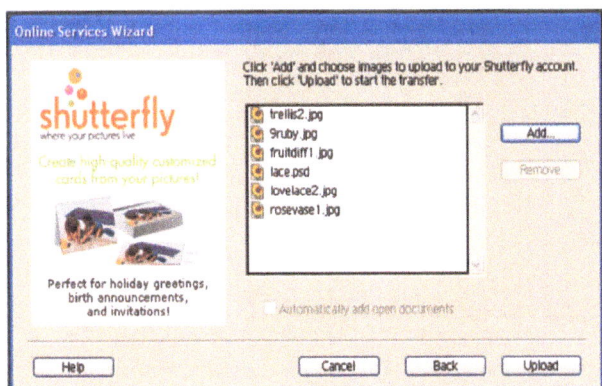

Shutterfly has some cool choices for you, in addition to just setting up a free online gallery. I particularly like their card-printing and mailing service!

32. Creating a PDF slideshow

A PDF Slideshow can be a fun and efficient way to share your photos with family or friends. I envision this as a good way to show work to clients, too. The only software that your viewer will need is Adobe Acrobat Reader, a free program, readily available from www.adobe.com.

Here is how to create a PDF Slideshow.

1. Select File > Automation Tools > PDF Slideshow.

2. In the dialog box, click **Browse** and find all the images you want to use. If you have several files in one folder, you can choose more than one of them:

3. To select several, hold **Ctrl** as you click your choices.

4. To select several in a list, click the first one you want and then **Shift+click** the last one.

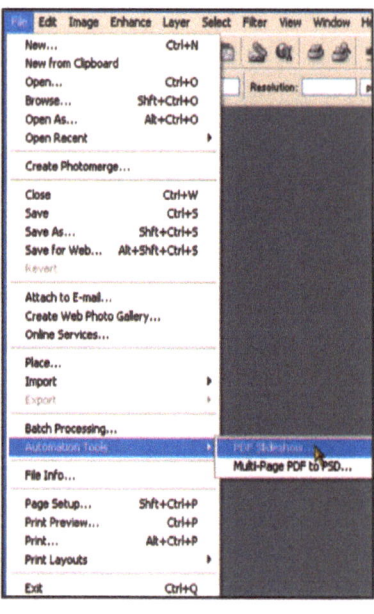

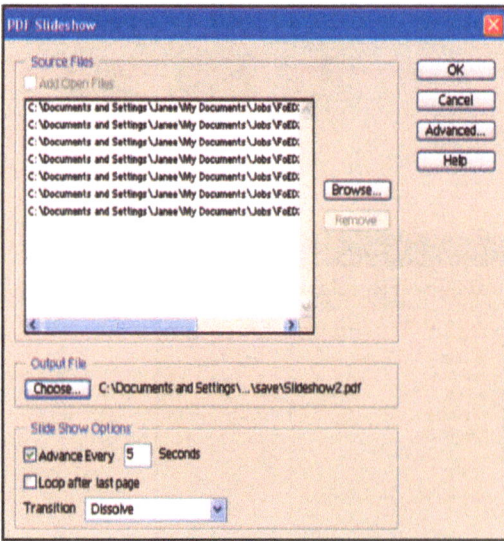

5. Choose your options at the bottom. The Transition option gives you many choices of ways you can make your slides transition from one to the next. You can also choose, in the Advanced... option, how much pause you get between slide changes.

6. To sequence your slides, in the PDF Slideshow dialog box drag the slides in the list to the position you want them.

The slideshow will probably come on in full-screen mode to play. If you want, though, you can view it at your own leisurely rate. Whilst in full-screen view, hit the **Esc** key. This will put you into the view you see here. To get the thumbnails on the left, push the Show Navigation Pane button just to the right of the binoculars.

I hope that in this chapter you have discovered some exciting ways to use your images, as well as some ideas for making the practical necessities of saving a little less tedious. In the next chapter, we will carry the "what to do with your images" thread a bit further, with some cool ideas for your own website!

Website nuts and bolts

1. Pick the right content
2. Think of your audience
3. Make your site easy to navigate
4. Consider download times
5. The differences between GIFs and JPGs for web use
6. Saving for the web
7. Making thumbnails
8. Making a web photo gallery

Creating images for your site

9. Keeping the background in the background
10. Making a seamless tiled background
11. Making a patterned page border
12. Making a transparent GIF
13. Matte? What's that?
14. Say it with a banner
15. Creating animated GIFs
16. Quick animation tips
17. A shortcut for making a capsule-shaped button
18. Rollover buttons
19 Saving the files for each button in each state
20. Installing rollover buttons into your site

Chapter 8

Winning Web Images

A website will usually have at least these three elements: text, images, and a navigation system. The text is handled with a text editor. Navigation can be either by linked text, or by linked images. The images? That's where Elements comes in!

But just having pictures and text tossed onto a page will not give you a good website. So before we start talking about your site's images, we should consider some aspects of good website design. Then I'll offer some tips on making your photos work well on the web. We'll look at topics like file type, file size, load times, and file quality. Then we'll be creating a Web Photo Gallery! Finally, we will get into how you can create some special images made just for your website: animated GIFs, transparent GIFs, rollover buttons, and seamless patterns for site backgrounds.

1. Pick the right content

When putting together your site, strive to have useful, interesting and entertaining content in a comfortable, attractive, and easily navigable format. So you work for excellence in these four areas:

- Content
- Comfort
- Navigability
- Attractiveness

Each of these four objectives is critical to having a good site. In many sites you see, there might be good information, but it is hidden in a labyrinth of jumbled links. Or maybe a site is just so ugly or confusing, that you don't stay around long enough to see what information it offers!

When you start your site, begin with a clear idea of where you want to take it. Your site cannot be all things to all people.

Strive to have content that is appropriate for your site's visitors. If your site is for your business, having personal writings about your exploits in your college fraternity may not be appropriate, for example.

Remember that you will need to update your site to keep it current and alive. You will only want to do this sort of work with subject matter that you love, and which fascinates you.

Don't try to make your site do too much. That will leave you with a shallow site that is not gratifying to you or useful to others.

If your site is a personal site, choose topics for which you have passion. Your website can be a wonderful experience for you, a journal of your progress, a testament to your growth.

2. Think of your audience

You want your visitors to feel comfortable on your site. Of course, you want your site to be usable, too, but comfort goes a step beyond that. Usability is a complex topic which relates to issues such as accessibility to the visually impaired. There are many very good websites and books with information on this, like our Flash Usability Guide. A Google search on "website usability" yields several.

If you have surfed around the Internet a bit, you certainly have been to a site that made you want to leave. Everyone has their own pet peeves about websites. Personally, I don't like a site that has too much going on; a bunch of flashing graphics and things that move bother me. Music that comes on as soon as I enter the site will make me hit the Back button very fast. What you do to make your site comfortable for your viewers will depend upon the purpose of your site and who your intended viewer is.

Pop-ups or banner ads ... I know that they are a necessary evil for some sites, but most people don't like them. Especially when you are using free webspace, you may have to put up with them. But as soon as you can get your own host, do, and lose the banner ads.

"Comfort", of course, may be defined differently, depending upon your site's intended audience. These tips are general guidelines, though, and they are appropriate to any audience.

It is usually best to keep a consistent design for all of your pages: same header, footer, background, and fonts. This gives your site a unified feel, and your visitors will know that they are still on your site.

Keep the number of fonts to a minimum. Having too many fonts leads to a cluttered page.
Consider readability.

This font has serifs.

This font is san-serif.

It has been shown in numerous studies that dark san-serif font on a light background is easiest to read, with black on white being the easiest.

Black text against a gray background has been shown to be easy to read, too.

This text is easy to read for a title or label.

But if you have a good deal of text, it becomes tedious to read it against the dark background.

Dark gray text against black? It may look cool at first glance, but it is not comfortable for most of us to read.

If you have music or other sounds on your site, make them "opt in", so that your guests can push a button if they want the sound.

Please leave out the "under construction" GIFs. I was as guilty as anyone, using a cute little animated steamshovel on my site, until it occurred to me finally: a good website is *always* under construction. You are never finished. Either your design is evolving, you are updating content, or both!

Leave the visitor's browser under their control. Sites that enlarge the site window to full-screen are particularly annoying to me and other people who multitask. Changing the viewer's pointer is another thing that you may wish to reconsider. Your viewer may have chosen a particular pointer for their computer, because of vision limitations.

Under Construction

If you use a background pattern, be sure it enhances the theme of your site. Cutesy or busy backgrounds can be distracting or annoying.

If you are going to put text directly on the background, make the background pattern very light and your text dark, so that it is easily readable.

If you use moving graphics, be sure that they work well with your message, rather than just being distracting.

Banner ads are annoying for most people. If you have to have them, use as few as you can. The same is true for pop-up ads. Flickering or glaringly flashing ads are particularly awful.

3. Make your site easy to navigate

I should state first that you should have navigation. You should begin site construction with a plan. If your site is to be about gardening, for example, you might begin your site by laying out your topics like this:

Don't put too much on the first page of your site. Your first page can be a page where you welcome your visitors with a look into what your site is about. If you have, on this first page, a list of places to go within your site, your visitors can get right into the site. Once in there, they should be able to make sense of your navigation system.

In your initial "where to go" links, a long list of choices is confusing, so keep to main topics on your first page. Allow your guests to click into your site for more detailed listings.

Make your design consistent with your purpose. For example, a kids' site should have bright colors and simple graphics.

Avoid link images which don't give clear clues about what they mean.

Instead, have visible labels on your buttons, so that your visitors will know where they're headed. The buttons should also contain ALT-tags, text indicators describing the graphic. (These tags enable your visitor to make sense of your page, even if s/he is visually impaired, or if the graphic does not load. You can create these ALT-tags in your web-editing software.)

4. Consider download times

It is usually good to keep your webpages short. In general, a webpage should contain no more than what would fit on a couple of typewritten pages. Of course, your mileage may vary. If your page has information that would be awkward to break up, or your viewer would find it more convenient to have it all on one scrollable page, then longer pages may be better.

Images will usually be the slowest part of your page to load, so be sure that they contribute something meaningful for your visitor. If you are using many images, such as in a photo gallery, you will want to use thumbnails, to speed up your download time. Then your visitors can click on only the ones they want to see. Similarly, if you want to show a single large picture, you can display a smaller version of it on your site, with a link to a larger version.

Be mindful of image sizes. Different screens have different resolutions, so what shows nicely on your screen may not all fit on another's. A good rule of thumb is to make images no wider than 800 pixels, because that will take up much of the width of most screens, although with larger moniters available now, this may appear small in the near future.

Save your images appropriately, usually either in a JPG or GIF format at 72 ppi. Most screens will display only 72 ppi, anyway, so don't save at more than that when it is for the web.

Experiment with manipulating the quality of your images in the Save for Web dialog box. Sometimes a little reduction in quality can amount to a huge difference in file size.

There will be times that you care more about having a moderate file size than you do about maintaining the integrity of each pixel. While many of us are blessed with DSL or Cable Internet connections that can download sites at a blinding 4 – 10 Mbps, there are still many users who are on a modem, running at 56 kbps. If you put images with large file sizes on your website, even the most dedicated modem-user will leave before any of them load.

And yes, the large majority of American surfers are still on a modem (87% as of September 2002, according to CableDatacomNews.com), and worldwide, the percentage of surfers not on modem is still well below 10% (TurboAds.com).

I have heard different "rules" for how large a web page "should" be, including all graphics. Of course this depends upon the audience for your website and what it is that you are offering them. If your 179K graphic is a bad photo of your dog, chances are good that you will irritate, rather than charm, your visitors!

5. The differences between GIFs and JPGs for web use

JPEG (or JPG): JPEG (which actually stands for Joint Photographic Experts Group) is one of the file formats you will see most on the web, because they can be made in relatively small file sizes. This format allows for unlimited color display and is, therefore, best for images which use continuous tones.

Just Photos and Gradients

The disadvantage to this format (as mentioned in the previous chapter), is that it is lossy, that is, it compresses the file with each repeated save. Therefore, you do not want to edit a JPG, save it as a JPG, and repeat this. You will notice a reduction in the quality of the image after just a couple of repeated saves!

GIF: GIF is another file format which you see for images on the web, because they can be made in small file-sizes. GIF is not lossy; repeated saves will not reduce image quality. If you need to have the background transparent for a web graphic, you will likely use GIF. Also, if you want to make an image on your website move, you may want an animated GIF.

Because GIF works by saving images in only a limited palette of colors, up to 256, it is a particularly good format for graphics like this one which have limited colors.

But because of this color indexing, GIF is generally *not* a good format for photos, or images with gradations of colors.

So what if you want to save a photographic image, and need the background to be transparent? You need to save as a GIF. A process called "dithering" is what Elements uses to combine two colors to approximate another. This enables you to get reasonable approximations to your colors, even when you do save a photo as a GIF.

Saving as a GIF with or without dither can also be a way to make a different kind of art from your photo. Experiment with these settings and see what they can do for you!

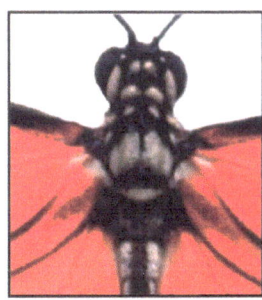

| GIF no dithering | 100% dithering | Saved as JPEG |

6. Saving for the web

Here is a nifty timesaving feature for you: **Save for Web**. Elements has it, and you should use it. Save for Web does several things for you.

Save for Web does not affect your original document. The image you are creating is a *copy*.

Whatever resolution your original document is, Save for Web will make this copy at 72 ppi - appropriate for the web.

Another timesaver is Save for Web's image sizing. You can size your image, see what it looks like in the preview window, and see how large the file is before and after your resizing.

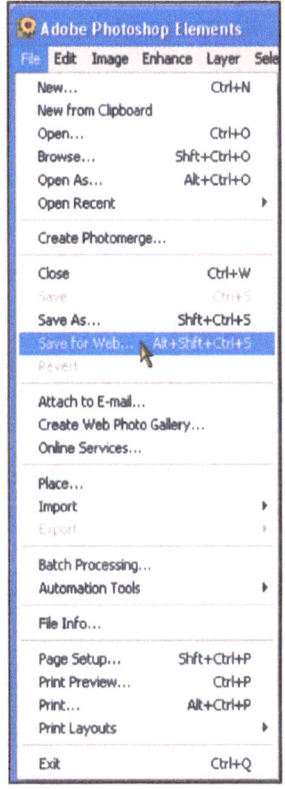

In this dialog box, you can pick your desired file format. If you are using JPG, you choose the quality you want for the image. If you are working with a GIF, you choose how many colors you want to use in the palette. The higher the quality, or the more colors, the bigger the file size will be.

After you have chosen all of the parameters in the Save for Web dialog box, you click **OK**. Another dialog box will come up so you can tell Elements where to store this new copy of your image.

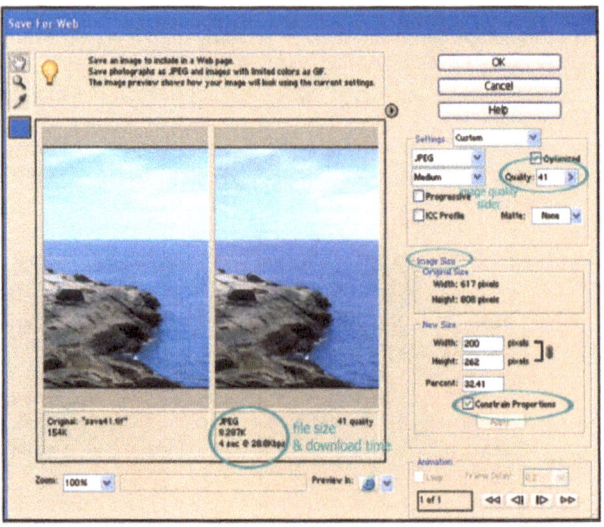

7. Making thumbnails

Use thumbnail images, smaller versions of your image, on your pages, especially when you have many images to show. You then link these to full-sized versions, so that your site's visitors can click only those they want to see in more detail. If your visitor just wants to see one or two images, he won't have to wait for all of the images to load full-size <yawn>. A page of thirty 2K thumbnails can load as quickly as *one* full-sized image that is 60K!

Clicking the thumbnail takes your visitor to the larger image.

If you have several images ready to put into a gallery format, Elements' Web Photo Gallery feature will enable you to create thumbnails from your photos quickly. You will read more about this feature in a minute.

You can make thumbnails in the Save for Web dialog, too, after you have saved your full-size image. Use the Image Size box there to create the thumbnail. Be sure to check Constrain Proportions. I like my thumbnails to have 100 pixels for the longer side, but you may have other ideas.

8. Making a Web Photo Gallery

Elements has a very nifty feature which makes it quite easy to put together a photo gallery for the web. You can choose from several designs for your gallery. Your site's visitors will be able to see your thumbnails when they get to the page. Then, if they click a thumbnail, they will see the larger image. And the nice thing is that Elements does all the hard part for you, once you find the command. It is almost hidden in the File menu. Here's how to make a Web Photo Gallery.

Move all of the files you want to use into one folder. Image size or file type can vary, but you will want to have them large enough so that you when you resize them, they will not be enlarged. Enlarging your images will compromise their quality.

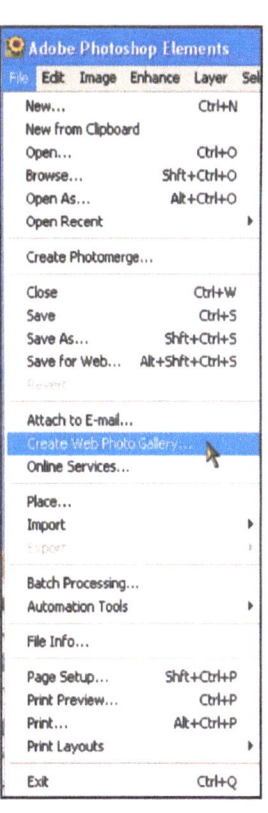

1. Select **File > Create Web Photo Gallery**.

2. In the dialog box, for Folders, use the **Browse** button to choose the folder for the source of your images, and use the Destination button to choose the folder where your finished pages and images will go.

3. Choose the style you want, what you want your banner to say, the sizing for your thumbnails, etc.

4. Choose whether to resize your large (display) images, whether to constrain both width and length, or just one of them, and to what pixel dimension. Then choose the quality for your JPEGs, and whether you want a border.

5. Next, you have the option of including copyright information, a title, or other text superimposed over your large images. Choose your font, color, opacity, and positioning.

6. Click **OK**.

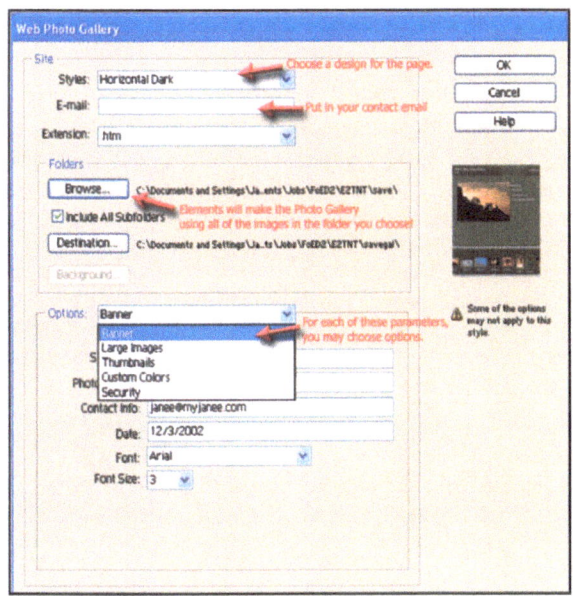

Your Web Photo Gallery will be constructed for you in flashes, as you watch! Then your browser will open, showing you your finished Web Photo Gallery.

This is not online yet, though; you will have to install it to your website. Elements will have made some pages for you, though, all ready for you to use, or customize in your HTML editor. The destination folder will look something like this:

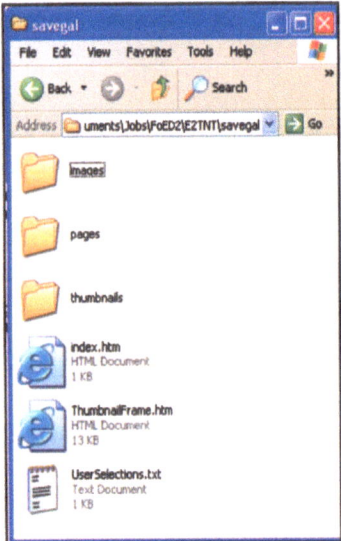

A word about copyright

There are some mistaken notions that, if something is on the web, it is yours for the taking. It can generally be assumed that, unless something is specifically said to be "in the public domain," it is copyrighted. To use it without permission, therefore, is illegal. So don't steal other people's stuff from their sites. Making your own is more fun anyway! Take your own photos and make your own graphics. You have the right software now, in Elements!

Of course there may be others who like your images and want to use them. There are some safeguards you can use to make it more difficult for people to use your work, such as using low-resolution work on the web, placing prominent copyright notices on the work, watermarking, or slicing your images and installing them in pieces. However, nothing will make your images completely safe from poachers. So as a general rule, if you have something that you do not want to have taken, you shouldn't put it on your site.

Creating images for your site

Aside from photos, there are other images which you can make for your site, now that you are working with Photoshop Elements. These are the fun things in a site: buttons, banners, interface designs, rollovers, patterned backgrounds, transparent GIFs, and animated GIFs. Along with your own photos, these design elements will help you to make your site your own!

9. Keeping the background in the background

I am not usually a big fan of patterned backgrounds. I think that part of the reason for this is that I've seen so many bad uses of patterns on the web. The background of your pages should be just that: the background. Patterns should be used to enhance your content, not to grab attention from it. Anything that is against your background should be clearly visible. No one will stick around to try to pick text out from a busy background! So design your background to be... a background!

One way to make the background less obtrusive is to lower the opacity on the tile.

10. Making a seamless tiled background

Background patterns can easily detract from, rather than enhance, your site's content. If you want a patterned background, though, there are some things you can do to make it work better. If you are using it with text, it is best either to use a plain background panel for the text, or to make your background pattern very light, almost like a watermark.

You can make a tiled background either from scratch, or from a design or photo you have already made.

1. Create a new file, with dimensions **an even number** in both directions.

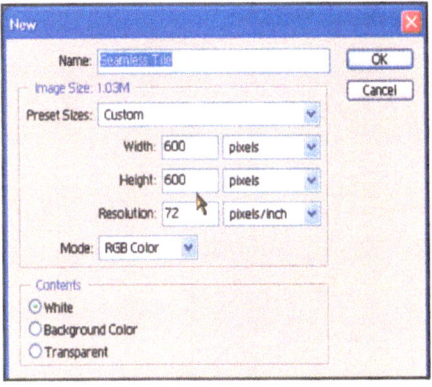

2. Make the design for the background.

   If you choose to make a patterned background for your site, you probably want it to be seamless. That is, you don't want to be able to see the edges of your tile.

3. To make the tile seamless, we will turn this tile inside out, in a sense, and then we fill in the middle to make the seamless effect.

Here's one way to do this:

4. **Filter > Other > Offset**. For Horizontal, put in half of the pixel width of your tile. For Vertical, put in half of the vertical height. Click OK.

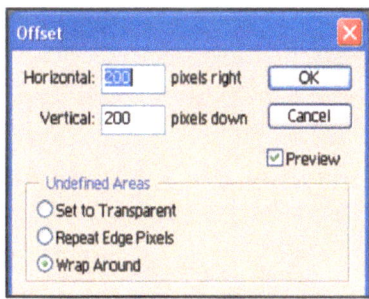

5. Now you need to smooth out the seams, where the lines are in the middle of the picture. Your method will depend upon the nature of your tile. You might use the Clone Tool to make the seams blend in, or you may use Liquify or another method. For this tile, I used the same brush that I used to create the tile, and added more grass in the middle.

6. Define the tile as a pattern as above: (**Ctrl+A**, then **Edit > Define Pattern**).

7. Make a new file and fill the canvas with your new tile to test it.

Though this pattern is probably too busy to put text directly over it, we can use a plain background panel for the text quite effectively.

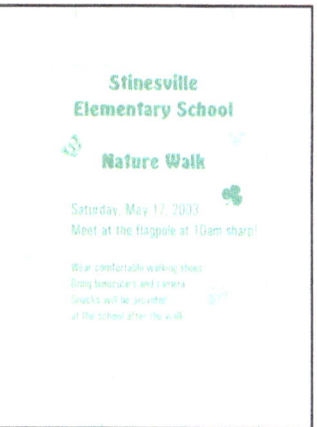

11. Making a patterned page border

I like making web pages with the background as a border around the page. This allows the page to have the "personality" of the border, but leaves the page easily read.

This page below is made by defining the tile image for the background. Then, in your web-creation software, you position a table in the center of the page, and all the content goes into this table.

I started with a leaf background. Then, I placed a table on that. The background of the table is a seamless tile in a crosshatch pattern. Finally, I put the page content in that table.

12. Making a transparent GIF

Suppose you want to put a picture on a patterned background and have it seem to float there, in other words, without its background? For example, in order to put "duckprints" onto this grass background, we need to save the image as a transparent GIF. Because its colors are limited, this is a good candidate for saving as a GIF anyway.

Here's how to make a transparent GIF:

1. Turn off the visibility eye for the background. Your object will be against the checkerboard.

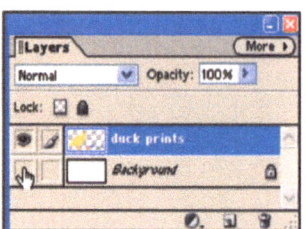

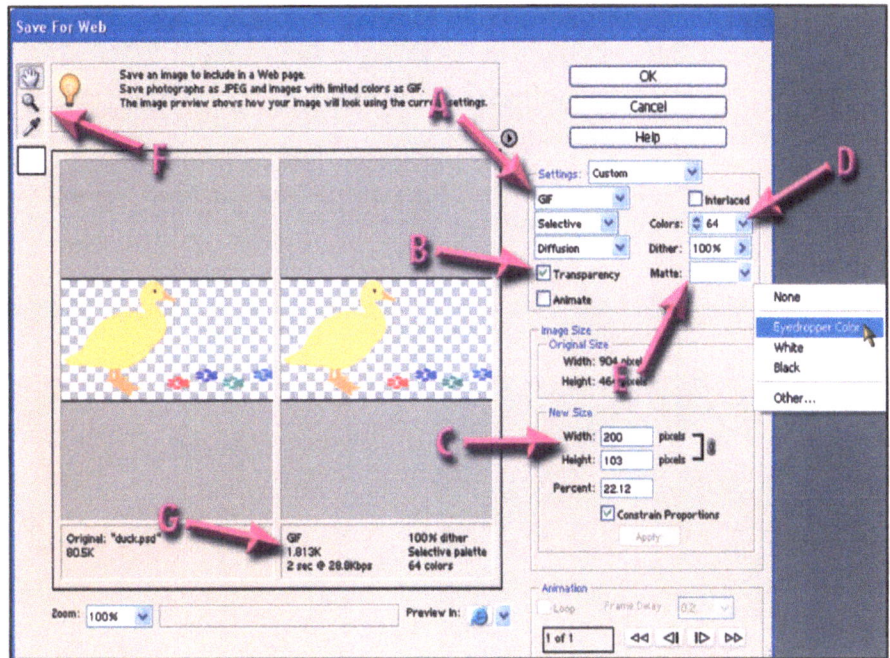

2. **File > Save for Web**. In the dialog box, choose the size you want for your finished image **(C)**, and choose GIF for file type **(A)**.

3. Be sure that Transparency is checked. **(B)**

4. Click on the color chip at **(E)** to choose a color for your Matte. You want to choose a color which is closest to the main color against which the GIF will sit. In this case, I chose white.

5. At **(D)**, choose the number of colors you need, in order to display your image well. You will notice at **(G)** that the file size increases as you increase the number of colors.

6. To look at certain parts of your image up close, you can use the Save for Web Tools. **(F)**

7. When you are finished tweaking your options, click **OK**.

13. Matte? What's that?

One of the options in the Save for Web dialog box is the Matte color. Matting lets your image blend in better with the background of your site. Here's how it works.

Photoshop Elements is a raster graphics program. This means that your art is based upon pixels, what color they are, and whether they are opaque, transparent, or semi-transparent.

Pixels are square. Because of this, in order to approximate the look of a curve or a diagonal, Elements will make some of the pixels around the edges semi-transparent. These illustrations show what happens with a semi-transparent red pixel when it is placed against different backgrounds:

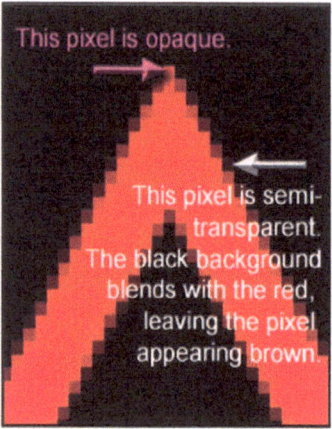

But when you save an image for the web, you cannot have pixels that are semi-transparent! They are either on or off. So what do we do about these edge pixels which are semi-transparent? We need to tell Elements what the main background color will be for the background of our graphic. This is the Matte color. Then Elements blends this color with those semi-transparent pixels.

For the first two examples, I saved with a blue matte:

And these two examples were saved with a white matte:

Notice how the duck blends in far better when the matte color matches the main background color.

14. Say it with a banner

Advertising-style banners have become ubiquitous on websites. You may want to create a banner you can offer to other sites to link to yours.

There are several standard sizes for these banners. For the large ones, 468 pixels x 60 pixels is the norm. You also see smaller "micro-button" banners, which are 88 x 31, as well as other sizes.

There are many considerations when it comes to constructing an banner ad, and there are plenty of fine resources with detailed information on this. At www.marketingterms.com, for example, there is a lot of information on banner ads and other web-marketing strategies.

Since space is limited, plan your design carefully to include what is essential. It is helpful to make your background for the banner in the proportions that you will need for the finished banner, but in a much larger size. Make your rectangle a fixed size in the Shape Options drop-down menu. In this screenshot, 440 x 155 represents the proportions for an 88 x 31 microbutton, multiplied by 5.

When you are done with the banner, crop the canvas to fit: **Ctrl-click** the banner layer in the Layers palette. **Image > Crop**.

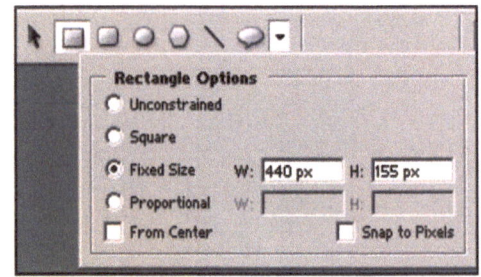

File size for banners is important. Usually, for example, a site will limit a 468 x 60 banner to 12K.

15. Creating animated GIFs

Animated GIFs are so fun to make that you may be tempted to put *lots* of them on your site. Actually, I hope that you *do* put many on your site, but please put them in an "Animations" gallery, not spread out over your site. I say this because animations, used to excess, are very annoying.

In Elements, you create an animation with layers, with each frame of the animation on its own layer. Elements plays the frames beginning at the bottom layer, and moving up. In this animation here, for example, the face starts out smiling. He slowly pokes his tongue out, then brings it back in, winks, then is left smiling.

After you get all the layers made, you create the animation in **File > Save for Web**.

This is done just as with saving any other GIF, except that you check the Animation choice. Then you choose what you want for all of the options in the Animation box. Experiment with these! The time needed for each frame will vary, depending upon the nature of your animation.

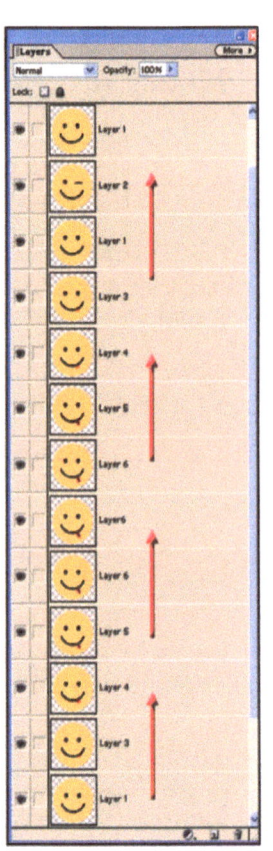

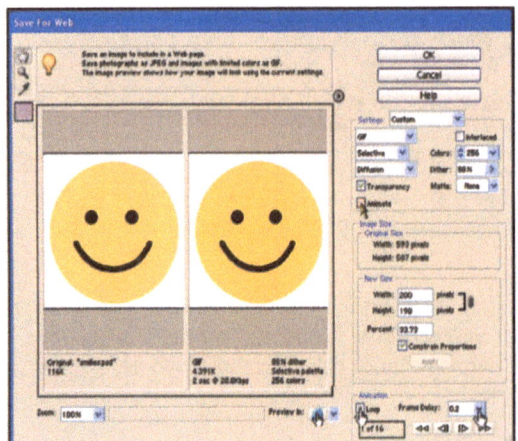

16. Quick animation tips

Making it easy to make your frames. It makes it easier to do the animation if you copy the first layer and alter it to make the next frame, and so on.

Adding more frames can make the animation go more smoothly, but it will also make the file size somewhat larger. To add another frame, you can click the Create a New Layer icon and create the new frame there. Alternatively, you can drag an existing layer (frame) to that icon and then modify it as necessary.

Keeping it going. If you want the animation to repeat, you can click the Loop option in the Save for Web dialog.

Previewing the animation. To see the animation, you have to open it in a browser, such as Internet Explorer. You can even do this through the Save for Web dialog box! Click the little browser button at the bottom of the box.

Clearing the jaggies. If your animation shows jaggy edges, there is a fix for this in the Save for Web dialog. Under Matte, choose a color which is the color your object sits against for the longest period of time.

Other ways to make animations. If you are really enjoying making animations, you may want to learn about making animations in Flash. Flash is Macromedia software which helps you to create moving graphics with smaller files and smoother animations. Friends of Ed is the premier publisher on Flash, and the website at www.friendsofed.com has all the information you could want about Flash books.

17. A shortcut for making a capsule-shaped button

A capsule button is attractive and can be sized to hold whatever text label you want to put into it. So these have attained a well-deserved level of popularity.

The secret to making a quick and perfect capsule is in the Shape options.

1. Choose the Rounded Rectangle Tool.

2. Then in the options drop-down menu, choose Fixed Size. For height (H), choose the height you want for your finished button.

3. Next, set the radius in the options to *half* of what you chose for the height. This will make the ends of the rectangle into perfect semi-circles, giving you a perfect capsule!

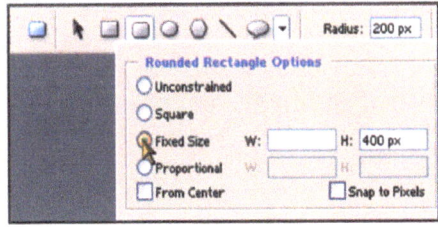

4. Back in the Options bar, check the Style. Click the drop-down arrow and then, in the flyout, choose Glass buttons, then Plum Glass, to copy my "Wine" button.

5. Depending upon the size of your button, you may have to adjust the Style settings. You do that by double-clicking the little **f** for that layer in the Layers palette.

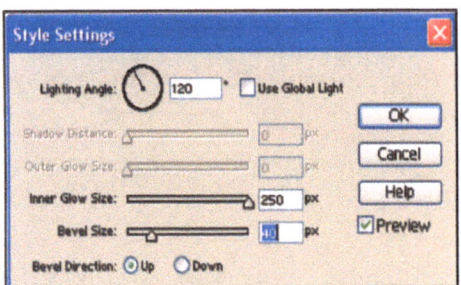

6. Choose the Type Tool and type the text for the button. I used Vivaldi font.

7. I applied a Sharp Inner Bevel Layer style to the type layer and, in the Style Settings, chose Down for Bevel Direction.

If you save this file in layered PSD format, with your button and your type layer separate, you can quite easily change your button's color later or make it say whatever you want. Since the text effect is done with a Layer Style, this type even remains editable!

To edit this label, click the type layer in the Layers palette, and choose the Type Tool. Highlight the old text, and type in the new.

18. Rollover buttons

I am asked nearly every day, "How do you make rollover buttons? You know, the ones that change color or light up when you put your mouse over them?" For the rollover buttons, also known as "mouseovers", on my site, I went to Jon Hughes from Vortex Design. On his site, Jon has some tidy tutorials for doing some beginning web page operations, including making rollovers.

For this example, the buttons are purple in their normal "off" state. When the mouse rolls over them, they turn pink, as if they are lighting up.

So let's do it!

19. Saving the files for each button in each state

What we'll do is to make one master PSD file from which we will make all six of the buttons. (There will be one for each "off" state, and one for each "over" state.) Because this file will be in layers, and the text will remain editable, new buttons or changes in these buttons can be easily done.

1. Begin by making the first button base. I used the button that I made just above. Label this layer "Capsule off," or something equally clever. I used the same Layer Style as above, then added a drop shadow.

2. Add the text label. For the font, I chose Vivaldi, one I find particularly appropriate for this vineyard web-site. Crop the button as closely as possible, but not so closely that you chop off any of your shadow's fuzz.

3. **File > Save As...** Save in PSD format, and name the file something that tells you that this file is for *all* the buttons in this collection, not just Wines.

4. Then choose **File > Save for Web**. Size the button appropriately in this dialog (remembering what size you use), choose the rest of your options here, and click **OK**.

It is important that you name this file something that tells you that this is the off state for this particular button, for example, I might name this one `winesoff.jpg`.

5. For the rollover version, duplicate the "Capsule off" layer, label the new one "Capsule over," and turn off the visibility eye for Capsule off. For the Capsule over layer, I used the Pink Glass Layer Style. I did not add the drop shadow to this version. Then in the Style Settings, I changed the bevel direction to Down and adjusted the bevel size.

6. **File > Save for Web**. For this one, name it something like `winesover.jpg`, telling you that this is the "over" state for this "Wines" button.

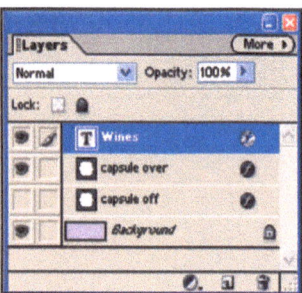 

7. Continue in this way. For my three buttons, each having two rollover states, off and over, I should have saved six separate files.

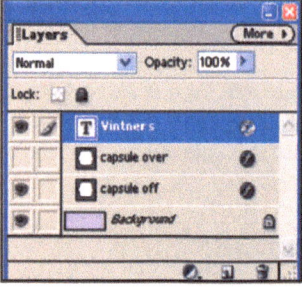 

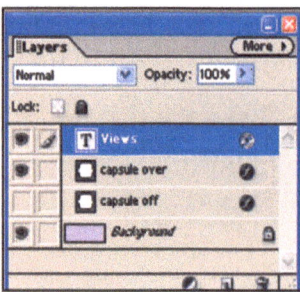 

Rollover buttons can be either JPGs or GIFs. If you are going to use these against a patterned background, you will want to save them as transparent GIFs, as above, using an appropriately colored matte.

20. Installing rollover buttons into your site

Extensive website-building or coding is beyond the scope of this book, but if you, like me, are a bit in awe of all of this, it is appropriate that we take a glance at how this works.

You can actually have very nice rollover buttons on your site, even if you have no experience coding. What you do is to point your browser to the page for this book on the friends of ED website. Here you will find coding for making 2- or 3-state rollover buttons.

- The NORMAL state is what the button looks like when the visitor first arrives at the site.
- The OVER state refers to the appearance of the button when the visitor rolls their mouse over the button.
- The DOWN state is what happens to the button when your visitor clicks the button.

Be sure that your button files are each named so that you know at a glance which one is which, and then insert your filenames into the code, in the appropriate places.

Rollovers are good fun and can add interest and an interactive, lively feel to your site. I hope that you will give this a try.

If you have a website already, I hope that you are excited about the possibilities that Elements gives you to make it in your own style. And if you don't have a site yet, step up to the plate! Get a web editing package and put yourself out there!

Preferences

1. General Preferences
2. Saving Files
3. Displays and Cursors
4. Transparency
5. Units and Rulers
6. Grid
7. Plug-Ins & Scratch Disks
8. Memory & Image Cache
9. Status Bar – Scratch Sizes

Color Management

10. Switching Color Pickers
11. Color Matching and Sample Painting
12. Hex Values and HTML
13. Activating Color Management
14. Saving Color Profiles with your Documents
15. Color Management in Print Preview

Hardware Configurations

16. RAM – the more the better
17. Monitor Setup
18. Graphics Tablets
19. Camera Pixels – when enough is enough

Chapter 9

Set Up

The tips and tricks in this last chapter differ from those in the rest of the book, in that they are unlikely to be used again and again – they are intended as advice on setting your preferences and additional hardware you might want. Nevertheless, once you've optimized your settings and found out what works well for your set up, you will save a lot of time by reducing the number of error messages you get, and processes being dealt with more efficiently.

Preferences

Significant improvements in performance and workflow can often be gained from tweaking key options in Elements' Preferences. I've included my Preferences as a guide, highlighting important preferences – remember though, your mileage may vary. Explore Elements' Preferences and set them in a way that best matches your situation.

1. General Preferences

To access the preferences go to **Edit > Preferences > General** or hit **Ctrl+K**. These general preferences and the other specific dialog boxes can significantly help improve the performance of Elements on your machine, and reduce the amount of hair pulling you need to do!

Need a quick way to open Preferences? Double click in the Ruler area around your image.

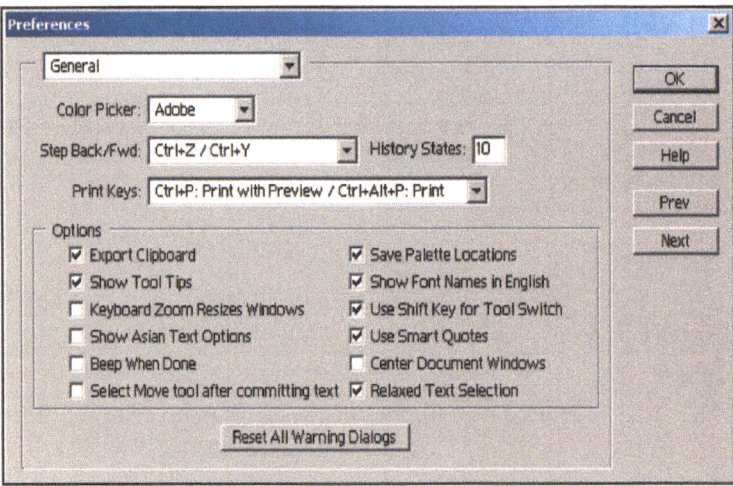

Hold the cursor over a preference option to view additional information about that option.

Most of the options in General Preferences are self-explanatory and are a matter of personal choice. Don't be afraid to change them, most changes are effective immediately, but a few won't come into effect until after you restart Elements.

By default Elements remembers twenty **History States**. Each History State requires system resources - either RAM or the Scratch Disk. If you are working on large files, high-resolution files, files with many layers, or on a machine with limited resources, reducing the number of History States may yield an improvement in performance. Obviously, there's a price to pay, but depending on the type of tasks you regularly carry out, ten or twelve History States may serve your purposes.

2. Saving Files

If you are primarily saving your images for use on the web, **File Extension** should be set to Use Lower Case to maximize compatibility with web servers, some of which require lower case extensions. **Maximize Compatibility for Photoshop Files** saves a flattened version of your file along with the layered version, potentially making the file significantly larger. **Image Previews** saves a thumbnail of your image into the file. There is a small file size penalty, but Image Previews are just the thing you need for quick browsing later on.

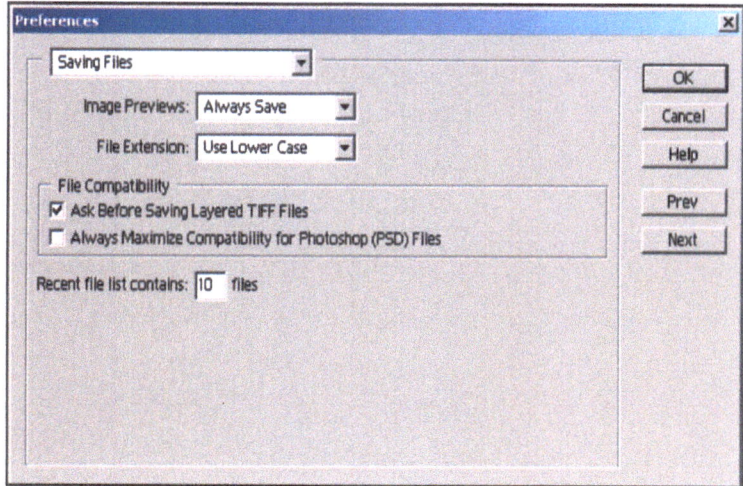

The **Recent file list contains** up to 30 files – increasing it from the default of 10 may help save time when going back to files you've just worked on, rather than having to navigate through folders.

3. Display and Cursors

Pixel Doubling speeds up an image preview by temporarily doubling the size of the pixels by halving the resolution of the preview. If your Filter Previews are taking too long, check it!

I prefer to have both **Painting** and **Other Cursors** set to Precise, where a cross hair is displayed making it easier to do accurate sampling – this may not be your preference as it doesn't show the size of brush you're using. I can then toggle to Brush Size while using tools by using the **Caps Lock** key. When your cursors are set to Standard, Caps Lock will toggle between Standard and Precise.

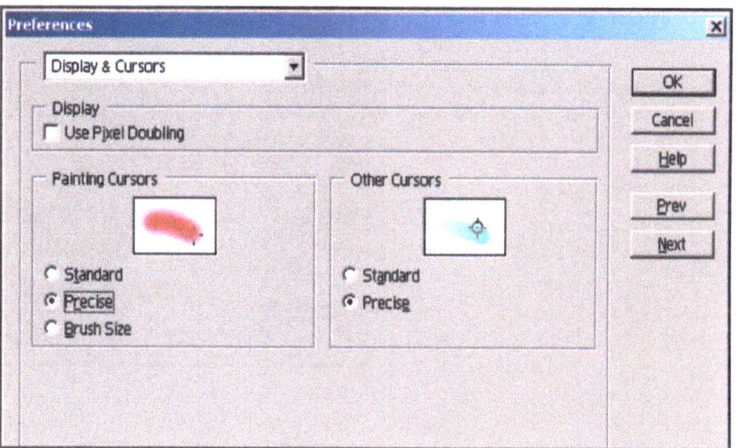

4. Transparency

The default display for Transparency should work well for the majority of the images you work on, though some find it can be distracting. If you are working with predominantly white on a transparent background, it may be very hard to see the content against the gray checkerboard – this is certainly a case when changing the colors of the grid will help you work more efficiently.

You can customize both the size and color of the grid that Elements uses to display transparent areas of layers.

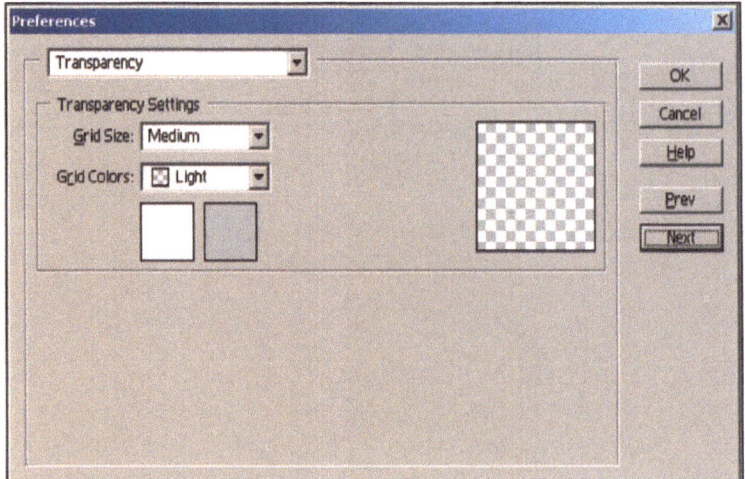

5. Units & Rulers

It's always worth setting your Rulers in **Units** that match the project you are working on. If you are working on images for the web, pixels will be much more useful as the units displayed on your rulers, rather than inches, centimeters or millimeters.

You can also adjust **Preset Resolutions** for new documents. Elements' default settings are right on the money, so unless you have a specific reason, leave them as they are.

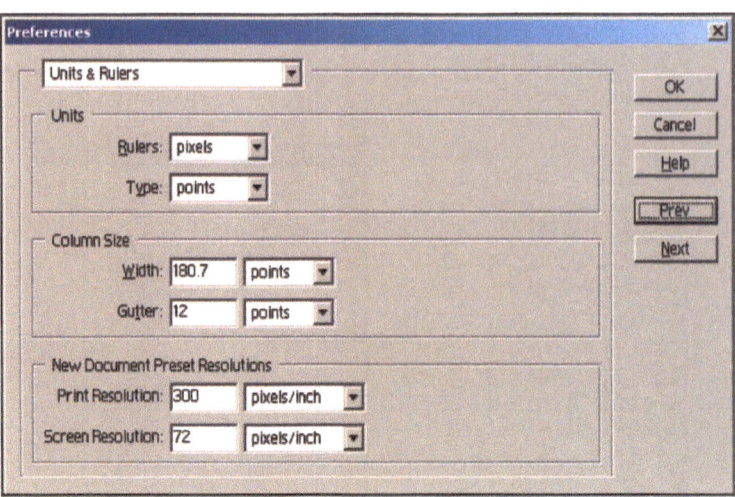

6. Grid

These settings are very much a matter of personal taste, a particular color may be to your liking, or may be unsuitable for an image that contains a lot of the same color as the grid you're using. If you are working on a document that requires precise placing of the elements (like a web page), then customizing the grid for that operation can be an extremely useful guide to positioning them correctly.

You can customize the Color, Style and frequency of Elements' **Grid**, which can be toggled off and on under the View menu. Most of the time, the default settings work great for me!

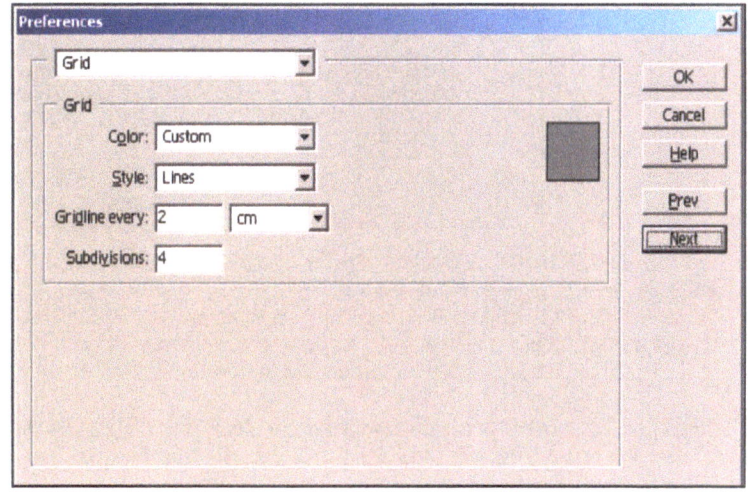

7. Plug-Ins & Scratch Disks

Scratch disks is a key option in Elements Preferences, one that can make or break Elements performance-wise. Elements uses Scratch disk files when there is insufficient RAM available for editing an image. It reads and writes temporary files to your hard drive, using the drives as virtual memory. The more Elements needs to use its Scratch disks the slower your work will be – your hard drives are the bottleneck, and this needs to be minimized.

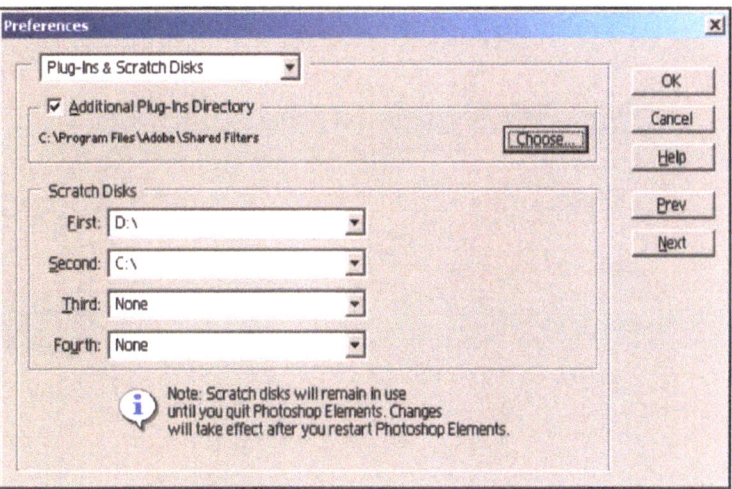

Ideally you should have a large, fast, unfragmented dedicated hard drive designated as your primary Scratch disk – physically separate to both the drive your operating system is installed on and the drive your Elements' files are located on. If this is not possible, set aside a large partition on your drive specifically for use as the Scratch disk, and defragment it to ensure Elements has a large contiguous space to work with for its Scratch. You can designate up to four Scratch disks, up to a total of 200GB – that's one big itch!

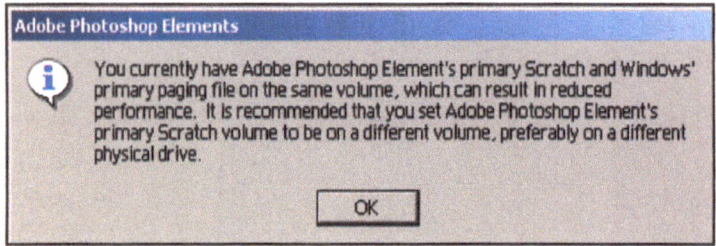

You may have received a notification when opening Elements for the first time that its primary Scratch disk was set to the same drive as Windows' primary page file, i.e. the drive it uses for its virtual memory, by default C:\ – the same default as Elements. This is part of the same problem – Elements performance when running off the Scratch disk will improve markedly if you designate a different physical hard drive as Elements' primary (first) Scratch disk, and let your operating system have a drive for its own virtual memory requirements.

If none of the above is possible on your system, don't worry! Elements will keep working until it runs out of Scratch disk and will let you know when that occurs. Whichever way you choose to go with setting up your Scratch disks be sure to defragment your drives regularly.

You can also specify an **Additional Plug-Ins Directory** Elements should check on start-up. I have several programs that use plug-ins so have created a Shared Filters directory and placed common filters there.

8. Memory & Image Cache

Memory Usage is a key setting. Elements is a resource intensive program – it needs RAM and lots of it. Adobe recommend having at least 3-5 times the amount of RAM as the file size you are working on, but throw in Layers and History States, and even with large amounts of RAM available, before long you are running off the Scratch disk.

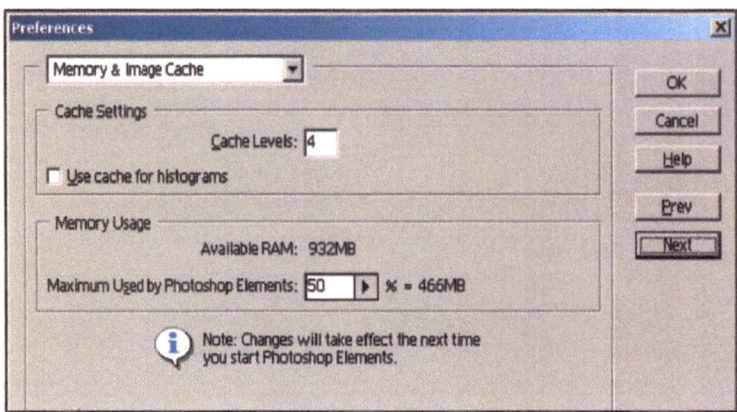

It sounds like setting the maximum RAM at 100% would be a good idea, but don't forget - you must leave ample RAM for your operating system and any other software you have running, otherwise your system will slow down or worse, crash! I typically run several other RAM hungry applications so leave my Maximum Elements' RAM conservatively set at 50% - Adobe recommend going no higher than 75%.

Cache Levels can be set as high as eight, but four should provide a good balance between speed and accuracy. Enabling **Use cache for histograms** is unchecked by default. With caching enabled, histograms such as Levels will be drawn more quickly, but less accurately. Given how important histogram data is and how quickly it is typically drawn, there's not much of a case for enabling histogram caching.

9. Status Bar – Scratch Sizes

Elements Status Bar is packed with useful information, none more so than **Scratch Sizes**. Click on the small triangle on the left side of the Status bar to view available options:

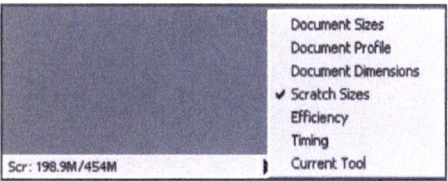

*If you can't see Elements' Status Bar it can be turned on by selecting **Window > Status Bar**.*

Scratch Sizes displays the total amount of RAM available to Elements on the right, and the amount of RAM required for the current file on the left. This screenshot was made immediately after opening a 17MB file – and already close to 200MB of Elements' RAM is being used! How can that be? The reason is the file has 10 layers. Run a filter on one layer, BOOM! It's up to 276MB, and so on. Having the Scratch Sizes visible lets me see at a glance how things are going. Do I need to use Elements Purge command? Should I reduce the number of History States? How heavily is Elements running on the Scratch Disk? Do I need to allocate more RAM to Elements? How much more RAM would get me by most of the time?

Document Sizes is another very useful display. Ever wondered how much each new layer adds to the size of your PSD file? Document Sizes displays the approximate flattened size of your file on the left, e.g. the size file that would be sent to the printer, and the approximate size of the PSD file on the right, including layers.

Color management

The number of colors the majority of screens now display means that the old Web Safe palette (limited to 256 colors) is redundant for most, but just because your monitor displays millions of colors, it doesn't mean that your image will appear exactly the same on your friend's monitor, or when it's printed. Color management is a large and complex area – we're just scratching the surface here...

10. Switching Color Pickers

In Elements you can use the Color Picker (show below) to select colors, but both Windows and Mac based systems have their own native color picker tools, which you may prefer.

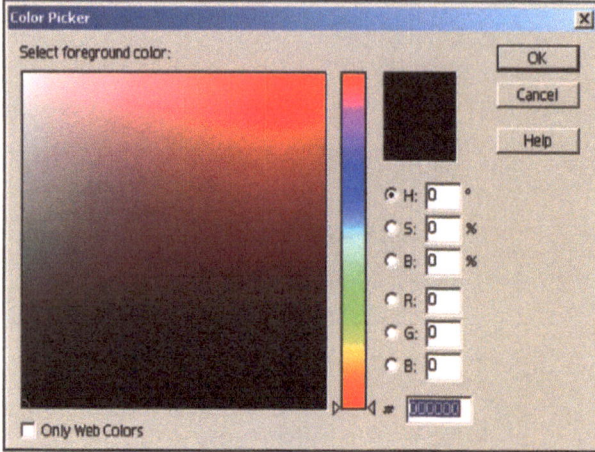

If you want to use one of them instead, choose **Edit > Preferences > General**, and select your respective operating system from the **Color Picker** drop-down menu. Below is an example of the Windows native Color Picker tool:

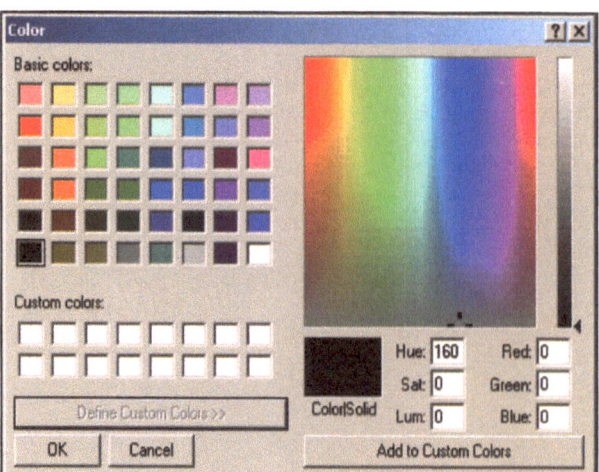

11. Color Matching and Sample Painting

If you need to match a color in an image, use the Eyedropper Tool, that's its sole purpose. You can find it at the bottom of the toolbox. It's the fastest and simplest way to exactly match the color you want.

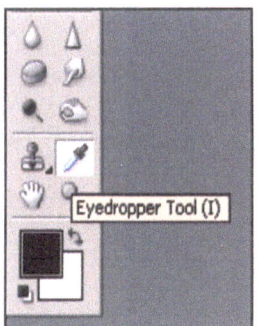

A number of other tools (Brush, Pencil, Gradient, Paint Bucket, etc) make use of the Eyedropper Tool while you hold the **Alt** key when they are active. This is known as "Sample Painting". Many digital painters will setup their own in-document swatch palette much like the traditional painter would use a palette. Switching between colors when painting is then as easy as **Alt+clicking**.

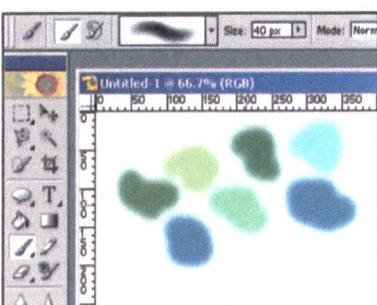

12. Hex Values and HTML

Hexadecimal values are used to define color in HTML. When designing a web site you'll most likely want to have a color theme to work by. If you've created your main interface in Elements, and want to use the same colors in your layout, you can copy the hexadecimal values from the Elements Color Picker.

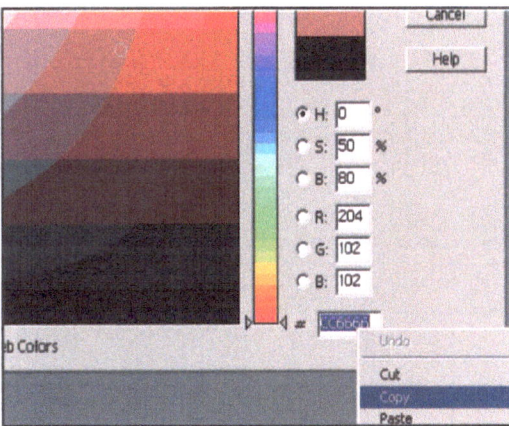

First you need to match the desired color (use the Eyedropper Tool). Next copy the hex value; select the value in the # field, right-click, and choose **Copy**. Now you can paste that value in your HTML editor and you will have the exact same color as you used for your interface.

13. Activating Color Management

Color management is a high-end tool that many professionals shy away from, as it can be a very complex area – we are not going to look at this in depth, just a quick tip. If you are preparing a lot of pictures on your computer for print then you should consider using color management, this will help ensure that the colors you see on your monitor match what you see in print.

Once you have an image open, use **Edit > Color Settings** to reveal this dialog box:

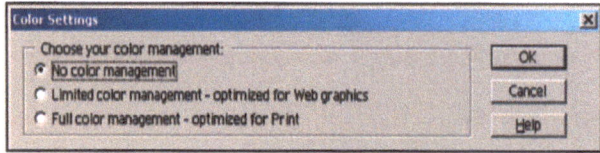

Choose **Full color management – optimized for Print**, and press **OK**. You've now tagged a color profile to your image that your printer and other devices will recognize.

Assigning color profiles to documents ensures that colors look the same when passed between hardware devices. This is because each device will use the color profile's settings to display colors accordingly.

14. Saving Color Profiles with your Documents

Once you activate **Full color management**, any document you open from then on will use color management. If you close Elements, it will default back to **No Color Management** when you re-open it. So when you save your document, be sure to check the **ICC Profile** box to keep the color profile attached to your document.

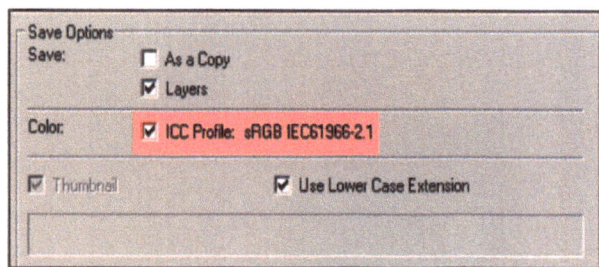

15. Color Management in Print Preview

If you go to **File** > **Print Preview**, select **Show More Options**, and **Color Management** from the drop-down menu, you'll see this:

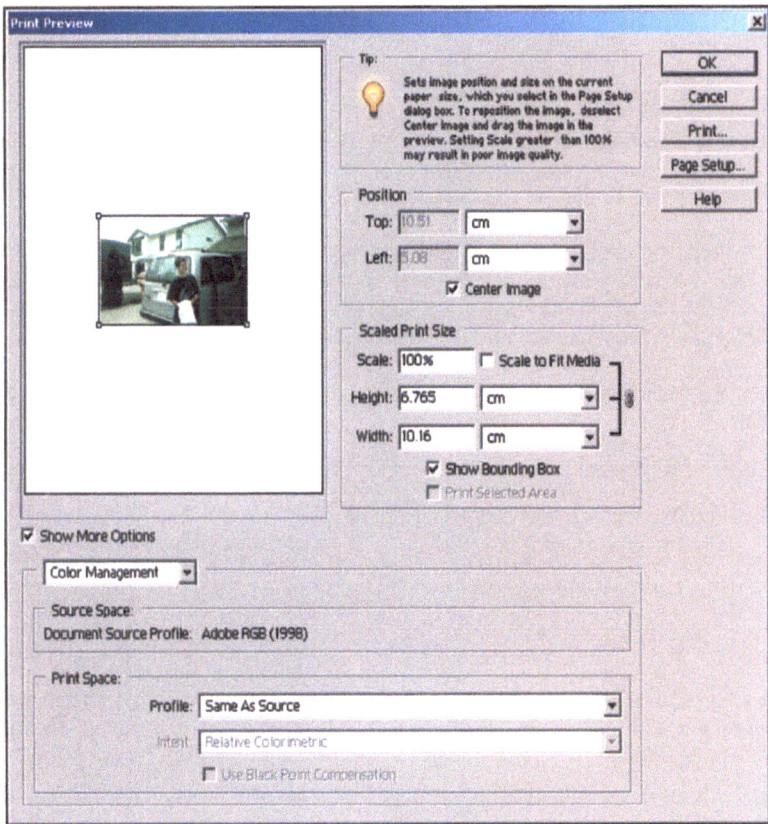

If a predefined color profile was installed for your printer when you installed the drivers, select it from the **Profile** drop-down menu for the best results. You can use **Same As Source** if you want to use the current color profile when printing (no profile conversions will take place). Use **Printer Color Management** to use the printer driver for color conversions, this will hopefully mean that the colors you see in print are the ones you want!

Hardware Considerations

There is an endless supply of accessories that could enhance your experience with Elements and some are considerably cheaper than they used to be; you can pick up 256MB of RAM for less than fifty dollars and a graphics tablet for under a hundred. These final tips may help persuade you to make that purchase and get even more out of Elements.

16. RAM – the more the better

Photoshop Elements loves RAM! Having an optimal configuration for your Scratch disks is important, but for obtaining the best performance from your system nothing beats RAM, and lots of it. Adobe recommends your system has no less than 128MB of RAM, but in reality that is not enough.

Before doing anything on your computer, your operating system and any other applications running in your system tray (e.g. Anti Virus software), have already used up a good slice of your computer's resources – anything up to 100MB of RAM! Start Elements without any files open and you've used another ~40MB of RAM already. Suddenly 128MB of RAM doesn't seem like much at all, ouch!

For an enjoyable experience in Elements, a more realistic minimum requirement is 256MB – anything you can afford above that, the better!

> *Motherboards have a limited number of slots for RAM. If you're buying a new system, rather than fill all the slots initially with small sticks of RAM, buy the biggest sticks of RAM you can afford, leaving as many slots free as you can for future RAM additions.*

There are many types of RAM available at a range of different speeds. Discussing all of the RAM options available is beyond the scope of this chapter, but the general rule for intensive applications like Elements is buy the fastest RAM you can afford.

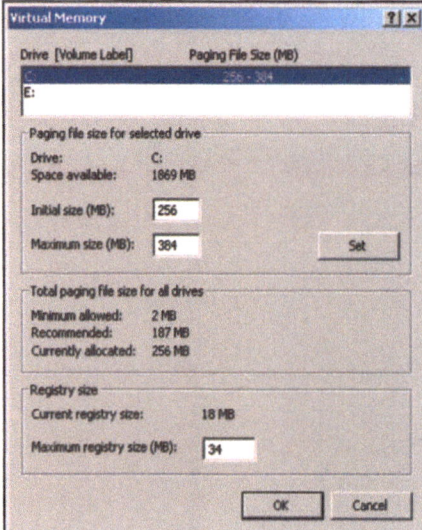

> *Not all RAM will fit and/or work on all motherboards. Before you buy RAM be sure to check the specifications of your motherboard.*

17. Monitor Setup

Elements loves screen real estate! Let's look at several ways you can give yourself more room to move in Elements.

Increase your Screen Area/Screen Resolution

Increasing your screen area lets you display more information on your screen. Palettes become relatively smaller leaving more screen space to access and work on your images. The best way to understand the benefits is to try it out!

Example 1: Elements Workspace – Screen Area set to 800x600 pixels:

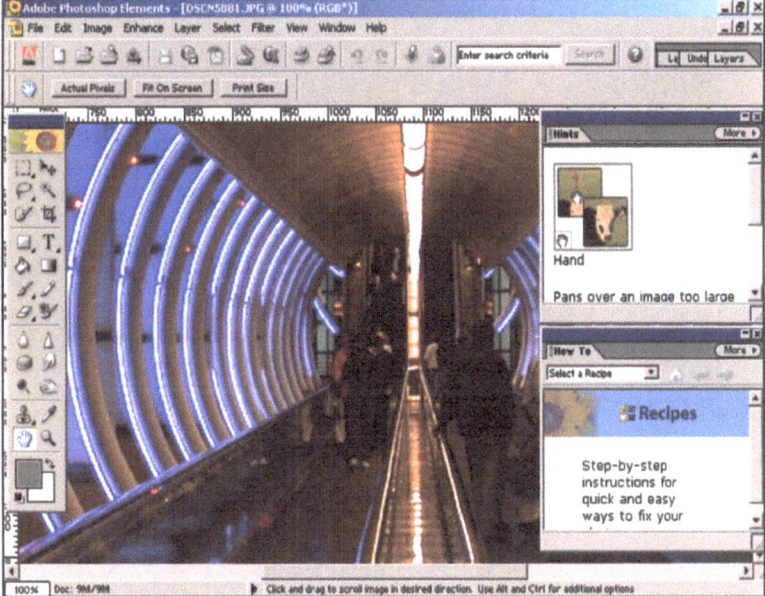

Adobe recommend a minimum screen resolution of 800x600 pixels and you can see why – with only two palettes open the screen is already cluttered, and access to your image file is limited.

Example 2: Elements Workspace – Screen Area set to 1280x1024 pixels:

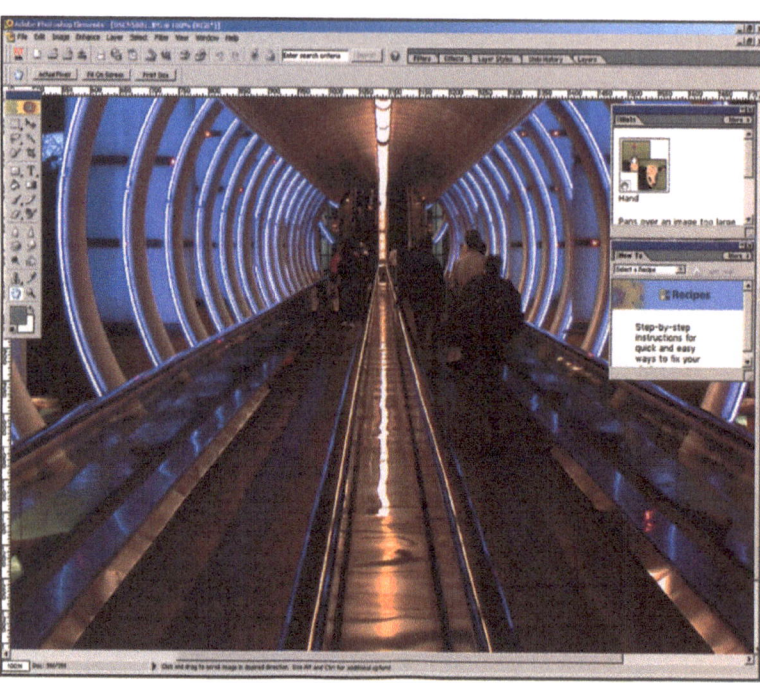

What a difference! Same monitor but with the screen resolution increased to 1280x1024 pixels. There's now ample access to the image, even with additional palettes open.

> *Look after your eyes! Too high a screen resolution can make palettes on the screen very small and difficult to read, leading to eyestrain and headaches.*

Windows' users can access Screen Area settings by right clicking on the desktop, clicking **Properties** and selecting the **Settings** tab.

Drag the Screen Area slider to the right. Click **OK** to apply. Experiment with different settings.

> *What Screen Area is best for you? That's a personal decision and will be influenced by the size and quality of your monitor, the capabilities of your video card, and your eyesight! 1024x768 pixels is a good starting point.*

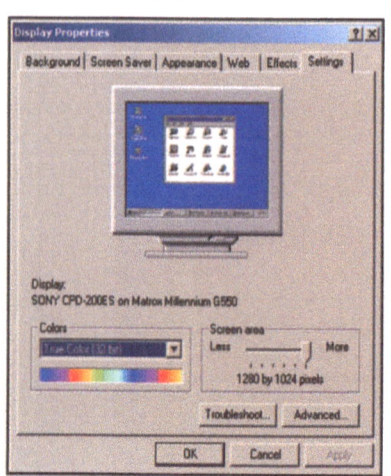

Monitor Size
The physical size of your monitor's screen can make all the difference with a palette-based program like Elements. For an uncluttered workspace you need to set your screen area/resolution to a screen area of at least 1024x768 pixels, but you still need to be able to easily read palettes, menus and the like. Much will depend on your personal preferences, but if you intend spending large amounts of time working with your images in Elements do your eyes a favor and use a 17" monitor or larger. A larger monitor set at a reasonable screen area gives you the best of both worlds – an uncluttered workspace that doesn't strain your eyes.

Dual Monitors
With the price of CRT and LCD monitors falling a workspace solution that is growing in popularity is having more than one monitor. The benefit being, you can have your image and main toolbar on your main monitor, your palettes open and easily accessible on the second – no more shuffling things around! Not all video cards support more than one monitor, so be sure to check yours before purchasing a second monitor. Your desk may start to look like the control center for a space mission, but if you have the need, the room, and the cash, dual monitors are a solution worth investigating.

18. Graphics Tablets

If you enjoy drawing, painting, or working with images in Elements, one of the most satisfying hardware upgrades can often be the purchase of a pressure-sensitive pen tablet such as those made by Wacom. With tablet support enabled, all of Elements' brushes will respond to the pressure applied to the pen much like drawing and painting in the real world. If you've been mouse-bound it's a revelation that might take some getting used to!

To enable Tablet support:

■ With any tool that uses a brush selected, click on the **More Options** icon in the shortcuts bar and check the 'Tablet Support' box.

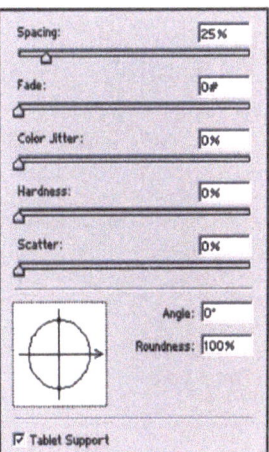

■ Select the Pen Pressure Brush group from the Brushes drop-down menu.

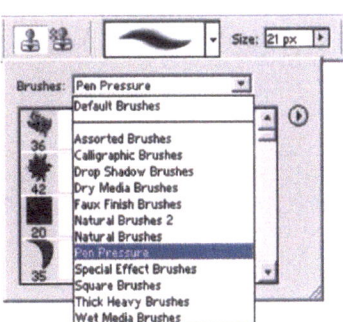

- Select a brush and get to work! As you paint and vary the pressure on the pen, properties of the brush vary dynamically, very nice.

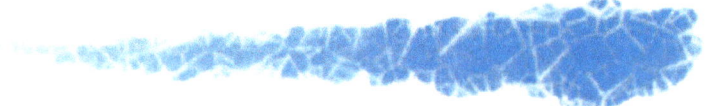

Made a mistake? Many pens come with an eraser at the top - flip it over and rub the mistake out – something you definitely can't do with a mouse!

R.I.P Rodent?
Once you're comfortable using a pen tablet there may be no going back to using a mouse. For those still attached to their rodent, most tablets support the use of mice directly on the tablet, some even come with a special mouse designed for this purpose. You can always leave your existing mouse plugged in and functional and use it as needed.

Pen Tablets come with their own driver – a small piece of software that allows you to configure the behavior of the pen and tablet. Refer to the documentation that came with your tablet if you need assistance.

19. Camera Pixels – when enough is enough

All current megapixel cameras generate images that are suitable for use online, but when it comes to printing images taken with your digital camera, how many megapixels are enough? Use this table as a guide:

Megapixel	File Size (MB)	Quality Print 200 pixels/inch
1	~2.5	Up to 4x6"
2	~5.5	Up to 6x8"
3	~9	Up to 8x10"
4	~11	Up to 8.5x11"
5	~14	Up to 9x13"

Most digital cameras allow you to take photos at a range of sizes up to the camera's maximum resolution. If storage permits, always shoot at the maximum resolution and quality. Refer to the documentation that came with your camera if you are unsure how to do this.

- File Size refers to the size of the uncompressed file generated by the camera.
- After many tests the majority of online users agree that 200 pixels/inch is the minimum resolution for reliable quality inkjet print output (higher for better quality printers).

You can use Elements' **Image Resize** (**Alt+I+R+I**) to increase the resolution and output size of an image file, but better results will be obtained by capturing more information at the time of taking the photo. There's no substitute for capturing as much information as possible at the moment when you originally take your picture – this gives you the maximum number of original pixels to work with when you do your image editing.

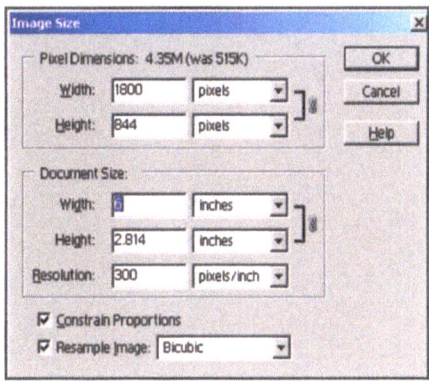

Appendix

Appendix A
Commonly used shortcuts

We've gathered together the most useful shortcuts in Elements. For a fuller list please refer to your Elements' Quick Reference Card – if you haven't lost it!

Toolbar
Cycle through hidden tools	Alt+Click tool
	Shift+ press tool shortcutkey*
Cycle through open documents	Control+Tab
Toggle cursor display	Caps Lock*
Default foreground/background colors	D
Switch foreground/background colors	X

* Behavior can be modified in Preferences.

Viewing
Fit image on screen	Double click Hand Tool, Control+ 0
Zoom to 100%	Double click Zoom Tool, Alt+Control+0
Zoom in	Control+ +, Control+Spacebar
	Control+Spacebar+drag over image
Zoom out	Control+-, Alt+Spacebar
Zoom into specific area	Control+drag over preview in Navigator
Scroll Image with Hand Tool	Spacebar+drag

Selecting and Moving

Move selection marquee	Any marquee+Click+drag (if Options set to New Selection), Arrow keys
Add to selection	Shift+Any selection too l
Subtract from selection	Alt+Any selection tool
Constrain marquee to circle or square	Drag+Shift
Draw marquee from center	Drag+Alt
Constrain to square or circle and draw from center	Drag+Shift+Alt
Switch to Move tool	Control (except when hand is selected)
Move selection (and contents)	Control+drag
Copy selection	Control+Alt+drag

Painting

To sample foreground color	Any paint tool+Alt+Click in image
To sample background color	Eyedropper+Alt Click in image
Set opacity, pressure or exposure	Number keys
Cycle through blending modes	Shift+ + or -
Fill section/layer with foreground color	Alt+Backspace
Fill section/layer with /background color	Control+Backspace
Display Fill Dialogue	Shift+Backspace
Paint straight line	Any painting tool+Shift
Connect points	Any painting tool+Shift+Click

Type Editing

Select 1 character at a time, left/right, or 1 line up/down	Shift+Arrow keys
Select 1 word left/right	Shift+Control+Arrow keys
Designate new text starting point over existing text	Shift+Click
Increase/Decrease selected text size in 2 pt/px increments	Shift+Control < or >

Palletes

Show/hide palettes, toolbox, shortcuts and options	Tab
Show/hide palettes only	Shift+Tab

Brushes

Increase/decrease brush size	[or]
Increase/decrease brush softness/hardness	Shift+[or]

Free Transform

Transform from center of box	Alt
Constrain to original ratio	Shift
Transform from center and constrain ratio	Alt+Shift
Distort	Control (can also be used in conjunction with Alt and Shift)

Skew	Shift+Control
Change Perspective	Shift+Control+Alt
Apply transformation	Enter
	Double click within bounding box
	Select another tool
Cancel	EscControl+ .

History

Step forward	Control+Y
Step backward	Control+Z
Toggle current and previous	Control+Alt+Z

Layers

Merge linked layers	Control+E
Merge visible layers	Shift+Control+E
Merge copy of visible layers to target layer	Shift+Alt+Control+E
Move target layer up or down	Control+[or]
Move target layer to top or bottom	Shift+Control+[or]
Load layer as selection	Control+Click layer
Add layer to selection	Shift+Control+Click layer
Subtract layer from selection	Alt+Control+Click layer
Toggle target layer transparency lock	/
Make Layer active	Control+Right click over image

Appendix B

Plug-Ins

Plug-ins are software modules that extend the capabilities of Photoshop Elements and other programs that support Photoshop-compatible plug-ins.

The most common types of plug-ins for Elements include:

- Filters and Effects
- Automation
- Import and Export

Plug-ins come in many shapes and sizes, ranging from basic filters with no options or preview through to complete suites of tools and effects with their own unique interface. Plug-ins are typically accessed from the **Filter** and **File** menus.

Elements ships with well over 100 plug-ins, but there are also many additional free and commercial third party plug-ins you can install to expand your creative options even further.

Original Image – Water Show, Bellagio Hotel, Las Vegas

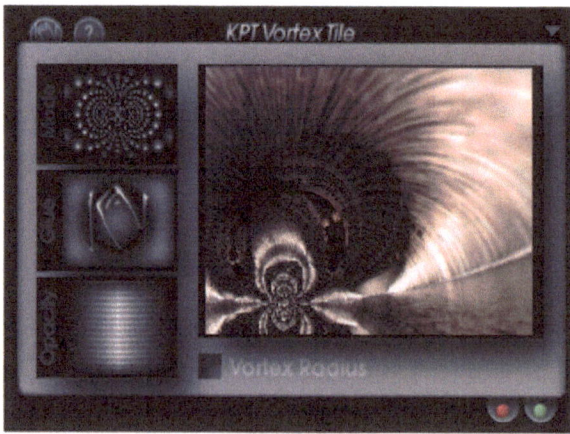

KPT Power Tools – Vortex Tiling

To see the full list of active Plug-ins in Elements select **Help > About Plugin.**

The default location on your hard drive for Elements' plug-ins is:

C:\Program Files\Adobe\Photoshop Elements 2\Plug-Ins\

The path to your plug-ins may vary depending on your installation and platform.

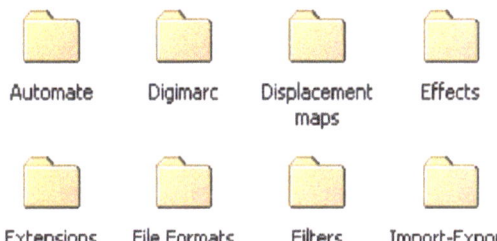

This is also the directory in which new plug-ins will be installed – usually automatically by the installer program. You'll need to restart Elements before new plug-ins can be used.

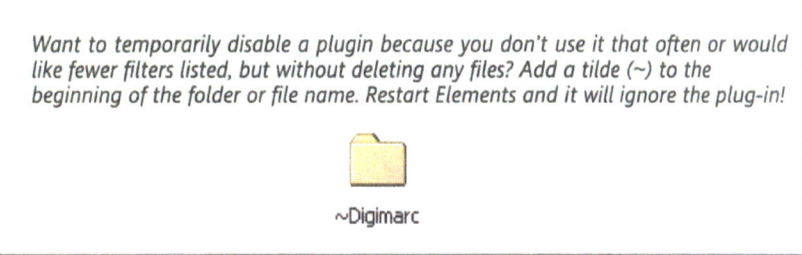

Want to temporarily disable a plugin because you don't use it that often or would like fewer filters listed, but without deleting any files? Add a tilde (~) to the beginning of the folder or file name. Restart Elements and it will ignore the plug-in!

You can also access plug-ins from other directories on your hard disk by using the **Additional Plug-Ins Directory** option of the **Edit > Preferences > Plug-Ins & Scratch Disks** dialog box. This is useful when other applications, such as Adobe After Effects, have compatible plug-ins in their plug-ins directories.

Online Plug-In Resources

Free and commercial plug-ins are available online, most are developed for the full version of Photoshop. Before purchasing a plug-in be sure to check it is compatible with Photoshop Elements and your operating system.

There are a lot free plug-ins available that vary in quality, but even some of the more commercial sites, listed below, offer freebies you can take advantage of:

www.extensis.com
www.lizardtech.com
www.andromeda.com
www.autofx.com
www.alienskin.com
www.xaostools.com
www.procreate.com/go/kpt
www.thepluginsite.com

Recipes

Recipes are located in Elements' How To palette. Recipes guide you through common tasks - Elements may even occasionally do the work for you!

You can check for and download new recipes any time you are online:

1. Select Download New Adobe Recipes from the drop-down menu in the **How To** palette.

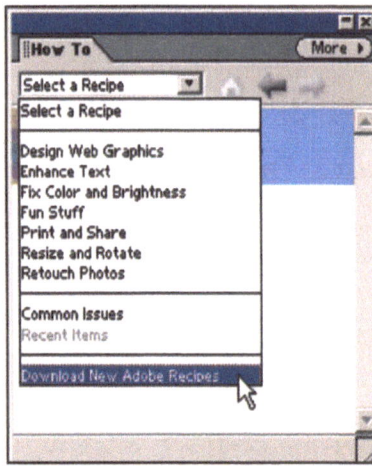

2. Select the new recipes you wish to download from the Online Services Wizard.

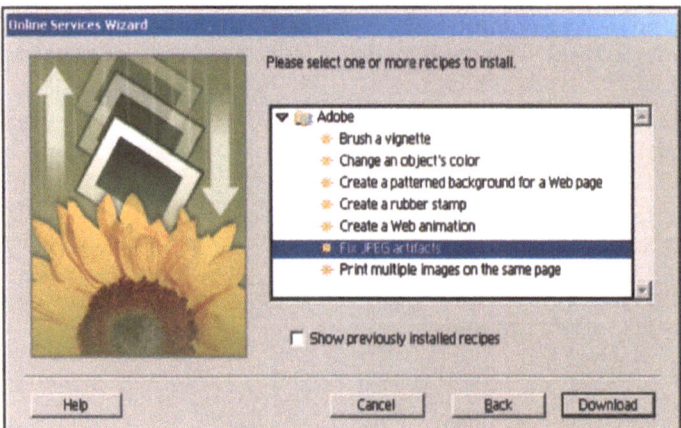

3. Click Download.
4. Click Finish.

The recipes will be installed on your computer and can be found in Elements How To palette under Recent Items.

Layer Styles

Layer Styles allow to you apply non-destructive effects to Layers. The creation of new Layer Styles requires the full version of Photoshop. Free and commercial Layer Styles compatible with Elements can be found online. Installing them is a snap.

1. Once you have located a Layer Style you want online (e.g. http://graphicssoft.miningco.com/cs/photoshopstyles/), download the Layer Style's ASL file.

2. Place it in Elements' Preset\Styles directory. The default location is: C:\Program Files\Adobe\Photoshop Elements 2\Presets\Styles. The path to your Styles folder may vary depending on your installation and platform.

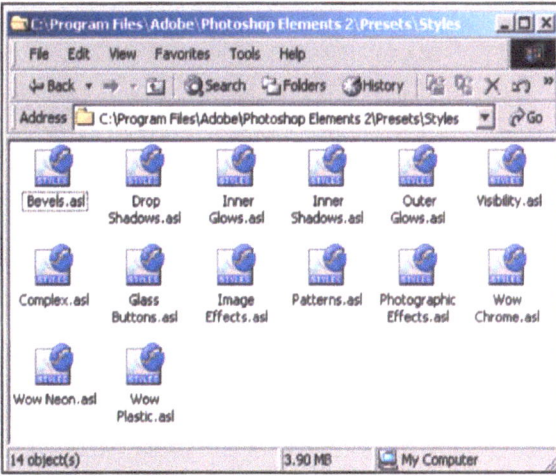

3. Restart Elements and the new styles will be available in the **Layer Styles** palette.

For more information on plug-ins, recipes and layer styles a search using your favorite search engine should provide a good list of sites for you to explore. Photoshop has a large number of dedicated followers that produce a lot of tutorials and other resources - these can be extremely helpful for Elements users, as well as the increasing number of sites dedicated solely to Elements.

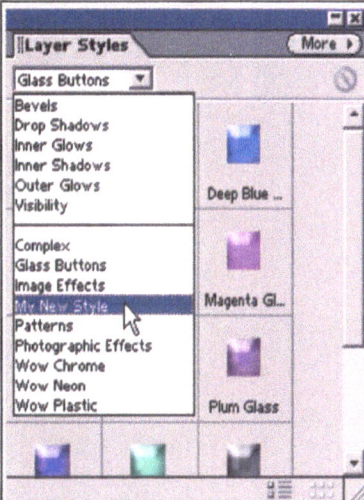

Index

The index is arranged hierarchically, in alphabetical order, with symbols preceding the letter A. Many second level entries also occur as first level entries. This is to ensure that you will find the information you require however you chose to search for it.